Included in Communication
Learning Climates That Cultivate
Racial and Ethnic Diversity

Judith S. Trent, editor

Wenshu Lee, Mark Lawrence McPhail, and Dolores Valencia Tanno, associate editors

Orlando L. Taylor, consulting reviewer

Carolyn Vasques-Scalera, AAHE project editor

A publication of

**AMERICAN ASSOCIATION
FOR HIGHER EDUCATION**

Published in cooperation with the National Communication Association

Published in cooperation with the National Communication Association

The National Communication Association is a nonprofit organization of Communication educators, practitioners, and students, with members in every state in the United States and 25 other countries. It is the oldest and largest national association promoting Communication scholarship and education.
1765 N Street, NW
Washington, DC 20036
http://www.natcom.org/

Included in Communication: Learning Climates That Cultivate Racial and Ethnic Diversity
Judith S. Trent, editor
Wenshu Lee, Mark Lawrence McPhail, and Dolores Valencia Tanno, associate editors
Orlando L. Taylor, consulting reviewer
Carolyn Vasques-Scalera, AAHE project editor

AMERICAN ASSOCIATION FOR HIGHER EDUCATION
One Dupont Circle, Suite 360
Washington, DC 20036
ph 202/293-6440, fax 202/293-0073
www.aahe.org

10 9 8 7 6 5 4 3 2 1   ISBN 1-56377-051-2

Contents

PART TWO: INSTRUCTIONAL PRACTICES

APPENDIX

Foreword

The American Association for Higher Education is pleased to publish this most timely volume, *Included in Communication: Learning Climates That Cultivate Racial and Ethnic Diversity*, the first of three volumes that will showcase innovative teaching and learning strategies, provide faculty in selected disciplines examples from their peers as to how they can make a difference in the success of students of color in introductory and gateway courses, and promote conversations in departments across the nation about the importance of diversity and the opportunity it brings to explore innovative pedagogy and revitalize learning in classrooms.

The 21st century is the time for higher education to rise to the occasion to serve the most diverse student population in history. For more than 30 years, AAHE has been the premier higher education association to lead faculty to achieve teaching and learning excellence. For the past decade or so, colleges and universities around the country have been trying to determine the impact of diversity on curricular and cocurricular life. In 1999, AAHE's Board of Directors officially adopted a statement on diversity in which they pledge: "AAHE will continue through its projects, conferences, and publications to assist campuses to increase access and diversity for students, faculty, and staff, as well as in curricula and programs." This publication builds on that pledge.

The three volumes (in Communication, Sociology, and English Studies) also represent AAHE's continuing commitment to collaboration on two levels. First, they bring together AAHE's own work in assessment, faculty roles and rewards, teaching and learning, and diversity in new ways. Second, AAHE is also collaborating with disciplinary associations — the National Communication Association, the American Sociological Association, and the National Council of Teachers of English, respectively. All three books are produced under the leadership of Dr. Carolyn Vasques-Scalera, AAHE's director of diversity initiatives, and disciplinary colleagues, with funding from the Knight Foundation.

Research shows that the success of students of color ultimately depends on the transformation of faculty who teach them, as well as institutional and departmental climates that value the presence of diverse students. AAHE as a praxis organization is committed to taking research and operationalizing it through exemplary practice, as modeled through this publication.

Yolanda T. Moses
President, American Association for Higher Education

The Diversity Framework Informing This Volume

Carolyn Vasques-Scalera

This volume is one of three in a project funded by the Knight Foundation. Each asks the question how can we create learning climates (in Communication, in Sociology, and in English Studies, respectively) that cultivate racial and ethnic diversity and promote the success of *all* our students?

The concept for these disciplinary monographs emerged from two important realities. First, despite gains made in access to higher education, numerous studies show that students of color remain underrepresented at every degree level and in many disciplines. Second, despite all we have learned about effective teaching and learning and about the importance of diversity in general, we haven't done enough to translate that general knowledge into specific disciplinary and teaching practices. These volumes are an attempt to make more intentional the connections between diversity and teaching/learning and to provide faculty with concrete strategies for enacting those connections in their discipline. To that end, there are several critical questions that must be considered:

What are our assumptions about who learns and how? Do we enact practices that suggest that there is only one way to teach and learn and belong to a disciplinary community? Do we send the message that only some students are capable of learning; that students are somehow deficient if they fail to learn under the conditions set explicitly or implicitly by the discipline? Do we adhere to elitist "weed-out" notions of success, that students who fail to succeed simply did not belong? Do we think of diversity in terms of excellence, or diminishment? Why should disciplines care about diversity?

The Framework's Elements

"Diversity" is a term that has been used widely and loosely with very different meanings and implications for practice. The questions posed above reveal some important insights about the particular diversity framework informing this volume and its companion two volumes to come.

1

These volumes challenge the deficit model of diversity, in which difference is equated with deficiency and seen as a challenge rather than as an opportunity for learning. *All* students and faculty bring a wealth of tradition, information, and experience to their understandings of the world, and that wealth can contribute in meaningful ways to the learning process. Furthermore, to focus on how some students are different, or to assume that *different* means "deficient," is to leave unexamined how the learning experience is set up to the benefit of particular groups by rewarding their culture-specific ways of knowing and doing.

2

These volumes move beyond a singular focus on access and representational diversity — the *numbers* of students of color in our classes and campuses — to examine the experiences students face once there. It's not enough to recruit diverse students if we do nothing to retain them; that is, if we don't offer a teaching/learning environment where they are genuinely included and are expected to succeed.

3

In thinking about students' experiences, these volumes expand the conversation beyond the usual focus on content — *what* we teach — to a discussion about the impact on students of process — *how* we teach. The volumes don't advocate an additive approach to curriculum, in which diverse perspectives are simply tacked on to the content of courses. Rather, they prompt us to think deeply about what it means to be included in classroom and disciplinary communities, and the ways in which we create, intentionally or not, barriers to meaningful student learning and participation in those communities. The volumes ask faculty to examine the hidden messages in our pedagogy, and they provide some alternate ways of teaching that are more inclusive and conducive to the success of diverse students.

4

These volumes challenge the notion that diversity is solely or primarily the responsibility of certain faculty (usually faculty of color); involves particular students (usually students of color); and is relevant only to certain areas of the campus (student affairs) or to specific disciplines (humanities and social sciences). The issues they raise and the practices they advocate illustrate not merely the relevance but the absolute *centrality* of diversity to teaching and learning. Their essays challenge not merely pedagogical practices but the epistemological foundations upon which each discipline rests. Each volume makes diversity relevant to that disciplinary context and raises important questions about what it means to engage in a disciplinary community that truly values diversity. They make clear that teaching and learning *about* diversity is not the same as engaging diversity and diverse learners in the learning process. As such, they model for other disciplines how to take up these issues.

5

While these volumes primarily address students of color and gateway courses, the issues raised apply to other forms of difference; the practices described transcend specific courses; and because the volumes are essentially about enhancing pedagogy and engaging diversity, the benefits extend to *all* students. An important theme concerns not simply making curriculum and pedagogy more relevant to students of color, but helping all students (and indeed, faculty) become more culturally aware and multiculturally competent. A growing body of research documents the benefits of having diverse learners and of engaging diversity issues — not just for the success of students of color, but for all students.

6

Finally, while the focus is mainly on classrooms, these volumes include essays and instructional practices that situate the classroom within its larger departmental, institutional, and disciplinary contexts. A meaningfully diverse classroom climate is a necessary but insufficient criterion to achieving the goals outlined above. Students also need to see themselves reflected in the curriculum and in the faces of faculty and administrators. Students need to experience an inclusive campus climate and disciplinary community. Individual faculty members enacting good practices in their classes is not enough; we need departmental, institutional, and discipline-wide support for diversity.

A Prompt for Conversation and Change

Thus the title of the volumes, *Included in* — which reflects that it is not enough to recruit students of color into higher education and into the disciplines if, once there, their progress is blocked by teaching/learning practices that exclude them. Nor is it enough to focus on persistence and success if, by that, we mean success only in the academy's dominant ways of thinking and learning. To their credit, many students of color have succeeded in higher education and will continue to succeed despite too-often unwelcoming climates and other barriers. But the title reflects the larger outcome we all desire; that is, for students of color to feel *included* in a discipline, to feel a sense of ownership and empowerment in the learning process, the discipline, the academy. The subtitle — *Learning Climates That Cultivate Racial and Ethnic Diversity* — reflects the means for getting there, that we must intentionally *cultivate* diversity (in all its forms). To do that is not simply a matter of letting people in, it means opening up the knowledge-creation process. The result is a more vital and viable discipline.

The use of the word *cultivate* is very intentional. These volumes present a fundamental challenge to the weed-out mentality that says only some students can learn and those who fail don't deserve to be there. But neither do the volumes assume that to succeed, students simply need to learn better study skills. They are not about changing who students are or how they learn. Rather, these volumes are intended to encourage faculty to examine our assumptions about who students are and how they learn, and the ways in which our pedagogy either contributes to or inhibits the inclusion and success of all our students.

These volumes are not intended as the final or definitive word on cultivating racial and ethnic diversity in the disciplines. Nor are they meant to be cookbooks for doing so. We risk perpetuating the exclusion and marginalization of students of color if we equate *identity* with *learning style*, or apply unreflectively the instructional practices that work well in one context with one group of students to all contexts and groups. Instead, the volumes are intended as a resource for conversation and examining assumptions, and they provide some guidelines for practice. But we must think carefully about who our students are, and enact multiple forms of teaching and learning that provide opportunities for all students to be genuinely included.

Clearly the issues raised in this volume and the ones to follow point to the need for more research in the scholarship of teaching and learning that explicitly investigates diversity questions. My hope is that you will find the monographs — individually and collectively — stimulating and empowering in furthering such work in collaboration with colleagues on campus, at your disciplinary meetings, and at AAHE events. I invite you to visit the AAHE website (www.aahe.org) for further resources and for venues in which to share your progress.

These are issues about which I care deeply, and with which I continue to struggle in my own teaching. It is exciting and illuminating to learn how different disciplines are grappling with these issues and bringing discipline-specific research to bear on pedagogical practices.

Acknowledgments

I would like to express my thanks to the editorial team from Communication, led by Dr. Judith Trent, of the University of Cincinnati, for their hard work in bringing this volume to fruition under such a tight timeline; also to our colleagues at the National Communication Association, particularly James Gaudino and Sherry Morreale, for their support of this collaboration. Many thanks to Bry Pollack, director of publications at AAHE, for her keen editorial eye.

This volume (and those in Sociology and English Studies) would not be possible without the generous support of the Knight Foundation and the guidance of Rick Love and Julia Van.

Most especially, thanks go to the faculty members in Communication who willingly and ably raised some critical issues and shared exemplary practices by which we might create more-inclusive disciplines, and indeed, a more-inclusive academy.

Introduction

Judith S. Trent

The primary purpose of this volume, produced collaboratively by the American Association for Higher Education (AAHE) and the National Communication Association (NCA), is to describe effective pedagogical strategies for increasing the participation and success of students of color in the Communication major. Specifically, the volume intends to:

- encourage conversations about inclusive teaching and learning and the importance of diversity issues in Communication pedagogy;

- provide Communication faculty with concrete teaching and learning strategies with which to promote the success of students of color in the gateway courses — that is, the courses that most often lead to a Communication major (Public Speaking, Interpersonal Communication, Group Communication, and the hybrid or combination course[1]); and,

- encourage discipline-wide action to remove any barriers to the success of students of color in Communication.

To achieve these three objectives, this volume includes two kinds of contributions. Part One contains 10 essays that focus on pedagogical, curricular, and administrative issues, examining a variety of factors that affect the success of students of color in the four basic Communication courses. Part Two describes exemplary instructional practices focusing on diversity and teaching and learning in the basic courses.

National Communication Association

When NCA's executive director, James L. Gaudino, and associate director, Sherwyn P. Morreale, asked me to develop and edit this volume, I agreed to do so largely because of the longtime commitment of the Association and its leaders and members to issues of diversity. I had worked with Jim and Sherry when, while I was president of NCA in 1997, we developed a Summer Conference on Racial and Ethnic Diversity.

The National Communication Association was founded in 1914 (for more, see Work and Jeffrey 1989). Almost 90 years later, the field of Communication is a large and vigorous one, marked by advancements in the study, criticism, research, teaching, and application of the artistic, humanistic, and scientific principles of communication. Now the oldest and largest academic society of Communication scholar-teachers in the world, NCA has grown from 17 to 7,100 members. Their research interests span all forms of human communication, ranging from face-to-face communication in dyads to mediated communication reaching large public audiences. The U.S. Department of Education's *Classification of Instructional Programs-2000* defines "communication studies" as a "group of instructional programs that focus on how messages in various media are produced, used, distributed, and interpreted within and across different contexts, channels, and cultures, and that prepare individuals to apply communication knowledge and skills professionally."[2]

Approximately 4,100 NCA members meet annually at the NCA national convention to present the results of their research. In addition, the Association convenes national and international conferences on specific foci in the Communication field.

NCA's membership comes from all 50 states in the United States, plus the District of Columbia, Puerto Rico, and Guam. In addition, individuals from 25 other countries are NCA members. Affiliate organizations currently include Communication societies from Israel and South Africa, and ongoing contacts with organizations in Latin America, Russia, and the People's Republic of China. NCA's membership affiliates with a number of divisions that focus on specific research topics. Currently, those units include African American Communication and Culture; American Studies Commission; Applied Communication; Argumentation and Forensics; Asian/Pacific American Communication Studies; Basic Course; Communication and Aging; Communication and Law; Communication and the Future; Communication Apprehension and Avoidance; Communication Assessment; Communication Ethics; Communication Needs of Students at Risk; Critical and Cultural Studies; Environmental Communication; Ethnography; Experiential Learning in Communication; Family Communication; Feminist and Women Studies; Freedom of Expression; Gay, Lesbian, Bisexual, Transgender Studies; Group Communication; Health Communication Division; Human Communication and Technology; Instructional Development; International and Intercultural Communication; Interpersonal Communication; Intrapersonal Communication and Social Cognition; Language and Social Interaction; Latina/Latino Communication Studies; Mass Communication; Organizational Communication; Peace and Conflict; Performance Studies; Political Communication; Public Address; Public Relations; Rhetorical and Communication Theory; Semiotics and Communication; Spiritual Communication; Theatre; Training and Development; Vietnamese Communication; Visual Communication.

NCA publishes seven scholarly journals, including *Communication Education*, which is solely devoted to Communication pedagogy; two annuals, one on freedom of expression and the other on intercultural communication; an index to journals in Communication; a series of books arising from the research of the discipline; and a serial publication of teaching activities, a quarterly called *The Communication Teacher.*

In addition to growing membership and breadth and depth of publications, scholarship, and pedagogy, recently NCA has extended its national influence in other ways. The Association belongs to several societies that promote scholarship (e.g., American Council of Learned Societies, Consortium of Social Science Associations, National Humanities Alliance). The Association's professional staff as well as individual members have also cultivated external alliances with other disciplinary societies (e.g., American Historical Association, American Political Science Association, American Psychological Association, American Sociological Association), with interdisciplinary organizations (e.g., American Association for Higher Education, Association of American Colleges and Universities, Council of Graduate Schools), and with funding agencies (e.g., The Carnegie Foundation, National Science Foundation, Pew Charitable Trusts). Throughout this period of expansion, the Association and its members continued to honor their core value of diversity in their research and pedagogy.

NCA and Diversity

This volume represents a watershed in the evolution of NCA's history of commitment to diversity. Since its founding, the Association has demonstrated, through both its policies and its actions, that Communication is a field that views diversity as an advantage to an academic discipline. Therefore, it came as no surprise that Communication was among the first disciplines approached by AAHE to develop a publication totally devoted to examining ways to encourage and retain undergraduate students of color.

During the 1960s, NCA was one of the first disciplinary societies to establish a member-based caucus devoted solely to the scholarship of and issues of importance to its black members (see Daniel 1995). In 1968, NCA established an ad hoc Committee on Social Relevance, which held its first meeting at the NCA 1968 national convention. According to one of the founders of the NCA Black Caucus, that meeting was an early indicator of NCA's interest in issues of diversity:

> We were treading in very unfamiliar waters, and hence there was no way to anticipate what "went down" at the December 28, 1968, Open Meeting on Social Relevance at the Sheraton Hotel in Chicago. The event was a true 1960s "happening." All Association members were invited to attend. The extra large meeting room was packed, wall-to-wall, standing room only, with approximately 2,000 long-haired White folks, a small handful of bushy-headed Black folks, and other folks who felt "a deep need to get involved." (Daniel 1995: 5)

That Social Relevance Committee evolved into NCA's Black Caucus. Meetings of the Caucus at the national convention frequently overflow room capacity, and its members annually convene a national summer conference as well.

Today, NCA boasts an Asian/Pacific American Caucus, Black Caucus, Caucus on Disability Issues, Caucus on Gay and Lesbian Concerns, La Raza Caucus, and Women's Caucus. Each serves as a meeting place for persons from underrepresented groups in the Association. These caucuses promote initiatives and present convention programs featuring research on topics related to the group served by the caucus. The caucuses also represent the political agendas of their constituents to the Association as a whole. This is often done through NCA's Affirmative Action and Inter-Caucus Committee, which reports directly to the Association's national governing bodies.

With the members of its Black Caucus as a starting point, in the 1980s NCA initiated a working relationship with a number of the historically black colleges and universities (HBCUs) in an effort to familiarize their faculty and students with the goals and teaching and research programs/activities of the Association. In 1996, I appointed a national task force on racial and ethnic diversity. That group developed a major research agenda for the purpose of better understanding and, where necessary, redirecting the Association's programs in support of diversity.

Specifically, the task force, Jim Gaudino, and I surveyed all Communication departments in an attempt to identify the racial and ethnic profiles of Communication faculty and students, the frequency and nature of recruitment and retention practices of Communication departments, and the perceptions of students of color of the climate within the Communication discipline. The results of this first questionnaire suggested that although most Communication departments participated actively in institutional efforts designed to recruit faculty and students of color, underrepresentation remained a problem.

A questionnaire, sent to each of the students of color who had been identified by his or her department, sought to learn more about departmental and institutional climate — i.e., whether, from their experiences as undergraduate Communication majors or as graduate students in Communication, the discipline was hospitable to students of color. Although a majority of respondents believed that their department was more supportive of diversity generally than was their campus, they felt that at both levels there was more rhetoric about diversity than there was action. They said, for example, that although the issue was frequently discussed, there were no really significant efforts to recruit students of color. They also noted that there were so few faculty of color that students tended to feel lost. And that while white faculty supported diversity rhetorically, they did not show a behavioral commitment to recruit additional students of color or to build sufficient supports programs within departments.

In response to these findings, in 1997 NCA convened a summer conference focused on racial and ethnic diversity in the field of Communication. That conference generated guiding principles and action plans for addressing four topics essential to the success of any diversity initiative for a department or a campus: criticism and research; pedagogy and curriculum; administration, recruitment, and retention; and campus and departmental climate and culture. (The proceedings of the conference, *Racial and Ethnic Diversity in the 21st Century: A Communication Perspective*, was published by NCA in 1997.)

The 1997 conference also resulted in the creation of an action plan that addressed all aspects of the Association's support for diversity in Communication research and instruction. For example, the plan called for efforts to increase the diversity of editorial boards and to make NCA's journals more sensitive to scholarship that had previously been marginalized. The plan also included an Association-funded grant (which was awarded twice) to departmental programs targeted to increase diversity.

More recently, the Association undertook an effort to forge better relationships between urban universities, HBCUs, and majority-white academic institutions. NCA's studies clearly demonstrated that while the discipline as a whole is underrepresented in terms of students and faculty of color, some Communication departments at urban campuses and HBCUs have large numbers of students of color. However, the study also suggests that the HBCU programs offer primarily undergraduate degrees and that the students typically do not go on to study Communication at the graduate level. NCA's current efforts are designed to forge closer relationships between undergraduate programs at the HBCUs and the graduate programs at majority-white institutions.

About This Volume

Developing and editing this volume has been, from beginning to end, a joyous and enriching experience. First, we were fortunate in putting together an editorial board that would be the envy of any editor. Wenshu Lee, from San Jose State University; Mark Lawrence McPhail, from Miami University; Dolores Valencia Tanno, from the University of Nevada, Las Vegas; and consulting reviewer Orlando L. Taylor, from Howard University, made helpful suggestions about the overall direction the volume should take and later made knowledgeable and perceptive recommendations regarding the manuscripts. And they did everything in a necessarily brief time period. (A truly awesome group of people.)

Second, when we put out the open call to all NCA members for essays and instructional practices, we received more than twice the number than could be used. Third, all contributors had the final copy of their manuscript to us by the day it was due. (Surely this must be a record.) And finally, being a part of this volume has been a pleasure because the ideas, advice, and examples that are this book will facilitate the intellectual growth and development of our skills as more culturally aware and sensitive Communication teachers and professionals.

The volume is organized into two major sections, essays and instructional practices for promoting the success of students of color in Communication. Within each, the contributions move from general principles to specific strategies.

In Part One, 10 essays provide a scholarly look at pedagogical, curricular, and administrative issues. In the first essay, Thomas J. Socha and Kelly Fudge Albada argue that the communication environment in academic departments is a component critical to the success of students of color. Importantly, they offer examples of successful departmental climate-warming activities. Next, Olga Idriss Davis, Jacqueline M. Martinez, and Thomas K. Nakayama maintain that students of color recognize that traditionally structured and presented Communication courses have little relevance to their everyday lives. The authors urge a revision in the research and teaching of the discipline that would foreground communication as a phenomenon of experience linked to time, place, and circumstance. Cheryl D. Gunter is concerned with the formulation of criteria for the successful completion of classroom activities. Because students of color can present with distinctive communication traits, the author urges instructors to develop appropriate evaluative criteria for all students. Dorthy L. Pennington focuses on promoting the success of African-American students in predominantly white Communication departments and asserts that success must be viewed holistically — the whole campus environment in which the students of color must operate. Mary E. Triece, Patricia S. Hill, Kathleen D. Clark, Yang Lin, and Julia A. Spiker argue for a teaching process and a learning environment based on pedagogies of empowerment. These authors discuss teaching philosophies and suggest classroom activities and learning communities that contribute to pedagogies of empowerment.

The next five essays in Part One offer more specific discussions for improving selected Communication introductory or gateway courses. In "Reshaping Rhetorical Rivers: Climate, Communication, and Coherence in the Basic Speech Course," Mark Lawrence McPhail, Ronald B. Scott, and Kathleen M. German discuss the way in which the intellectual and institutional climate of colleges, universities, and academic departments affects students of color in basic Communication courses. The authors suggest some specific curricular strategies that can transform the atmosphere and therefore the outcomes for students in the Public Speaking course. Next, Linda G. Seward argues that even though universities traditionally study nonwhite, non-male cultures in isolation, the Interpersonal Communication course, because it focuses on concepts rather than groups, can be developed to counter intellectual segregation or omission. Suggestions for creating a concept-oriented class are offered. Nanci M. Burk focuses on the basic course experience of Native-American students, suggesting storytelling as one pedagogical methodology to improve classroom discussions of diverse cultures. Victoria O. Orrego, Patricia Kearney, and Timothy G. Plax explain and advocate a holistic teaching strategy in the basic Public Speaking course. They discuss the ways in which lectures, class activities, and alternate teaching tools can be used in diverse classrooms. Finally, Ronald L. Jackson II, Carlos D.J. Morrison, and Celnisha L. Dangerfield recommend the "cultural contract" paradigm as an approach to diversity. They provide strategies for empowering students of color in the basic

Public Speaking course and argue that the inclusion of cultural diversity in the Communication curriculum is a way to retain students of color in the discipline.

In Part Two, eight instructional practices provide substantive and eclectic information for Communication instruction in diverse classrooms in the basic courses. As in Part One, the contributions in this section progress from the general to the specific. The first contribution, by Katherine G. Hendrix and Aparna S. Bulusu, describes a workshop for the preparation of graduate assistants to teach in a multicultural classroom. The second, by Dale Cyphert, has as its focus the inclusion of cross-linguistic speaking to help students who have English as their second language or who have strong dialects.

The last six instructional practices present specific useful and creative teaching activities for the diverse classroom. Cynthia Berryman-Fink explains an exercise that helps students explore their personal prejudices. Heather E. Harris writes about an exercise she calls "Learning About 'Others,' Learning About Ourselves." The activity presented by Diane M. Monahan involves the use of music in the Interpersonal Communication classroom; while Ann Neville Miller's activity advocates the use of group ceremonial speeches in the Public Speaking classroom. Theresa Bridges and Tara Lynn Crowell explain a semester-long exercise that gives students the opportunity to create personal repertoires of intercultural skills. And Roy Schwartzman and Bayo Oludaja provide an activity that promotes student investigation of ethnic, racial, and cultural backgrounds — their own and those of other individuals.

Taken together, the essays present a wealth of innovative ideas available for Communication instruction in the basic courses.

Acknowledgments

The concept for this book (and those that might follow in other disciplines) originated with the American Association for Higher Education. The National Communication Association and I have had the pleasure of working with the series editor, Carolyn Vasques-Scalera, director of diversity initiatives at AAHE, from the early thinking about the volume through its completion. The association with AAHE and Carolyn has been a positive experience.

Working with the NCA professional staff, once again, has also been a distinct pleasure. I especially want to thank Jim Gaudino for his enthusiastic support of the volume and Sherry Morreale for her skilled advice and help in this project from beginning to end. In fact, Sherry led the successful collaboration between NCA and AAHE that was key to Communication's being selected by AAHE to contribute a volume on promoting the academic success of students of color.

I also want to thank two other very important people without whom we could not have sustained the initial interest in the volume among NCA members nor met the publication deadlines. Evelyn Crothers, my 83-years-young mother, did all of the initial correspondence with potential contributors who answered our call for manuscripts; and Lisa A. Connelly, a University of Cincinnati graduate assistant in the Department of Communication, very conscientiously and carefully helped in the preparation of the final manuscript.

Finally, I thank my Communication colleagues — the authors of the essays and instructional practices. I have learned much from them and appreciate their enthusiastic participation in this important project. I believe the expertise they have shared will be of great benefit to all of us — and, more important, to all of our students.

Notes

1. These four courses were selected for primary consideration in the volume because they represent the four most popular orientations to the course identified in a series of national surveys conducted of the basic Communication course, beginning in 1969 and most recently in 1999 (see Morreale et al. 1999).

2. This definition and a categorical description of *Communication, Journalism,* and other related fields, Section 09, was developed for the U.S. Department of Education by the National Communication Association, in collaboration with the member associations of the Council of Communication Associations.

References

Daniel, J.L. (1995). *Changing the Players and the Game: A Personal Account of the Speech Communication Black Caucus Origins*. Washington, DC: National Communication Association.

Morreale, S., M. Hanna, R. Berko, and J. Gibson. (1999). "The Basic Communication Course at U.S. Colleges and Universities: VI." *Basic Communication Course Annual* 11: 1-36.

Work, W., and R. Jeffrey. (1989). *The Past Is Prologue: A Brief History of the Speech Communication Association*. Washington, DC: National Communication Association.

Part One
Pedagogical Issues

Toward Good Global Warming

Improving the Interracial Communication Climate in Departments of Communication

Thomas J. Socha and Kelly Fudge Albada

O vert racism might be on the decline, but all facets of the university, especially academic departments, face the challenge of creating a welcoming environment for students of color. Departments of Communication, in particular, have made (or are well-positioned to make) progress in warming chilly racial climates. This essay extends previous theoretical work on the problem of the "chilly climate for women" (Hall and Sandler 1982, 1984) to the problem of the chilly climate for students of color in Communication. First, we review the literature from the discipline of Communication Studies and allied fields that have examined the concept of chilly communication climate. Next, we develop an outline of points to consider when assessing a Communication department's racial communication climate (e.g., faculty knowledge-ability, representation in classroom readings, and so on). Finally, we highlight examples of successful interracial-climate warming in two Communication departments, including students' assessments of class readings and textbooks.

Chilly Communication Climate

Communication scholars have studied communication climate in the contexts of organizations and organizational relationships (Falcione 1974; Fink and Chen 1995; Follert 1980), departmental and college training programs for graduate students (Andrews 1983), groups (Gibb 1960), and classrooms (Rosenfeld 1983; Rosenfeld and Jarrard 1985). This work has generally defined communication climate as "the social/psychological context within which relationships occur" (Rosenfeld 1983: 167) and has highlighted the importance of developing supportive, welcoming communication environments if successful communication and satisfying relationships are to develop.

According to Fink and Chen (1995), communication climates are multidimensional and consist of at least three levels:

> Psychological climate is the individual member's cognitive representation of . . . the prevalent values, norms, and expectations in his or her organizational environment. . . . Organizational climate is a set of attitudes and beliefs that is shared and collectively held by organizational members

11

as a whole. . . . Finally, group climate is the elaboration of organizational climate that permits group members to reinterpret the organization [within organizational groups]. (495)

Psychological communication climate can be experienced differently among individuals in an organization, and the organizational climate (i.e., shared perceptions) could be more or less shared and more or less understood among different groups of people in the organization (e.g., management employees, white employees, black employees). However, Fink and Chen (1995) found that the more time colleagues spent communicating, the greater the convergence between psychological climate and organizational climate (i.e., increased similarity between how the individual sees the organization and generally shared perceptions of the organization).

Psychological climate and organizational climate can take on positive or negative qualities, or in Gibb's (1960) terms, become "supportive" or "defensive." A communication climate that takes on positive qualities that foster trusting, cooperative, and friendly communication would be considered supportive. In contrast, a defensive climate takes on negative qualities that "limit preconceptions about appropriate and expected behaviors, abilities, . . . [and] personal goals . . . based on [negative] sex roles [or racial stereotypes] rather than on individual interests and ability" (Hall and Sandler 1982: 4).

Both defensive and supportive communication climates can vary in degree as well as in level of explicitness or openness. That is, psychological and organizational communication climates can vary in degrees of supportiveness-defensiveness (e.g., a "hostile" communication climate is one that is viewed as extremely negative/defensive) and be more or less explicitly or openly supportive or defensive. For example, a defensive communication climate (psychological and organizational) can be experienced subtly and referred to as "chilly." A chilly climate is characterized by a general and subtle feeling of "unwelcomeness" that people experience when interacting in this particular context. That feeling might be shared widely and regarded as an aspect of organizational climate as well as be an aspect of the psychological climate for particular individuals.

Previous research on the "chilly" climate has focused primarily on the experiences of women, but also it has examined the experiences of ethnic minorities in organizations. That past work attempted to operationally define qualities of defensive and supportive climates. For example, Fink and Chen (1995) adopted a Galileo approach that relies on a series of questionnaires that ask about attitudinal similarity, belief similarity, and climate-perception similarity, with an eye to examining the co-construction of climate. In classrooms, climate has been measured using the Communication Climate Questionnaire (Hays 1970) and the Classroom Environment Scale (Trickett and Moos 1973). These scales directly (see Hays 1970) or indirectly draw on the work of Gibb (1960) and incorporate his defensive-supportive elements of communication climate: openness, descriptiveness, provisionalism, positiveness, and equality.

Research has found that defensive climates in the classroom develop in various ways. For example, a professor's messages could be perceived as sexist and/or as unsupportive (Rosenfeld and Jarrard 1985). Students experiencing a defensive communication classroom environment, according to Rosenfeld (1983), might respond with "coping mechanisms" to manage their feelings of defensiveness. "Active mechanisms" can include verbally resisting a professor's influences, retaliating against the professor, or forming alliances; "passive coping mechanisms" include hiding feelings, not doing what the professor asks, or daydreaming. Similarly, Ellis and Fisher (1994) argued that since a group's communication climate arises from its members' communication and perceptions of their relationships, changing a negative communication climate involves reducing defensiveness in the talk, specifically giving people ways to save face, avoiding accusatory and intimidating messages, and focusing on common needs and goals.

Chilly Interracial Classroom Communication Climate

This discussion of the general qualities of the chilly communication climate also applies to interracial communication on campus. According to Hall and Sandler, "Minority students frequently find the general campus climate at predominantly white institutions to be *the* major barrier to intellectual and personal development and to the completion of degree work" [emphasis in original] (1984: 11). Further, minority students who drop out "cite a general academic, social, and cultural climate that makes them feel like unwelcome guests, where simply trying to survive day-to-day uses up an inordinate amount of energy" (11). Hall and Sandler (1984) also noted that minority students' efforts to create supportive environments by bonding with other minority students sometimes can be misperceived and responded to defensively by the dominant group.

The interracial communication literature offers examples of chilly interracial climates encountered by students of color. According to Henderson (1999):

> Daily we witness the negative effects of racial prejudice. It creates inequalities, exclusions, and an atmosphere of rejection that prevent some groups of people from being allowed into mainstream American life. Prejudice is like a terrible cancer, engulfing the entire body, mind, and spirit, often defying the skills of those who wish to intervene. (xv)

Cose (1993) adds to this description by commenting on the "perceptual chasm separating so many blacks and whites" (13). According to Cose, "the problem is not only that we are afraid to talk to one another, it is also that we are disinclined to listen. And even when the will to understand is present, often the ability (gained through analogous experiences) is not" (13).

Given that communication and perceptions of relationships are key locations for the creation of chilly interracial climates for students of color, an important context to examine is the classroom. Speaking about the chilly interracial communication climate in university classrooms, Henderson (1999) identified 10 questions that black students ask (consciously or unconsciously) that help assess an interracial climate's temperature. For example, "Is the teacher able to put students at ease?" "Is the teacher able to empathize with and show understanding of the students and convey positive expectations?" (117-118). Questions such as these highlight the aforementioned general aspects of climate. However, a unique question raised by Henderson that points to a dimension not addressed in communication climate literature asks, "Is the teacher sincerely committed to teaching black students?" (118). This question speaks directly to the attitudes of the teacher (Cose's "willingness to listen") and to the teacher's ability to communicate genuine interest in students of color. That is, in order to build a supportive interracial communication climate, the ability to convey interest coupled with some sense of cultural understanding is necessary. Henderson (1999) reinforces this point when he proposes that among the many solutions for warming chilly interracial communication climates a key element is "personal involvement that emanates from feelings of outrage at the behaviors of hateful people, from the need to communicate grievances, and from the need to get rid of injustices" (182). In short, to communicate to all students, "there's room at the table" (187).

Beyond showing a genuine interest, faculty must feel comfortable and be knowledgeable about the various cultures represented among the students they teach. Socha and Beigle (1999) surveyed professors and instructors of Family Communication about their knowledge of African-American and African cultures and about their levels of comfort in communicating this information to mixed-race classes. Results showed low-to-moderate levels of knowledge-ability and low-to-moderate levels of apprehension in communicating information about cultures other than one's own to multiethnic classes. Yet, faculty reported a very high degree of openness to learning about African-American and African cultures.

Socha and Beigle (1999) also found that Family Communication textbooks presented a limited cultural picture that reinforced whiteness. Cultural representation in texts is an important component of a communication climate. All students should be able to envision themselves in readings and faculty members' examples, as well as in their department's curricula and extracurricular activities.

Examples of Good Global Warming

To move toward warming chilly interracial communication climates in Communication courses and departments calls for considering the various factors gleaned from the previous discussion of communication climate. In this next section, we highlight examples of some of the major elements of warming chilly interracial communication climates that involve faculty, classroom readings, and programmatic activities.

EAST CAROLINA UNIVERSITY

Introductory Communication classes, such as Communication Theory and Interpersonal Communication, are often the venues by which students are first exposed to the field, faculty, and department. As in the Family Communication classroom, for optimal learning to occur all students should be able to envision themselves in the readings, examples, department, and field. The Department of Communication and Broadcasting at East Carolina University (ECU) sought to assess the perceptions and experiences of students of color within an introductory Communication Theory course in order to determine the perceived classroom climate. The department also asked students of color to provide feedback on several Interpersonal Communication textbooks, as well as to relate their evaluations of and suggestions for the department and university. The students' responses were revealing of their psychological climates and the group and organizational climates.

The introductory Communication course is the first course that intended Communication majors and minors complete, and it fulfills a social science general-education requirement for all students. Some 480 students per year are exposed to the Communication department through this course; hence, it contributes significantly to the perceived climate of the department and typical Communication classroom. As stated previously, a chilly climate can be created if the instructor is perceived to be unsupportive or, more extreme, to be sexist or racist. These perceptions are based on the often subtle messages sent in classroom interactions and choice of textbook and instructional examples.

The textbook employed in the course is one that is adopted at many other universities, Griffin's *A First Look at Communication Theory* (McGraw-Hill, 2000). Though the students in this course are not assigned additional reading, instructors supplement the course with lecture material, examples, and video clips. This textbook's content and characteristics were rated by 21 students of color in the course on a seven-point scale (1=strongly agree, 4=neutral, 7=strongly disagree). Their responses follow:

- Applicable (M=2.8)
- Friendly (M=2.9)
- Informative about people who are different than I am (M=2.9)
- Inclusive of diverse perspectives (M=3.1)
- Includes me (M=3.3)
- Warm (M=3.4)
- Appealing (M=3.5)
- Includes examples/cases about people who are similar to me (M=3.5)
- Includes research that is relevant to me (M=3.5)
- Related to my experiences (M=3.5)

- Includes research that employed people who are similar to me (M=4.0)
- Informative about people who are similar to me (M=4.3)
- Pictures people who are similar to me (M=4.3)

On average, the students of color in this course perceived that the textbook had something to offer them (e.g., "applicable," "informative about people who are different") and was not unapproachable or antagonistic (e.g., "friendly"). Most of their responses fell in the midrange of the scale (between 3 and 5), suggesting a tepid climate.

Especially interesting to note is that the items that scored higher (i.e., closer to "strongly agree") were general characteristics and in many cases not necessarily even related to diversity per se (e.g., "friendly," "applicable," "appealing," "warm"); items related specifically to students of color (i.e., "informative about people who are similar," "pictures people who are similar," and "includes research that employed people who are similar") received the most-negative assessments. Thus, a friendly or even inviting textbook is not necessarily an inclusive one.

To further determine the importance of textbooks in relation to perceived climates, students responded to similar items for three Interpersonal Communication textbooks: Verderber and Verderber's *Inter-Act: Using Interpersonal Communication Skills* (Wadsworth, 1998), Wood's *Interpersonal Communication: Everyday Encounters* (Wadsworth, 1999), and Devito's *The Interpersonal Communication Book* (Longman, 2001). It was part of a class assignment to read and review these Interpersonal Communication texts. Of these texts, *Interpersonal Communication* faired best in terms of perceived warmth, applicability, inclusiveness, and visual elements. One student noticed that "diversity is actually integrated, not made to stand out," while another student commented, "I really enjoyed the 'Communication Notes' and 'Student Voices' sections. They provided different perspectives (i.e., diversity as well as everyday applications)." However, all three of the Interpersonal Communication texts scored higher than Griffin's *Communication Theory* textbook, perhaps due to the wider appeal of the topic of interpersonal communication and the narrower focus of such books. That is, Interpersonal Communication textbooks present theories and then delve into various applications and contexts of those theories; Communication Theory textbooks often take broad strokes toward the study of communication. At East Carolina University, the Interpersonal Communication class is offered in smaller sections than the Communication Theory course; thus, class discussion and small-group exercises can be more readily employed in the former. As a result, student involvement in that material is greater. The students themselves suggested the importance of this classroom characteristic:

- "[Instructors should] get more student participation, as there are so many diverse cultures involved."
- "The professors answer our questions and give us help. [One] should express yourself by voicing your opinion."

■ "[We need] more interactive activities."

Students also noticed whether "diversity" stood out or was integrated in the textbooks. Most contemporary authors recognize and address cultural diversity to some extent in their textbooks, yet they sometimes do so in ways that portray cultural variations in communication as exceptions to the rule, afterthoughts, or marginal. In such textbooks, communication variations due to culture are often highlighted in shaded boxes, placed as case studies at the end of the chapter, queried in discussion questions, or summarized in a diversity chapter at the end of the text. The students of color detected those techniques and indicated a preference for the integration of "cultural diversity" within the textbook. They appreciated the inclusion of a wide range of minority groups (e.g., people with disabilities), and responded positively to textbook features that encouraged interaction or multiple perspectives (e.g., "Student Voices" sections).

Moreover, the students of color noticed the difference in a textbook between substantively taking on diversity and superficially taking on diversity. That is, including people of color in photographs or using ethnic-sounding names in examples is perhaps an initial step toward inclusion, but comparing different ethnic or racial groups in terms of the theories and concepts is a much larger step. One student of color explained:

> I would love to see more examples of minority cultures represented in relation to theories and practical experience. The class text tends to present the adult/majority opinion — very sterile. [I] must make inferences to apply to my particular situation. The lecture is more representative of the student perspective but is lacking in the minority. . . . [Instructors should] look at perspectives other than the standard; does this theory hold true for all groups of people? What are the discrepancies? Include everyone in the analysis so there is not a blatant assumption, especially by students who have not experienced different cultures.

Students also suggested "researchers should include more diverse samples" and "[statistics] should be broken down by race also, because all information is not relevant."

If such material is not provided in textbooks, then instructors must supplement the course to address racial communication variations. Though most Communication instructors supplement their course reading list, this is not always an easy task, for many instructors have not been trained in interracial communication or intercultural communication. Or if they do include readings, such as research on language use, they might neglect nonverbal communication or small-group interaction. However, as suggested by the students above, one way to circumvent this problem is to get the students involved in the material, to be "interactive." By drawing students into the discussion or by asking them to bring relevant material into class or both, instructors can overcome their limitations in training while improving the experience for all students in the classroom. Although the students of color did not always agree on the solution, they provided additional suggestions for improving their experiences in the Communication classroom:

- "[Instructors] should talk about cultural differences more. . . . Not really all cultures, but just black and white because that's the most 'hot' topic. Explain what makes us so different as far as how we communicate."

- "When students/faculty/staff think of minorities, they always think of African Americans . . . maybe when [they] talk about culture, [they should] be more specific instead of so general."

- "Use examples. Ask questions inclusive of communication in non-European, American, or East Asian cultures."

- "Our lectures as well as examples have opened my eyes to different cultures and have also helped me to relate to my own. I think asking for special treatment would go against everything that we have been working towards; however, I think we should be included in some examples other than being shown in stereotypical roles."

- "I like the fact that my professor shows minority (positive) clips for examples as well as others."

- "Use more media directed towards people of color."

- "Classes could include more cultural opportunities in our projects."

- "I would like to know more about people of color who have made great accomplishments in the area of communication."

- "I feel the Communication and Broadcasting department should express more openly that these areas of education are not only for people of light skin shades. . . . In the beginning of each semester, express to the class that Communication is a very diverse field."

As suggested in the communication climate literature, students of color are looking for demonstrated commitment and personal involvement from their faculty, and this commitment and involvement comes through in our textbook selection, pedagogical tools, and classroom interaction. However, the students also pointed to issues outside of the classroom when assessing its intercultural climate. Specifically, they were also assessing the intercultural communication climate of the department.

In the organizational literature, Morrison and Von Glinow (1990) delineated three phases of workplace development in terms of cultural diversity. First-order affirmative action organizations are in compliance with the legally mandated racial diversity requirements only. Second-order affirmative action organizations are in compliance with legal mandates as well, but they focus more on supporting and retaining people of color. Multicultural organizations go further in this pursuit and recognize that racial, gender, or cultural diversity is an asset to an organization. Cox (1991) argued that a multicultural organization is characterized by full structural and informal integration of ethnic minorities, absence of prejudice and discrimination, low levels of intergroup conflict, and a pluralistic form of acculturation; that is, that "both minority and majority culture members adopt some norms of the other group"(35). The students of color in the Communication Theory course raised issues that approximate the concepts of structural and informal integration and pluralistic forms of acculturation.

For instance, students recognized problems with structural integration at the university and departmental levels:

■ "Nothing can be done because the school is not that diverse."

■ "[The university should] have professors and/or administrators of color present in abundance on campus."

■ "As a student of color, I am often discouraged at the number of [African Americans] that are in my classes. In some cases, I am the only black person in the entire class! [It] often makes me feel uncomfortable. Also, why is there only one African-American Communication teacher?"

An East Carolina University report on diversity, released in March 2000 by the Office of Research, Assessment and Testing, depicted an environment in which students of color were less satisfied socially and academically and possessed lower feelings of belonging than did white students. It seemed likely that contributions to their dissatisfaction were their experiences with prejudice and discrimination. According to the report, 38 percent of African-American students and 58 percent of white students reported hearing peers make racially offensive remarks at some point. Among all students, 16 percent reported hearing racially offensive remarks by faculty, staff, or administrators once or twice; 6 percent reported hearing such remarks three or more times. More than 40 percent of African-American students said that they felt discriminated against at the university, and 73 percent of them were likely to perceive race as the reason behind the discrimination. Although most students (85 percent) were reasonably comfortable befriending an "other," they were less comfortable dating outside of their race (31 percent). Moreover, 60 percent of the African-American students and 40 percent of the white students characterized their interracial friendships as superficial.

It is, perhaps, not surprising then that both the department and university were given an average performance ranking in addressing cultural diversity, and a lukewarm-to-warm climate assessment by the students of color surveyed for that project. Notwithstanding, the students noticed the university's recent efforts to improve the climate on campus. Said one student, "Many forums on campus hosted by minority groups and the university have been excellent. The Coffee in the Kitchen project is extremely beneficial to all students. I also enjoy presentations by the cultural awareness committee of the student union." This student was referring to the Chancellor's Initiative on Race — a year-long, collaborative effort that resulted in art, music, literature, speakers, and roundtable discussions and included faculty, staff, students, and community members. The activities afforded many opportunities for faculty to increase their knowledge and training and to demonstrate their commitment and involvement.

High-profile speakers offered training opportunities for faculty and students. For instance, ECU was visited by John Marshall, first African-American director of the U.S. Marshals Service; Jane Elliott, a nationally known speaker on prejudice; Dr. Bertie Berry, stand-up comic and expert on diversity; Dr. Mary Frances Berry, chair of the U.S. Civil Rights Commission and professor of American social thought at University of Pennsylvania; and Dr. Christopher Edley, senior adviser to President Clinton on race and a Harvard law professor. And "Diversity Yes!" was a series of brochures by the ECU Office of Equal Employment and Opportunity and the Department of Human Resources, with specific aims to increase faculty and staff knowledge on diversity.

Arts, culture, and holiday celebrations offered additional opportunities for faculty and students to get involved. Included were a performance by the Thespians of Diversity, a Pow Wow, a showcase of a gospel choir, a jazz concert honoring Duke Ellington, and a multicultural holiday celebration. Other awareness events dealt with "Living With the 'Other'" (adjusting to campus living), AIDS, sexual assault, Latino heritage, intercultural student leadership and peer mentoring, and racial profiling in the media. Future projects include the Internet Diversity Experience, a health initiative, and outreach efforts to local schools and other agencies. Finally, the three-phase "Coffee in the Kitchen" project recruited students, faculty, staff, and community members for focus groups and training on historical and present-day race-related issues.

The aforementioned events reinforce the notion of a systemic effort within an organization to become multicultural, as suggested in the organizational literature. We, as Communication professors and departments, are well-positioned to become involved in such efforts, and can improve the experience of students of color by doing so. Faculty involvement in these events can broaden faculty knowledge and training, which can inform their teaching. Encouraging student participation supplements course content and represents more active learning. Overall curriculum in Communication classrooms can be greatly enhanced by building such events into student assignments. For instance, students could help to create publications for the events, write for magazines or campus newspapers, critique the speakers, conduct their own research on race, or take on a race-related issue in a campus communication campaign. Assignments might ask students to reflect upon communication within their own culture or to learn about communication in another culture through community outreach projects or interpersonal interactions.

Communication faculty can further demonstrate their commitment to these issues by becoming personally involved in campus events as participants, planners, and critics. For instance, Interpersonal Communication scholars can help students discuss "superficial" interracial relationships; Media scholars could take on stereotypical images in the news or entertainment programming. Other strategies might include inviting Communication experts on race or diversity to campus or class, as guest lecturers or to team-teach classes.

Finally, for climate warming to take place, the efforts must be backed fully by "management." Thus, departmental policies, course offerings, and faculty recruitment efforts must support efforts by individual faculty members. In the Department of Communication and Broadcasting, for instance, we have adopted a language discrimination policy that simply states that we support the use of inclusive language by faculty and students in our classrooms. However, as seen in the students' comments, we must continue to improve our efforts if we are to warm the climate and develop into a multicultural organization.

OLD DOMINION UNIVERSITY

Old Dominion University (considered Virginia's international university) undertakes various formal and informal efforts to create warm, welcoming communication climates for all students. Similar to ECU, Old Dominion University (ODU) offers many programs for students and faculty targeted toward the goal of creating a learning environment that not only is welcoming but also values and celebrates diversity. (Some of these efforts can be viewed on the University's website at http://web.odu.edu/commthea.) For example, the Department of Communication and Theatre Arts runs an annual University-wide film festival that has been focusing on diversity in film and television. All faculty are supported to travel and study abroad.[1] Faculty can apply for funds to receive specific training in intercultural communication at places such as the Summer Institute for Intercultural Communication, in Portland, Oregon. Faculty can also apply for monies from the College of Arts and Letters to work on internationalizing their courses.

Among ODU's efforts are two successful activities unique to its Department of Communication. The initiatives might not immediately seem important tools for establishing warm, welcoming intercultural climates, but over time they have proven to be vital. First, the department supports an Undergraduate Teaching Assistant (UTA) program, in which undergraduates are provided coursework and experience in university teaching (see Socha 1998). Over the years, African-American undergraduates have been strongly encouraged to participate in the program (and many have). These teaching assistants become visible role models for all students, but for African-American students in particular, UTAs are visions of success. These best and brightest students have gone on to graduate school, and some now occupy faculty positions at universities.

The other subtle but significant example is the effort taken in the department to help all Communication majors discover their personal intellectual interests in the discipline of Communication Studies through multiple courses in Communication Research Methods. Students in undergraduate Communication Research Methods courses are encouraged to explore their own ideas by proposing and undertaking original research studies. Over the years, students of color in these methods courses invariably have chosen to explore racism, prejudice, and other communication issues of societal and personal significance. The import of these research projects stretches well beyond the sequence of courses.

For example, one Old Dominion University alum from Malaysia later went on to examine intercultural embarrassment in her M.A. thesis (see Ganesan 1998) and is pursuing a Ph.D. in Communication focusing on culture. An African-American alum, who recently earned a Ph.D. in Higher Education, returned to share with the Communication faculty his first published article on the relationship between black urban communities and universities (see Rowley 2000). The department is proud to have had a hand in Professor Ganesan's and Professor Rowley's development.

These concrete, but often invisible examples of making room at the table for a wide range of people and ideas are among the hallmarks of a welcoming communication environment that fosters genuine dialogue among diverse human beings.

Conclusion

It is clear that feeling welcomed, included, and genuinely respected goes a long way toward bridging the gaps of cultural diversity. This essay has emphasized that the communication climate is a subtle but potent factor in the success of all students, but particularly students of color. Faculty who show interest in ethnic culture, read beyond the boundaries of their own culture of origin and make certain that their students do so as well, and most important communicate their interest and understanding can serve as empowering forces for students of color.

Note

1. One of us (Socha) was supported, in part, through the ODU Office of International Programs and his University Professor Award funds to travel to South Africa with a delegation of faculty from the National Communication Association. This experience was incredibly valuable in helping to bridge the knowledge gap between American and South African Communication Studies faculty.

References

Andrews, P.H. (1983). "Creating a Supportive Climate for Teacher Growth: Developing Graduate Students as Teachers." *Communication Quarterly* 31: 259-265.

Cose, E. (1993). *The Rage of a Privileged Class.* New York: HarperPerennial.

Cox, T.H. (1991). "The Multicultural Organization." *Academy of Management Executives* 5: 34-47.

Ellis, D., and A. Fisher. (1994). *Small Group Decision Making.* New York: McGraw-Hill.

Falcione, R.L. (1974). "Communication Climate and Satisfaction With Immediate Supervision." *Journal of Applied Communication Research* 2: 13-20.

Fink, E.L., and S. Chen. (1995). "A Galileo Analysis of Organizational Climate." *Human Communication Research* 21: 494-521.

Follert, V. (1980). "Communication Climate: A Theoretical Framework for Accessibility." *Journal of Applied Communication Research* 8: 91-100.

Ganesan, P. (1998). *Communication to Reduce Embarrassment Between Individualistic and Collectivistic Cultures.* Norfolk, VA: Old Dominion University, Department of Humanities.

Gibb, J. (1960). "Defensive Communication." *Journal of Communication* 11: 141-148.

Hall, R.M., and B.R. Sandler. (1982). *Project on the Status and Education of Women.* Washington, DC: Association of American Colleges.

———. (1984). *Out of the Classroom: A Chilly Campus Climate for Women?* Washington, DC: Association of American Colleges.

Hays, E.R. (1970). "Ego-Threatening Classroom Communication: A Factor Analysis of Student Perceptions." *Speech Teacher* 19: 43-49.

Henderson, G. (1999). *Our Souls to Keep: Black/White Relations in America.* Yarmouth, ME: Intercultural Press.

Morrison, A.M., and M.A. Von Glinow. (1990). "Women and Minorities in Management." *American Psychologist* 45: 200-208.

Office of Research Assessment and Testing. (March 2000). *Diversity at ECU: Student Perspectives.* Greenville, NC: East Carolina University.

Rosenfeld, L.B. (1983). "Communication Climate and Coping Mechanisms in the College Classroom." *Communication Education* 32: 167-174.

———, and M.W. Jarrard. (1985). "The Effects of Female and Male College Professors on Students' Descriptions of Classroom Climate." *Communication Education* 34: 205-213.

Rowley, L.L. (2000). "The Relationship Between Universities and Black Urban Communities: The Clash of Two Cultures." *The Urban Review* 32(1): 45-65.

Socha, T. (1998). "Development of an Undergraduate Teaching Assistant Program in Communication." *Journal of the Association for Communication Administration* 27: 77-83.

———, and J. Beigle. (1999). "Toward Improving Life at the Crossroads: Family Communication Education and Multicultural Competence." In *Communication, Race, and Family: Exploring Communication in Black, White, and Biracial Families,* edited by T.J. Socha and R. Diggs, pp. 209-227. Mahwah, NJ: Erlbaum.

Trickett, E.J., and R.H. Moos. (1973). "The Social Environment of Junior High and High School Classrooms." *Journal of Educational Psychology* 65: 93-102.

Coloring the Communication Experience

Using Personal Narratives to (Re)define Success of Students of Color in Communication

Olga Idriss Davis, Jacqueline M. Martinez, and Thomas K. Nakayama

As authors, we bring different backgrounds and experiences together for our work on this essay. As an African American, a Mexican American, and an Asian American who teach and conduct research in performance studies, intercultural communication, and rhetoric, respectively, we bring an array of differences together in our professional lives at Arizona State University. Despite these many differences, however, we have come to recognize certain common circumstances within the Communication discipline generally that we think discourage students of color from continuing in Communication courses. In this essay we shall explore these circumstances and offer suggestions to remedy them, specifically focusing on the advantages of using personal narratives as pedagogy. Our objective is to help create a curricular and attitudinal context that can address the concerns and needs of students of color. Moreover, we shall argue that by creating such a context we improve the curriculum and discipline of Communication itself.

There are several ways in which the Communication curriculum tends to exclude the experiences and concerns of students of color. One of the most serious problems is its tendency to reduce "communication" to mean information located within a narrow context of the presumed norms of American culture, which is white. Moreover, few Communication courses take seriously the student's experiential knowledge of communication, community, and culture — a difference that is particularly relevant for students of color. In Public Speaking classes, for example, the general presumption is that students shall learn to speak within a frame that values certain kinds of knowledge to the exclusion of others. What counts as evidence, what constitutes arguments and effective organization are all culturally specific to a white cultural logic. With these presumptions in place, communication itself is reduced to a tool that is disconnected from the particular cultural norms lived and experienced by students of color but not by white students. Hence, white students more easily accept and identify with the frames presented in the Public Speaking course than do students of color.

A more radical approach would foreground that students already speak in a variety of public and private contexts and have specific cultural and experiential knowledge about effective communication within those contexts. Rather than impose a narrow and limited standard of "effective" communication, such an approach would examine the knowledge and understanding that students already possess in their home communities and cultures. This would shift the context from a presumed standard of public oratory to the fact of public and private speaking as it is already present in students' lives.

A similar situation exists in Intercultural Communication classes, where the emphasis is on the correct imitation of the daily habits of communication within a given culture. The presumption here is that successful intercultural communication is accomplished by learning the dominant norms of communication behavior of a given culture so as to be able to imitate them in actual interaction with persons from that culture. A more radical approach to intercultural communication would foreground that every person is *in-cultured*; and rather than teach a ready set of culturally specific communication behaviors, it would examine the ways in which their own cultures are already present in students' communication behaviors. With this approach to Intercultural Communication, students must examine the ways in which their own conscious experience is itself already driven by culture. To our predominantly white American students, such an approach is shocking, because American culture is individualistic and conceives of persons as autonomous. American (white) culture itself would have us believe that we are not in-cultured. Recognizing how everyone is in-cultured creates a much better foundation for understanding across cultures.

The communication experience in many of our university courses is based on the perspective of Western logic and white American standards of normative human communication behavior. Such perspectives, whether intentional or not, negate the historical and lived experiences of students of color. One way of coloring the communication experience is to use personal narratives so as to foreground the experiential knowledge that students of color and others outside of the white mainstream bring to their classroom study. Coloring the experience of communication challenges the dominant notions and assumptions about why students of color fail to participate successfully and achieve as Communication majors, and instead highlights the ways that the Communication curriculum has failed students of color. We argue that by *coloring* the communication experience, our gateway courses become a context of shared experience that embellishes, enhances, and enriches for all students the Communication major's success. In so doing, the gateway courses, irrespective of their titles, are transformed in ways that redefine the Communication classroom as a safe space for interrogating cultural norms and therefore also transforming lives.

Engaging Students of Color and Transforming Communication

Central to recruiting and retaining students of color in our gateway courses are the notions of *engagement* and *transformation*. By engagement, we mean creating a curriculum that teaches theory by talking from community. The historical, as well as contemporary, meaning of belonging to a community has tremendous significance for members of marginalized communities. Students of color are no exception. Communities are places of safety, but also rich sources of vernacular knowledge that give life to cultural identities. In our experiences with white students, community has little meaning to them. They prefer to stress the importance of individuality and autonomy. The discipline of Communication Studies has not been able to reflect these profound differences in the ways that people see themselves in relation to communities. Our relationships with communities form an inherent part of the complex relationships between culture and communication. The predominant norms of mainstream (white) American culture create an orientation away from recognizing this key aspect of communication particularly as it is lived in the lives of students of color.

By transformation, we refer to the ways in which narrative discourse can be a liberating, consciousness-raising experience of locating self in the meaning-making process of being in the world, and conversely of recognizing culture's meaning-making influence upon us. Because the histories of many cultural groups are not taught as part of the national story — "The History" of the United States as opposed to the histor*ies* of the United States — learning to open space for these muted narratives is central to a different consciousness and understanding about the world. Black feminist scholar Barbara Christian explains the role of personal narrative as epistemological in cultural experiences of the *other:* "People of color have always theorized — but in forms quite different from the Western form of abstract logic. . . . Our theorizing . . . is often in narrative forms, in the stories we create . . . in dynamic rather than fixed ideas" (1989: 336).

One of the major reasons that students of color seldom become Communication majors is because they see communication theory as not being rooted in the cultural practices of their everyday lives. Other Communication scholars such as Lawrence Grossberg (1997), in his book *Bringing It All Back Home*, see the operations of hegemony in our discipline, and reveal the ways in which Communication Studies operates as a master narrative. The lived experiences of students of color are often obfuscated in Communication courses, because their narratives are unheard and they are seen as inarticulate in critically expressing the happenings of their world. Contrary to that notion is the challenge of finding ways to create identification with and among our students of color while deconstructing the practice of hegemonic curricula. Through personal or experiential knowledge, students of color are engaged in talking about community and the identities and self-understandings they generate. This sort of engagement becomes the training ground, if you will, for personal and social transformation. A liberatory pedagogy in Communication courses can offer ways in which students deal with ethical concerns grounded in an epistemology that provides a practical process for change including experience, reflection, judgment, and action (James 1993).

Performance and Context in the Communication Experience of Students of Color

The notion of the classroom as a safe space for redefining success of students of color is a vital concept to consider. "Safe space," a term used by black feminist scholar Patricia Hill Collins (1991), refers to the space of liberatory struggle, which values marginalized social realities. This liberatory space opens the possibility for negotiating life performances and everyday social practices. The Communication classroom can be such a space for success of students of color by offering a context for invention, discovery, knowledge, and meaning-making in the cultural discourse of everyday life. The classroom offers a dynamic site of reflexivity between context and power relations in personal narrative.

As several critical educators and black feminist scholars argue, the critical classroom provides interesting ways to rethink issues of identity and subject formation (Freire 1996; hooks 1990; James 1993; McLaren 1994). Ogbu (1999) and others suggest that a critical pedagogy in which the classroom transforms the discursive and institutional formations that reproduce white, patriarchal, and Anglo supremacy is a classroom in which students are engaged in creating a culture of change. Creating a culture of change requires a recognition of the ways in which we are in-cultured and how we therefore perpetuate culture in our communication practices. Once we recognize how we perpetuate culture in our own communication practices, we then have the capacity to alter the terms in which we perpetuate culture and our location within it.

Change refers to challenging traditional humanism, or the master narrative, which embraces only the cultural values of white, Western, male hegemony — a culture wherein the teacher is the omniscient, rather than the catalyst, for the exchange of meaning-making among students and teacher. Effective change that promotes success of students of color comes from students on the margins who resist the master narrative with rhetorical and performative strategies other than the master's tools (Lorde 1984) found under the rubric of argumentation, empiricism-positivism, and so on. In order for students to see a difference in our discipline, they must first *see* a discipline that reflects their culture, experience, and activism for change. The Communication classroom that engages in performative strategies of resistance holds academic authority accountable when the cultures of students of color are ignored. Thus, a redefinition of the classroom and of the objective of Communication curriculum encourages a new vision for gateway courses to embrace students of color.

Personal Narrative as a Construct for Success of Students of Color

It is no revelation that personal narrative is a viable methodological tool for the study of communication (Langellier 1989; Peterson and Langellier 1997). According to Carilli (1998), "personal narrative has the potential to transcend all quantitative and qualitative research methods, and stand alone, giving epistemological information and insight into the communication process" (232). While traditional scholars might argue against the efficacy of personal narrative, it is essential to embrace its value for the success of students of color. As explained by Hantzis (1995), the personal narrative calls into question the relationship between identity and experience. Grossberg (1997) argues for a more experientially based paradigm within which to analyze the ordinary and extraordinary ways people use, challenge, and interact with culture in their daily lives. The dialectical tension between the personal narrative of lived experience and the master narrative of the discipline establishes a relationship of oppression, because the master narrative delegitimates the lived experiences of people of color. It simultaneously creates resistance, because students of color recognize (even preconsciously) that there is no space for their own experiences and cultures to be recognized, much less utilized as a pedagogical resource.

Through the performance of narrating lived experience, knowledge becomes a sharing of understanding rather than an expression of ego involvement (Carilli 1998). The personal narrative is liberating discourse — offering students of color a space to write their voices into existence, to own the marginalized, contested spaces of race, class, gender, ethnicity, or sexuality. Narrative as a liberating and transformative text provides the context of ownership that students of color need in order to feel connected to our discipline.

Experiential Knowledge as Pedagogy

Personal narratives are gaining more recognition as important communicative modes for research and teaching. Yet, many teachers shy away from featuring personal narratives as a primary mode of classroom work because of the difficulty of evaluating personal narrative writing. As teachers, it is obviously inappropriate for us to evaluate the content of a student's experience. Some students will have had life experiences that give them greater insight about their own personal, social, and cultural lives. Others will not. Some students will have a more natural literary style that is well suited to personal narrative work. Others will not. As teachers, we will necessarily relate better to the experiences of some students over others. None of these differences is a legitimate basis for evaluating the personal narrative produced by students in our classes.

Still another set of problems exists with personal narrative writing and performing as a pedagogical tool: the tendency to think that "because I experienced it this way, it is true." If we allow such a notion to remain present in our classroom work, we will create a context in which students are fighting for the accuracy and validity of their lived experiences.

Despite these very serious problems, we advocate the use of personal narratives as a tool for foregrounding experiential knowledge in the Communication classroom. If we approach communication as something that is embodied and in-cultured, then we can shift our taken-for-granted notion that personal narratives are a unique self-expression and instead accept the idea that what students actually come to experience is itself a manifestation of their particular location in a cultural, social, and historical time and place. The "truth" of each student's narrative is thus not a competing reality with others' but one that begs the questions "How did I get here?" "How did I come to say and experience *this?*" Rather than simply assign personal causes and effects to their experiences, we can investigate the very cultural, social, and historical terrain in which certain experiences have come to be what they are.

The writing of personal narratives themselves requires that students engage in a process of sharing their self-understanding. In that process, teachers encouraged students to lessen the investment of their egos in the actual narrative they produce and instead explore their community-based commonalities that validate their individual realities and shared social locations. In addition, students can be encouraged to explore a number of different accounts of their experiences. By rewriting one another's narratives, students explore the other cultural influences that the authors themselves might miss.

Liberatory Pedagogy in Practice

One example of this notion of liberatory pedagogy is demonstrated in a Performance Studies course at Arizona State University taught by one of us (Davis) that explores the performative nature of black female slave narratives. The notion of *engagement* created space for discussing the historical and contemporary contributions of black women's liberation struggles. Readings about the 19-century life of black women stimulated and challenged students to expand their experiential base. Reflections were expressed in journals, through essay papers, on field trips to museums exhibiting historical images of black women, and in small-group work where insights were shared. Considering dominant discursive structures and norms of the period, students wrote personal narratives from the perspective of personae in the pre-emancipatory period of American history. The critical writing of personal narrative experience was a way to inform, challenge, and resist the nexus of racist-(hetero)sexist-classist ideology of contemporary American thought and action to which the students had become victims or perpetrators or both. Through performance they learned about the self as a communication activist for change and educated audience member — experimenting with creating ways to redefine worlds, freedom, and liberation struggles of not only the 19th century but also, more important for their world, the 21st century.

Finally, ethical action came about by judging master narratives enculturated within institutionalized constructs of power and control. Students of color as well as white students located themselves in the continuum of history through the meaning of personal narrative. Transformation occurred as students *re-encountered* themselves, not as Communication majors and minors merely enrolled in a course, but as historically situated selves engaging and interacting in human experience in which they *entered into* the social reality of racism, (hetero)sexism, and classism. As a result, performance through personal narrative offered a space for each student to interrogate his or her social, cultural, and ethical responsibilities within the context of social relations of power while critically assessing the dialectic of social justice. It is our contention that the practice of personal narrative in Communication's gateway courses can offer a way to engage and transform students of color. By making space for self-reflection, for thinking and organizing to resist oppression, and for demonstrating communication as a pedagogy for self-development, we encourage students of color to become majors based on inclusive ethics and an active commitment to community liberation.

What's at Stake for Students of Color and for the Communication Discipline?

The history of Communication is not one that reflects sustained interrogation and understanding of how disempowered and marginalized cultural groups might speak and be heard. The strategic selection of the "roots" of rhetoric in ancient Greece reinforces a focus on dominant groups and domination. Plato and Aristotle, for example, came from privileged classes and did not reflect upon how "others" might engage rhetoric. The study of public speaking through the 19th and much of the 20th century continued to focus on the ways that white men might speak. It is only very recently that we as a discipline have turned sustained attention to the communication experiences of white women and, subsequently, even less attention to experiences of people of color.

The contemporary Communication curriculum needs to turn its attention more seriously to the realities of living in an increasingly multicultural society and global community. At the heart of this communication problematic is the question of how we might listen to others with very different cultural experiences and realities. Very little research has been done on how white people, for example, listen to people of color. Donald Rubin's (1998) studies on how white students hear accents from instructors with Asian features are only the beginning of the kind of exploration that we need to understand the ways that whites invoke communication strategies to dismiss the voices of others. Marsha Houston's (1997) work on white women and black women opens up important discussions about differences in communication styles that thwart understanding. Both authors reveal ways in which the normative (white) conditions of communication preclude genuine understanding across cultural differences.

While we advocate for the use of personal narratives in the Communication curriculum, we also recognize that not everyone will listen to the voices of others. This is the central quandary of communication in a multicultural society. Yet, personal narratives offer a significant first step in helping us to begin understanding the role that communication might play, as well as the problems to be confronted, in the bridging of cultural differences. So long as the Communication curriculum focuses on the assumption that our study is race-blind, we reinforce an assumption that communicators are white. Whether in interpersonal interaction or the public-speaking context, we make a serious error if we continue to ignore the reality of cultural diversity. Not only do we underprepare our white students for life in the 21st century, but we communicate to our students of color that Communication Studies is not for them.

Students of color must see that a Communication major offers liberatory strategies for creating identity and performing change. It is imperative that they see the study of human communication as a way to talk to and teach one another about the different social lives and cultural experiences each of us brings to our interactions. In this way, the discipline is advocating something much like what Maria Lugones describes as "world"-traveling. As she puts it,

> affirm this practice as skillful, creative, rich, enriching, and, given certain circumstances, as a loving way of being and living. I recognize that much of our traveling is done unwillfully to hostile white/Anglo 'worlds.' . . . Racism has a vested interest in obscuring and devaluing the complex skills involved in it. (1989: 275)

We all have to start traveling across cultural worlds. The Communication curriculum is one place where we should begin.

References

Carilli, T. (1998). "Verbal Promiscuity or Healing Art? Writing the Creative/Performative Personal Narrative." In *The Future of Performance Studies: Visions and Revisions*, edited by S. Dailey, pp. 232-236. Annandale, VA: National Communication Association.

Christian, B. (1989). "The Race for Theory." In *Making Face, Making Soul/Haciendo Caras: Creative and Critical Perspectives by Women of Color*, edited by G. Anzaldúa, pp. 335-345. San Francisco: Aunt Lute Foundation.

Collins, P.H. (1991). *Black Feminist Thought*. New York: Routledge.

Freire, P. (1996). *Pedagogy of the Oppressed.* New York: Continuum.

Grossberg, L. (1997). *Bringing It All Back Home: Essays on Cultural Studies.* Durham, NC: Duke University Press.

Hantzis, D.M. (1995). "Performing Experience(s)/Shiftings to Self." Paper presented at the Speech Communication Association Convention, San Antonio, Texas.

Houston, M. (1997). "When Black Women Talk With White Women: Why Dialogues Are Difficult." In *Our Voices: Essays in Culture, Ethnicity, and Communication,* edited by A. González, M. Houston, and V. Chen, pp. 187-194. Los Angeles: Roxbury.

hooks, b. (1990). *Yearning: Race, Gender, and Cultural Politics.* Boston: South End Press.

James, J. (1993). "Teaching Theory, Talking Community." In *Spirit, Space & Survival: African American Women in (White) Academe,* edited by J. James and R. Farmer, pp. 118-135. New York: Routledge.

Langellier, K. (1989). "Personal Narratives: Perspectives on Theory and Research." *Text and Performance Quarterly* 9(4): 243-276.

Lorde, A. (1984). *Sister Outsider: Essays and Speeches.* New York: The Crossing Press.

Lugones, M. (1989). "Playfulness, 'World'-Traveling, and Loving Perception." In *Women, Knowledge, and Reality: Explorations in Feminist Philosophy,* edited by A. Garry and M. Pearsall, pp. 275-290. New York: Routledge.

McLaren, P. (1994). *Life in Schools.* White Plains, NY: Longman.

Ogbu, J. (1999). "Beyond Language: Ebonics, Proper English, and Identity in Black-American Speech Community." *American Educational Research* 36(2): 147-162.

Peterson, E., and K. Langellier. (1997). "The Politics of Personal Narrative Methodology." *Text and Performance Quarterly* 17: 135-152.

Rubin, D.L. (1998). "Help! My Professor (or Doctor or Boss) Doesn't Talk English!" In *Readings in Cultural Contexts,* edited by J.N. Martin, T.K. Nakayama, and L.A. Flores, pp. 149-160. Mountain View, CA: Mayfield.

Difference Is Not Disorder

Diagnosis in the Basic Communication Course

Cheryl D. Gunter

Among their responsibilities, instructors of Basic Communication courses (for my purposes, those in which students learn to research, outline, write, deliver, critique, and analyze the audience for various forms of public presentations) must formulate evaluation criteria for a diverse assortment of learning tasks. That formulation of what constitutes successful completion should be grounded in a consideration of students' presenting communication patterns. Some students will present with what the Communication Disorders discipline considers "standard" dialects; some with what are considered "nonstandard" dialects *(communication differences)*. Still other students will present with communication patterns inconsistent with either standard or nonstandard dialectal variations — that is, *communication disorders*. Any time a student communicates in a manner different from the "cultural standard," the instructor's first task is to discern whether that student's communication pattern is a *difference* or a *disorder*. The next task is to formulate an appropriate response to that pattern in evaluation of student work, by implementing procedures and criteria that accept variations in communication pattern within the parameters of excellence.

Obviously, not all students who present with communication differences or disorders will be students of color; and not all students of color will present with a difference or disorder. But some likely will. It is for the benefit of those students that I offer below ideas for differentiating between communication *differences* and *disorders*, then discuss some issues that arise related to appropriate evaluation of student performance. The essay's discussion is organized on three key questions: What is the communication status of the student? How could the presence of a communication difference affect the performance of that student in the Basic Communication course? and What model of evaluation of student performance is now in place in the Basic Communication course?

1. What Is the Student's Communication Status?

As an initial step, the instructor of a Basic Communication course should be able to compare and contrast the central traits of the variations of communication with which students of color might present: standard American dialect, nonstandard American dialect (communication difference), and communication disorder.

DIALECT

Each person who learns a language, such as American English, learns a particular variation of rules of that language, referred to as a *dialect* (Owens 1992). Some persons with dialects have learned just the one language, the rules of which have been influenced by particular social, personal, and residential factors. This describes the dialects spoken by students for whom English is a first language. Some persons with dialects have learned more than one language, and to the influences on their first language have been added influence(s) of the second (or more) language(s); this would describe the English dialect of a nonnative student. Students of color could present with dialects of either variation, depending on their individual life circumstances.

Linguistic and Paralinguistic Aspects. A person's dialect influences multiple linguistic aspects of communication. An *accent* is the influence of a dialect on the production of speech sounds. But an accent is just one example. Another aspect is *topic choice*; that is, different dialects can vary in their parameters for which topics are appropriate for discussion in particular contexts and with particular conversational partners. A dialect can also influence *word choice*; for instance, students with different dialects could refer to the same item, person, or incident using an assortment of different terms. *Sentence construction* can vary among dialects, in terms of the order of modifiers and referents. A dialect also can influence *narrative production*; that is, a preference for topical order versus temporal order, and the emphasizing of various aspects of the narrative to the relative exclusion of others. And, of course, a dialect can influence *social interactions*, affecting the directness of comments and the distribution of conversational turns.

A dialect also can influence paralinguistic aspects of communication. Dialects vary in their *rate of speech, duration of words, intonation of voice, stress of words, and other temporal parameters* of communication.

Nonlinguistic Aspects. A dialect influences nonlinguistic aspects of communication too. One area of influence is *kinesics*; that is, body movements and facial positions of students with particular dialects could reflect their preference for a particular level of exuberance or expression. Another is *proxemics*, or the intimate, personal, and social distances students maintain as reflections of their values toward relative status and relationships. And *chronemics*, or attitudes toward time. Even the decor and other visible structures that students impose on their immediate environments can reflect dialectal influences.

STANDARD AND NONSTANDARD DIALECTS

Instructors also should differentiate between *standard* and *nonstandard* dialects of a language. Within American English specifically, particular variations of the language have been designated as "standard" dialects. The genesis of such standard dialects, as Hegde (1991) notes, can be as the version of language of the people who live in prestigious geographical areas, the people of a particular race, the people of a particular educational level, the people of wealth, the people in power, or even the most people — or some combination of these and additional factors. These "standard" dialects have been presented in textbooks as the formal or ideal variations of a language. Other variations of the language have been designated as "nonstandard" (also known as *vernacular*) dialects.

Among native speakers of English, there are dialects based on social factors (such as economic level) and personal factors (such as educational level), as well as those based on residential factors. Some well-known dialects are *midwestern, southwestern, southeastern*, and *northeastern* (based on broad areas) and *Boston, Appalachian, New York*, and *Bayou* (based on more localized areas). Then, among speakers of English as a second language, there are the numerous dialects that result from the influences on English of various African, Latino, Asian, and European first languages.

COMMUNICATION DIFFERENCES

As instructors become more familiar with the patterns of particular standard and nonstandard dialects, they should reflect on the interpretation imposed on the presence of such patterns. During the describing and differentiating of various dialects, some authors have equated "nonstandard" with "*sub*standard" and admonished instructors to view nonstandard dialects as conditions to be corrected (Warren-Leubecker and Bohannon 1985); that view remains prevalent in some circles. But in others, the discussion of dialects has evolved, resulting in a reconsideration of "nonstandard" dialects as *communication differences.* That is, students who present with nonstandard dialects are viewed as possessing language patterns that fall within the parameters of normal communication. For example, Edwards (1991) asserts that a "deficit" view of nonstandard language is incorrect, and that diverse variations of a language that have developed within language communities all can be considered accurate and capable of expression of communication functions. To reject this "deficit" view is crucial in our quest to provide the best possible conditions for success for students of color.

To the degree that America's increasing diversity is reflected in college enrollments, instructors of the Basic Communication course can expect to encounter increasing numbers of students who present with communication differences. According to the 1990 United States Census, the native-born population is some 12 percent African-American, 8 percent Latino-American, 3 percent Asian-American, and 1 percent Native-American (some of whom likely speak in dialects considered "nonstandard"); an additional 20 million persons are not native born (and likely learned English as a second language). Overall, some 14 percent of the population has a dominant language other than English.

Instructors would be well-advised to become familiar with the central traits of the dialects of both native and nonnative speakers of English. Increasing numbers of publications exist documenting the distinctive traits of particular dialects. Hulit and Howard (1997) and McLaughlin (1998) provide clear and concise overviews of the central traits of common dialects of native speakers of English. Descriptions of Spanish-influenced English are available from Kayser (1995) and Taylor (1986). Other authors describe particular variations; for instance, Penalosa (1995) summarizes the traits of Chicano English, and Wolfram (1995) the traits of Puerto Rican English. For Asian-influenced dialects, Cheng (1987, 1995) discusses Chinese English; Takada and Hanahan (1995) discuss Japanese English; and Hoi and Bich (1995) Vietnamese English. At the same time, however, instructors should remember that common features of communication cross over dialectal boundaries, and that within particular dialects students can present diverse interactional patterns. The point is that instructors should interpret all overviews of dialectal traits as general but not as stereotypical descriptions.

COMMUNICATION DISORDERS

To this point, I have addressed variations on normal communication (*communication differences*). In contrast, the skills of students with *communication disorders* do not fall within the parameters of normal communication. That is, the variations in such students' communication cannot be accounted for by the presence of a particular dialect. In general, students with communication disorders share one or more of the following traits: (1) communication that results from or leads to physical harm to the speech production mechanism, (2) communication that distorts the intention or information to be shared, (3) communication that is so distinctive that it draws undue attention or reaction to the student, (4) communication that diminishes the self-concept or creates an inappropriate emotional state in the student (Van Riper and Emerick 1990). Communication disorders can be mild (i.e., trained clinicians would notice them, but no one else) to severe (i.e., anyone would notice and react to them).

Research on the incidence of communication disorders in the United States has centered on children and older adults (see, e.g., Fein 1983; Gillespie and Cooper 1973; Leske 1981). But one overview has looked at the incidence of communication disorders in first-year university students. In it, Coulton (1986) reviewed speech screenings of more than 30,000 such students from 1971 to 1983, and estimated that 1.4 percent of them had disorders in speech sounds (various errors in the production or combination of speech sounds), 0.7 percent had voice disorders (problems related to vocal characteristics such as loudness, pitch level, or quality), and 0.3 percent of them had a disorder in fluency (abnormal speech rates or stutter or clutter behaviors that diminished the speech rhythm). He did not assess the presence of disorders of language; however, other research has estimated that 6.2 percent of pre-university adolescent students have language disorders

(Marge 1972). From these estimates, instructors can expect some 9 percent of university students to present with a communication disorder of unknown cause (idiopathic), who due to the nature of their disorder might or might not receive accommodation from campus disability services offices. (Additional students could present with communication disorders that have co-occurred with a disability such as deafness or blindness, and so are classified in their records as "disabled" and do receive services.)

Because this essay focuses on the dialects of students of color and whether those dialects are within the parameters of normal communication, I won't discuss the broader picture of communication disorders here. However, instructors of the Basic Communication course would do well to become familiar with which traits should prompt a clinical evaluation of a potential communication disorder — such as a stutter, non-normal voice production, or various other disorders that are independent of dialect.

At the same time that instructors focus on what *is* a communication disorder, they should also be focusing on what *is not* a disorder. A position paper from the American Speech-Language-Hearing Association summarizes the status of dialects:

> No dialectal variety of English or any other language is a disorder or pathological form of speech or language. Each social dialect is adequate as a functional and efficient variety of English. Each serves a communication function as well as a social solidarity function. It maintains the communication network and the social construct of the community of speakers who use it. (1983: 23-24)

ASSESSING COMMUNICATION STATUS

An instructor can ascertain the communication status of his or her students in collaboration with professionals from the discipline of Communication Disorders. In some cases, Communication Studies even shares an academic department with Communication Disorders. Even when they don't, campuses with a concern for student success will provide a home for the clinical services central to the Communication Disorders discipline, often in schools of Health, Communication, or Education. Clinicians from Communication Disorders would welcome such collaborative endeavors to stimulate discussion of communication issues, advance information on communication norms, and provide clinical services.

One model for the provision of clinical services is the assessment of the communication status of *all* students in the Basic Communication course prior to or at the start of the course as an inherent element of it. In such an assessment model, Communication Disorders professionals, in consultation with Communication Studies instructors, would determine which students (1) clearly *did* have skills within the scope of normal communication, (2) clearly *did not* have skills within the scope of normal communication, and (3) needed further evaluation.

This model allows the instructor to recommend appropriate accommodation, remediation, or both, based on each student's particular communication needs.

To schedule assessment prior to enrollment offers distinct advantages. Students are familiar with the concept of placement assessments from other academic areas, such as music or mathematics, so participation in a communication assessment would not be alien to them. Should the assessment reveal the presence of a communication *difference*, the instructor would be aware in advance of the need to establish evaluation criteria that accept variations of communication within established parameters of excellence; should the assessment reveal a *disorder*, the instructor would anticipate not only appropriate accommodations but also remediation activities, and could work with the student to seek clinical services.

A drawback to the approach is the resources it requires. Communication Disorders professionals conduct screenings of oral communication skills in their clinical practice, and some Communication Studies instructors include screening as a part of their initial overviews of the skill levels of students in their classes. The screening process involves the broad determination of whether a student appears to clearly present normal or non-normal communication skills or is in need of additional in-depth evaluation to determine the presence of a disorder. Even if a screening focused on speech-production skills and did not include the broader area of language skills, each interaction would take five to 15 minutes. And, since one aim of the assessment would be to identify both differences *and* disorders, professionals from the disciplines of both Communication Studies and Communication Disorders would need to participate collaboratively. If conditions precluded assessing students' communication status before enrollment, the instructor could conduct the assessment early in the semester, perhaps as one of a series of required class exercises. But the advance approach is still preferable, especially should a disorder be discovered that requires remediation. Also, sometimes the revelation of a communication disorder after the course has begun can negatively affect the student's attitude toward participation in course activities. Then, too, the pressures of time constraints in such a schedule can increase the chances for misinterpretations of assessment results.

For these reasons, some instructors prefer an alternate model of reactive, rather than proactive, service provision — that of assessment only when the instructor becomes concerned about the communication status of specific students. While this as-needed model reduces the drain on resources and allows more personalized attention during assessment to individual students, the potential benefits of having their communication status assessed is lost for the rest of the students in the basic course.

ISSUES TO ADDRESS

Whether all students have their communication status assessed, or only those who present with particular cause for concern, the intention remains the same: for the instructor to determine whether a student possesses standard, nonstandard, or disordered communication skills. That determination necessitates the addressing of five issues:

1. Is the student's pattern of communication consistent with a particular dialect? In an assessment, evaluators would collect information about the student's patterns of communication, then compare these with the patterns of standard and nonstandard dialects. Should a student's linguistic, paralinguistic, and nonlinguistic aspects of communication be consistent with the rules of a particular nonstandard dialect, then the student's skills would be described as *different*. However, if these aspects are inconsistent with any rules — that is, not even one intact rule-based communication system has developed — then the student's skills would be described as *disordered* and in need of intervention. (The aim of that intervention would be for the student to become capable of consistently comprehending and producing at least one dialect, whether standard or nonstandard.) Even if a student appeared to possess a dialect, the evaluators would proceed with additional queries to determine whether the student used that dialect for the most productive interactions.

2. Does the student's pattern of communication interfere with information or intention? Next, evaluators would assess whether particular aspects of the student's communication — even if consistent with the rules of a dialect — interfered with how well an audience could understand the student. For instance, might an audience unfamiliar with the dialect's rules for speech sound production find it difficult to understand the student's articulation of some words? Or might an audience unfamiliar with the dialect's particular idiomatic phrases find it difficult to understand the implication of those phrases? Evaluators also would assess whether particular aspects of the student's communication interfered with how well an audience could understand the student's intention. For instance, might an audience unfamiliar with the dialect's rules for sentence construction find it difficult to interpret the intention of a statement? Or might an audience unfamiliar with the facial expressions common in the student's culture misinterpret the connection of the expressions to the oral information? While evaluators would be hesitant to label these differences as disorders, the instructor could at least alert such a student to the potential of particular behaviors to interfere with communication, so that the student could account for these differences in his or her analysis of the audience for a speech.

3. Does the pattern of communication call undue attention to the student? Evaluators would assess whether particular aspects of the student's communication — even when consistent with the rules of a dialect — called undue attention to the student. Some amount of attention from other students is to be expected, as with distinctive personal traits; evaluators, however focus on the *nature* of that attention. Is the attention positive and indicative of curiosity toward the student and his or her distinctive cultural experience? Then the instructor can use that curiosity as the basis for course interactions that celebrate diversity among the class. Is the attention less than positive? Then the instructor must ascertain the locus of responsibility for that reaction and, as before, address the discrepancies with appropriate pedagogy.

    4. Does the pattern of communication evoke unpleasant or unproductive reactions in the student? Evaluators would assess the student's own reactions to possessing a communication difference. Sometimes common communication apprehension can account for a student's unpleasant or unproductive reactions, in which case the instructor has available the usual assortment of models of intervention for apprehension. If, however, the communication difference is in fact the basis, then the instructor and student would need to explore the student's eventual communication aims, and decide which educational means would best allow the student to achieve those aims, as well as explore values associated with the communication experience.

    5. Does the pattern of communication restrict the student's opportunities? Evaluators would honestly appraise whether the student's communication differences have restricted his or her curricular or extracurricular opportunities or both. Here, evaluators and the student must divorce themselves from the idealistic ("all opportunities are open to all qualified students") to confront the realistic. When restrictions are evident, the instructor is presented with an opportunity to commend to the student the merits of *bi-* or *multidialectalism* (command of two or more dialects); meaning, students expand their communication effectiveness by being capable of choosing among communication patterns to best address the needs of the particular social contexts.

    Once students with communication differences or disorders are identified, the time comes for the instructor to assess the appropriateness of particular elements of her or his Basic Communication course for those students with differences.

2. How Might a Communication Difference Affect the Student's Performance?

A communication difference can impact a student's performance of the activities that instructors of the Basic Communication course use to teach the skills needed to research, outline, write, deliver, and criticize various genres of public presentations. So, instructors should review their particular criteria for successful completion of those activities, and reflect on how the performance of a student with a communication difference might contrast with the performance of students who present with standard English dialects.

Which performance elements need review? The "Speech Performance Evaluation Form" (Iowa State University, 1995) used in the Basic Communication course at one Midwestern academic institution is representative of the criteria with which student performance is measured; and an overview of that evaluation tool reveals the elements instructors there consider central to the completion of various tasks. In the overview below, following each area on the list are examples of the potential effects of communication differences to which an instructor should be sensitive:

Area 1: TOPIC

Potential effects of communication differences include: (a) selection of topic, (b) selection of focus within topic, (c) selection of perspective for topic, (d) selection of pertinent information related to topic, (e) determination of appropriateness of topics for particular audiences, and (f) determination of appropriateness of topics for occasions.

Area 2: THESIS

Potential effects of communication differences include: (a) placement of the thesis within the structure, (b) expression of the thesis, and (c) selection of a thesis or purpose within the experience or the interest of the audience.

Area 3: DOCUMENTATION

Potential effects of communication differences include: (a) balance of supportive material, (b) sources of supportive material, (c) determination of authoritative nature of sources, (d) use of unfamiliar material, (e) use of material best interpreted in a particular cultural context, and (f) relation of material to particular purposes within a presentation.

Area 4: STRUCTURE

Potential effects of communication differences include: (a) choice of narrative structure imposed onto speech, (b) choice of temporal, topical, or combined format, and (c) structure of information within sections of presentation.

Area 5: CONTENT

Potential effects of communication differences include: (a) choice of words, (b) use of unfamiliar phrases, (c) use of idiomatic phrases, (d) use of humor, sarcasm, and other abstract constructions interpreted in a nonliteral manner, (e) use of cultural references, and (f) match of language to the status, seriousness, and intent of the occasion at hand.

Area 6: SPEECH

Potential effects of communication differences include: (a) articulation of particular speech sounds, (b) pronunciation of particular words, (c) construction of sentence structure, and (d) construction of narrative structure.

Area 7: PARALINGUISTIC BEHAVIORS

Potential effects of communication differences include: (a) rate of presentation, (b) variation in intonation pattern, (c) loudness of presentation, and (d) match of intonation pattern to sentence structure and intention of information.

Area 8: NONLINGUISTIC BEHAVIORS

Potential effects of communication differences include: (a) overall position and movement, (b) facial expression, (c) hand movement, (d) eye contact with audience, (e) distance from audience, and (f) coordination of visual aids.

This overview has pointed out how communication differences can affect particular dimensions of public performances. But instructors need not limit critique of their instructional practices to the criteria they impose upon student speeches. Similarly, instructors should review their criteria for student success across other activities in the Basic Communication course, to increase their awareness of dialect-sensitive areas of student performance evaluation.

3. Which Model of Evaluation of Student Performance Is Now in Place in the Course?

When students with communication differences (and even communication disorders) enroll in the Basic Communication course, instructors are faced with resolving two instructional aims sometimes at cross-purposes: how to maintain standards of excellence for student performance, while at the same time allowing variations within their definition of what constitutes excellence. On some campuses, instructors of the Basic Communication course agree to adopt an evaluation protocol that is applied consistently across multiple sections of the course. In such a protocol, some philosophical components of evaluation have been translated into practical application, with clear, consistent assumptions about excellence in place. Elsewhere, however, instructors are given the discretion to create their own individual approaches to evaluation. Instructors would be well-advised to honestly appraise their evaluation practices to determine which models of evaluation are implemented across their courses, then whether those models constitute best practices for students presenting with communication differences.

Instructors should evaluate their standards of comparison. For instance, some instructors use an "ideal" standard, which incorporates their assumptions about what constitutes excellence in communication, then compare the performance of individual students against that ideal. The "ideal" standard might reflect protocols that have been published, communication patterns that win speech competitions, or even the instructor's personal experiences with those who have demonstrated exceptional skills. Whatever its basis, the standard of comparison would be an absolute one, applied across all students across all instructional contexts.

Other instructors use context-specific standards. Rather than compare performance against an absolute ideal, for instance, they compare students against the ideal of that student's particular communication pattern, in effect asking: "What would constitute excellence (effectiveness) for a student who presents with this communication pattern, and to what extent has the student demonstrated that ideal?" In other words, a student with a dialect would be assessed in comparison with the linguistic, paralinguistic, and nonlinguistic rules of that particular dialect. Peterson and Marquardt (1994: 14) assert that "unless we understand the . . . structure and the function of the language we are listening to, we cannot judge the efficiency of the speaker's use of it." Instructors who compare students in context are attempting to assess effectiveness within dialect parameters.

Some instructors extend this context-specific approach to assess how effectively the student would be communicating both in the dialect's native context (that is, in a familiar context with persons who share that dialect) and also in its nonnative context (that is, in an unfamiliar context with persons who do not share the dialect). Here the question is, "How well has the student adapted to the elements of the communicative environment?" This way, the focus of evaluation centers not on the presence of particular dialectal traits, per se, but rather on the student's adaptation of communication for various purposes.

These are but a sample of the diverse approaches to evaluation of student performance that instructors might apply in the Basic Communication course. The important point is that instructors must become aware of their expectations for their students. Once their standards of comparison are apparent, instructors can then discern the rationale for the standards. If the rationale is consistent with the aims of the Basic Communication course, then the particular standards may be allowed to remain. If they are inconsistent, they must be changed. Regardless, instructors must address key issues such as these:

- Under which instructional conditions would the presence of a communication difference, by definition, impact the evaluation of a student?

- Under which instructional conditions would a student with and a student without a communication difference be evaluated inconsistently?

In the end, as instructors become more aware of what models of evaluation they are implementing in their courses, they can adapt those models to incorporate concerns for clear and appropriate criteria for excellence, as well as consistent standards of evaluation to the extent possible.

Conclusion

This essay has overviewed a three-part process that could contribute to the creation of an environment that would increase opportunities for success of students of color in the Basic Communication course. That is, (1) Communication Studies instructors, in collaboration with Communication Disorders professionals as needed, ascertain the communication status of their students, to inform the formulation of appropriate expectations for student performance. (2) Alerted to the presence of students with communication differences (and disorders), instructors then assess the course's instructional components, looking particularly at those tasks most likely to be influenced by communication differences, in order to delineate which aspects of student performance would or would not be cause for serious concern. (3) Finally, instructors evaluate the models of evaluation they apply in the course to discern whether these models reflect the philosophical and practical considerations most essential to the instructor and most effective in evaluating students. When instructors find inconsistent or inappropriate philosophies or practices, they reconstruct their models to reflect best practices in evaluation.

By participating in this three-part process, an instructor's awareness of and answers to issues that surround communication differences will be enhanced, as will be the experiences of *all* students in the Basic Communication course.

References

American Speech-Language-Hearing Association. (1983). "Position Paper on Social Dialects." *ASHA* 25(9): 23-24.

Cheng, L.L. (1987). *Assessment and Remediation of Asian Language Populations.* Rockville, MD: Aspen.

———. (November 1995). "Chinese-Influenced English." Paper presented to the Annual Convention, American Speech-Language-Hearing Association, Orlando, Florida.

Coulton, G.R. (1986). "Speech Disorders Among College Freshmen: A 13-Year Survey." *Journal of Speech and Hearing Disorders* 51(1): 3-7.

Edwards, J. (1991). *Language and Disadvantage: Studies in Disorders of Communication.* 2nd ed. London: Whurr.

Fein, D.J. (1983). "The Prevalence of Speech and Language Impairments." *ASHA* 25(2): 37.

Gillespie, S.K., and E.B. Cooper. (1973). "Prevalence of Speech Problems in Junior and Senior High Schools." *Journal of Speech and Hearing Research* 16: 739-743.

Hegde, M.N. (1991). *Introduction to Communicative Disorders.* Austin, TX: Pro-Ed.

Hoi, D.J., and N.N. Bich. (November 1995). "Vietnamese-Influenced English." Paper presented to the Annual Convention, American Speech-Language-Hearing Association, Orlando, Florida.

Hulit, L., and M. Howard. (1997). *Born to Talk: An Introduction to Speech and Language Development.* Boston: Allyn & Bacon.

Kayser, H. (1995). *Bilingual Speech-Language Pathology.* San Diego, CA: Singular.

Leske, M.C. (1981). "Prevalence Estimates of Communicative Disorders in the U.S. (Speech Disorders)." *ASHA* 23(3): 217-225.

Marge, M. (1972). "The Prevention of Communication Disorders." *ASHA* 15: 29-34.

McLaughlin, S. (1998). *Introduction to Language Development*. San Diego, CA: Singular.

Owens, R. (1992). *Language Development*. New York: Merrill-Macmillan.

Penalosa, F. (November 1995). "Chicano English." Paper presented to the Annual Convention, American Speech-Language-Hearing Association, Orlando, Florida.

Peterson, H., and T. Marquardt. (1994). *Appraisal and Diagnosis of Speech and Language Disorders*. Englewood Cliffs, NJ: Prentice-Hall.

Takada, N., and E. Hanahan. (November 1995). "Japanese-Influenced English." Paper presented to the Annual Convention, American Speech-Language-Hearing Association, Orlando, Florida.

Taylor, O., ed. (1986). *Nature of Communication Disorders in Culturally and Linguistically Diverse Populations*. San Diego, CA: College-Hill.

U.S. Bureau of the Census. (1990). 1990 Census. http://blue.census.gov.

Van Riper, C., and L. Emerick. (1990). *Speech Correction*. 8th ed. Englewood Cliffs, NJ: Prentice-Hall.

Warren-Leubecker, A., and J.N. Bohannon III. (1985). "Language in Society: Variation and Adaptation." In *The Development of Language*, 3rd ed., edited by J.B. Gleason. Columbus, OH: Merrill.

Wolfram, W. (November 1995). "Puerto Rican English." Paper presented to the Annual Convention, American Speech-Language-Hearing Association, Orlando, Florida.

Contextualizing the Success of African-American Students in Predominantly White Communication Departments

Dorthy L. Pennington

I have taught Intercultural Communication and Cultural Studies with a domestic (United States) focus — i.e., interracial communication — at a predominantly white university for more than 20 years. My teaching and research have centered around communication and cultural issues between blacks and whites, so I am more intimately familiar with the literature in that area than any other, not to minimize the importance of broadening the focus to include communication and cultural issues between or among the other groups that now make up multicultural America. I focus here on contextualizing the communication and cultural issues between blacks and whites as those issues manifest themselves in university or college classrooms. I argue that facilitating the success of African Americans in Communication classrooms begins in a much larger context: that of the campus and community environment and the cultural and social activities that occur therein.

In this essay, I begin with descriptions of four events that reflect a natural and spontaneous emergence of cultural expression and values by African-American students on my campus, and I then use theory to make sense of my observations and their implications for classrooms in Communication and Cultural Studies. Finally, I show how these events provide the larger context into which my class, Intercultural Communication: The African American, falls and operates, sharing what I hope have been successful activities and class procedures within that context. My observations are not necessarily related to one another, but there is an intertextuality among them that increases the likelihood that principally similar ones can be occurring on my campus or elsewhere. These observations, I hope, have heuristic value that extends beyond my essay. After each, I was left with a question or questions, which are subsequently stated. After the four observations, I present two separate statements, written to me recently by students, one black and the other white, explaining why they were absent from the same class. I pose questions after these statements, as well.

46

OBSERVATION 1

At a recent social dinner meeting between African-American faculty and African-American students, self-introductions were made. The majority of the students, many of whom were campus leaders, introduced themselves as having a strong identification with a black Greek organization. In the order of their verbal discourse, almost without exception, the name of the sorority or fraternity to which they belonged was stated following their name, as something of a high-priority identity marker. Students would say, for example, "Hi, my name is Jane Doe, and I am a member of Zeta Phi Beta Sorority," or "Hello, I am John Doe, and I belong to Kappa Alpha Psi Fraternity." This order of information manifested itself throughout the introductions, with other information about the students, such as their major or other campus affiliations, being presented lower in the order.

Question: Why was there such a strong identification of these African-American students with Greek organizations as a part of their identity?

OBSERVATION 2

One of my students shared a videotape of a meeting led by African-American students held one evening to discuss issues of identity and identification among African-American students on campus, including perceptions of some of the problematized issues for the students. During the meeting, the students expressed different viewpoints on the need for, or likelihood of, African-American students on campus being able to derive a common identity, given the diverse socioeconomic backgrounds from which black students come; issues of intraracial and interracial rejection on campus; and relationships between black males and black females on campus. The public speaking of the students at this meeting flowed freely and undeterred, and each student who wanted to speak was given a chance to voice his or her opinion. The meeting was attended by students only.

Questions: Why did the students feel the need to arrange a meeting on this topic? Given the substantive and provocative nature of this discussion, why didn't the students ask a faculty or staff member to make a presentation or to facilitate the meeting?

OBSERVATION 3

The black student gospel choir gave a concert in a campus auditorium, which also featured other gospel singing groups from this region. At this occasion, the student choir would be recording live its first commercial CD. In the public announcement about the event that appeared in the local newspaper, the only reference made to a starting time was that the doors would open at 5:30 pm. The elaborate printed program issued to attendees at the door also did not list a starting time for the performance, which actually began around 6:45 pm. The printed program indicated the nature of the event as a full-fledged worship service titled "Crazy Praise," which included scripture reading, prayer, and an open invitation to Christian Discipleship to anyone who wished to come forward during the service. The printed program also revealed pertinent information on the nature and purpose of the black student gospel choir. As printed in the program, they are:

> . . . about glorifying God through music. We predominantly spend time singing and studying His word while developing a supportive Christian family. Singing for God means we are messengers for His word. Every time that we sing His word, we pray that someone will cry out "What must I do to be saved?"

> [The choir] is a very uplifting and spiritually motivating organization. We refer to [the choir] as one big family in Christ. To most of us, [the choir] is our home away from home. Members wait eagerly for choir rehearsal to give them that extra spiritual uplift they need to make it through the week. [THE CHOIR] IS MORE THAN JUST SINGING — it is Bible study, worship, and Christian fellowship.

The choir was directed by a fellow student; and the musicians, who played improvisationally, were also students. The entire evening, including the music sung by the choir, was affective, filled with pathos, spontaneous, expressive, interactive (engaging the audience), dynamic, rhythmic, and movement-oriented, with the choir and the student director moving about freely. The style and mannerisms of the director included not only body movements but also platform mobility (even while directing the choir) and verbal solicitation for audience involvement during the pauses between songs. The implication was that the audience members were not to simply listen to the music's message, but they were expected to internalize and act upon it. The ministers who offered the scripture and the prayer also encouraged audience participation. On this occasion, they showed that a stage performance event was merged with the personal when they extended an open invitation for anyone who wanted to give their life to God to come forward during the service. This event, in essence, represented the integration of forms, where a concert and recording session were blended with a worship service; the performance was merged with the personal; and the message given in music was not just informational, but it was expected to have life-application, as well.

Questions: What is significant about the choir serving as a "home away from home" for its members? What is significant about the cultural style of the concert/worship service, and about the blending of forms — i.e., a concert, recording session, and a worship service all in one — and being held on the campus of a state university?

OBSERVATION 4

In my Intercultural Communication class, students had been randomly assigned to small groups, each given the task of producing a skit to be presented in class illustrating a significant current or historical issue or problem in interracial communication. With there being a small number of African Americans in the class (nine out of 52), students were permitted to produce costumes that helped them to portray a member of a different race if they felt that to be necessary to enhance their presentation. (In years past, costuming had not been a provocative issue, because the classroom environment, which I often refer to as a laboratory, had been trusting enough for there to be interracial role playing. The prior establishment of a psychologically safe environment is important.) Some of the African-American students in the class took offense at a white student's portrayal of an African American in a skit, and they verbally expressed their anger in class. In addition to the issue that the skit was portraying (incompatible schema surrounding the flying of the Confederate flag), the perception of the costumes as offensive had to be resolved right away.

Question: In providing a classroom and campus environment that is safe for all students, especially those in underrepresented groups, what are the limits of classroom interracial interaction, even if it occurs in a laboratory-type learning environment? Is there a place for humor or satire?

TWO EXPOSITIONS

The first, explaining his absence from class, written by a white male student:

> Dr. Pennington, I wanted to let you know the reasons for my absences of the past 3 classes.
>
> Last Tuesday, October 17, I spent in St. Louis with other Green Party supporters. We all took a bus and participated in the 017 protests at Washington University. We got to see Ralph Nader speak twice, participated in 2 marches each having over 1,200 citizens, and protested the exclusion of Ralph Nader from the debates. Our protest included mockery (making big puppets of the presidential candidates), autonomous action (chants of "This is what democracy looks like!"), playground name calling ("Whose streets? Our streets!"), speeches, and downright civil disobedience.
>
> It was an amazing experience and I felt that my voice was being able to be expressed properly.
>
> As for last Thursday and Tuesday, I was in New York for the College Music Journal Festival. This included 1,000 bands and independent films and panels. This is why I love being a dj here.
>
> I saw some amazing music, including underground soul singer Sharon Jones (of which she danced with me and I got some of her lyric sheets) and political heroes Antibalas Afrobeat Orchestra which mixed African polyrhythms with direct political action lyrics.
>
> I had the opportunity to see some music panel discussions on the future of hiphop and the future of internet music. I also got to see Ellis Island, walk across the Brooklyn Bridge (a dream of mine) and hear street musicians throughout the subway.

> I had wonderful experiences but missed a lot of school in the process. Whatever I need to do to catch up, I will. I am almost finished with the Acculturation book and I can take the test tomorrow if you would like me to.
>
> I hope you understand how these events have helped enrich my life experience. The last 9 days have been hectic but enlightening.

The second, explaining his absence from class, was written by a black male student:

> Dr. Pennington, I have been going through some personal changes with my financial situation these past couple of weeks which played a major role in my attendance in class.
>
> I have not received my financial aid this semester because of verification. My people are not wealthy and I use my Pell grant to pay for my expenses. Recently my phone, gas, and water have been turned off. I've really been struggling and it's been a distraction to my studies.
>
> I hope that you can understand and if we could work something out, I'd like to thank you.

Questions: What is the difference between the college experiences of these two students? As the white student felt that his voice was "being able to be expressed properly," how can the voice of the black student be expressed properly?

Discussion

The task of making sense of these four seemingly unrelated observations and two written statements is facilitated by noting several transcendent propositions about African-American students on my campus:

■ They seek clearly reliable means of identification and support, and want to ensure and negotiate for themselves an academic community and classroom environment that are psychologically and culturally safe; the role of providing the support needed is played by peers and by a rather unique role of religion and spirituality.

■ They are attracted to academic fora that focus on diversity and other issues in which they are interested and can feel involved, and where they feel that their voices can be heard; the fora often have life-application meaning for them.

African-American students on predominantly white campuses are faced with identity issues that situate them along a range of experiences, from being assimilated to being marginal, and they practice different patterns of cultural adaptation. For many of them, life on a predominantly white campus is analogous to the transcultural adaptation experiences that any of us encounters when we engage in international adaptation. A profile of transcultural adaptations given by Mansell (1981) best describes what I observe about African-American students on my campus, especially as it pertains to expressive responses to an environment that is different from their home environments. Mansell shows how shifting emotional and affective states lead to varying degrees of *alienation, marginality, acculturation,* or *duality.* As far as cultural identity in a new environment is concerned, in *alienation,* there is a sense of loss or separation, where one remains monocultural; in *marginality,* there is a sense of division or split loyalties to a double bind; in *acculturation,* there is a sense of belonging and identification with the new culture to such an extent as to be monocultural with that group; and in *duality,* there is a sense of autonomy, biculturalism, and independence.

While my conversations with African-American students in Communication reveal that their backgrounds, exposure to, and assimilation in European-American culture vary from one extreme to the other (a diversity among black students, which was problematized in my Observation 2), for the most part a sizeable number of them exhibit behaviors that would indicate both *marginality* and *duality* of their identity on my campus. Perhaps their strong identification with Greek organizations indicates their attempts to find a sense of belongingness, and yet, a belongingness that represents biculturalism, since most African-American Greeks belong to black Greek organizations rather than to white ones, even on a predominantly white campus. Thus, differences are expressed in the two sets of campus Greek organizations. Black Greeks' sense of biculturalism and independence is demonstrated through unique performance rituals associated with black Greek activities, such as step shows, which take place on our campus several times during the academic year. Believing step shows to be unique to black Greeks, I asked members of my class, which contained black and white Greeks, if anyone knew of white Greek organizations that performed step shows, and no one did.

In addition to lending credence to biculturalism, or duality of African-American identity on a predominantly white college campus, performance events also call attention to the nature of support that is important to, and negotiated by, African-American students. In a study of high-risk high school students, which included many African Americans, based on income and family background, Rosenfeld and Richman (1999) made a link between social support mechanisms and school outcomes. In identifying various types of social support (including *listening support, emotional support, emotional challenge support, reality confirmation support, technical appreciation support, technical challenge support, tangible assistance support,* and *personal assistance support* (295), they found what I think are two intriguing, and yet explanatory, results for my observations. On the question of who provided specific types of support, these researchers found that for at-risk students, teachers were not listed as being either primary or secondary providers of the eight types of support listed. Instead, behaviors seen by teachers as supportive (those behaviors concerned with students' well-being) were, perhaps, seen by students as being a part of the class routine, or even suspect, according to Rosenfeld and Richman. The students in the study, on the other hand, reported receiving *technical appreci-*

ation support, technical challenge support, and *reality confirmation support* from their friends (1999: 303). While these were high school students, this study has relevancy here.

For the students in my Observation 2, I now better understand why they did not ask for faculty or staff members to lead their discussion of identity issues: because the forum was structured to elicit support for their position, their friends and peers, rather than teachers, were seen as providing the support that they felt they needed. And, likewise, the students in the gospel choir explicitly indicated that the choir was their "supportive Christian family," their "home away from home," and that they eagerly awaited their regular rehearsals to give them "that extra spiritual uplift they need to make it through the week." This indicates that the student gospel choir on my campus provides for its members emotional support (comfort and caring); reality confirmation support (sharing and viewing the world in the same way); and personal assistance support (providing service or help, such as a ride to rehearsals for those who needed it). The metaphor of the choir as being a "Christian family," expressed within the context of a large state university, is significant in upholding the view that African-American culture emphasizes having a holistic connection among religion, spirituality, and secular life, as explained by Daniel and Smitherman (1976).

The value placed on spirituality expressed by the African-American students in the choir resonated with the stated focus of the 1999 National Black Student Leadership Conference, attended by some 900 college students, on "ethical responsibility, spiritual growth, and preparing to lead in a global economy" (Fields 1999: 14). The choir clearly practiced duality of their transcultural experience, in that their concert/recording-session/worship was attended primarily by blacks, a reversal of the usual campus racial ratio; this was an autonomous, independent event.

Observations 2 and 3 clearly show a reliance on peer leadership among African-American students, in both the discussion leaders and the choir director. This is consistent with a successful diversity peer-education program started by students on my campus in 1995. Called the "Diversity Peer Education Team," these peer student-educators, through activities and open discussion, explore issues pertaining to diversity and multiculturalism and serve as a vehicle to foster multicultural awareness and sensitivity in the university community (Best and Edwards 1998). The Diversity Peer Education Team is not limited to African-American students; but their central involvement in it, along with the student-led discussion of identity and diversity issues cited in my Observation 2, points to the saliency of diversity issues among African-American students. In addition to informal fora of the type cited, the need is evident for more formal and structured environments for exposure to diversity, such as classrooms. Communication classrooms and curricula are especially suited for this, for several reasons. Carrell (1997) found that diversity in the Communication curriculum has a positive impact on student empathy, which is a central component in communication competence. Empathy was more greatly achieved by students who completed a full course in Intercultural Communication, as compared with students who had diversity infused in an Interpersonal course, or compared with students who were required to give only one speech on diversity issues in the Public Speaking course. Intercultural communication competence is a desirable goal. According to Carrell (1997), facilitating its central component, empathy, is important in Intercultural Communication classrooms and curricular offerings.

Achieving empathy as a part of intercultural communication competence in the Intercultural classroom is a challenge, but instructional lessons can be learned by using my Observation 4 and the two student expositions. The event described in Observation 4, which occurred in my Intercultural/Interracial Communication class, required an immediate resolution. In addressing the issue right away, I practiced teacher immediacy, which, according to Neuliep (1995), is something that African-American students expect, especially from African-American teachers.

In processing the anger expressed by the African-American students, in retrospect I had assumed (based on past classes) that the level of interracial trust in my class that year was higher than it actually was, and it was a learning experience for me to have clear barometers for measuring interracial trust and empathy in the future. Nevertheless, in preparing the class for the activity-oriented group skits, I had aimed to establish the proper context through the reading materials and small-group tasks covered earlier in the semester. In that Intercultural/Interracial Communication class, I combine a culture-general approach with a culture-specific approach. Students must read articles on culture in general, which contain a model on worldview and other cultural components including language, schemas, beliefs, attitudes and values, temporality, proxemics, religion, social networks, and interpolation patterns. Students then write a nongraded paper that describes their own culture and how these various components operate. Next, they read articles that give general descriptions of various culture types, learning the communication values and characteristics of each culture. For this, I prefer to use readings that identify two basic culture types as *oral* and *literate* and that show how the two types foster different values. For example, oral cultures value face-to-face communication, communalism, sharing, spontaneity, and a relaxed regard for time, while literate cultures foster technological communication, competition, individualism, sometimes-circumscribed interaction, and a stricter regard for time. My students are offered these as theoretical possibilities, not as absolutes, for understanding culture. I complement the readings with videotapes that extend the comparisons between cultures to those between Western and non-Western cultures. We then apply the cultural types to the students in the class, showing that African Americans historically have had oral culture values.

With the culture-general background established, I then move the course to a culture-specific level, focusing on African-American culture and on interracial communication in the United States. Topics covered include African-American identity, core cultural values and symbols, communication style, and cultural interpretation. For the Interracial Communication portion, I begin with a historical reconstructionist approach, requiring students to read a historical article that describes race relations in early America and how racism and racial hierarchies were formed. Students, especially European Americans, are amazed at the arbitrariness with which race and physical distinctions became permanent markers and symbols affecting human relations and communication. While many historical sources are available for this assignment, I prefer an account titled "The Breaking of the Bond" by L. Bennett, Jr., in *Confrontation Black and White* (Penguin, 1965). With this historical foundation laid, I then go full-fledged into Interracial Communication readings that cover issues of race, stereotypes, prejudice, language, power, beliefs, attitudes and values, perception, normalization, interracial communication competence, and prescriptions for improving interracial communication.

To guide students through the readings, with an eye toward application, I use case studies, usually of current events taken from newspapers, and videotapes that show an unresolved interracial communication problem. I assign students to small groups to discuss the cases and to apply principles and terms from their readings to identify a problem, explain it, and suggest solutions. The small-group format allows the voice of each student to be heard, as well as for intragroup closeness, sharing, teamwork, and negotiating opinions. Moreover, these same small groups produce the skits presented toward the end of the term, so group members have an established relationship with one another. Each group reports the summary of its case analysis to the class, contributing to a general discussion. I find that the general discussion is a time of openness and information sharing that places the cases within a larger social context. Often students will relate a similar experience that happened to them, especially African-American students. This type of discussion of the readings gives each student a voice, and it gives my class a sense of currency, something that seems to appeal to them. One of my African-American senior Communication majors indicated that my class had more African-American students than he had seen in any one class during his four years at the university (the number is relatively small though, just nine out of 52).

The prescriptions for improving interracial communication include openness, trust, equality, assuming mutual responsibility for the communication outcome, and "relational empathy," as discussed by Broome (1991), which includes provisionalism, negotiation, process, and building shared meaning. At the same time, however, I find that in order to make my class a productive one that enhances interracial communication, I must process and channel class discussions in a way that strikes a delicate balance between relational empathy among students and making room for the impact of historical facts and legacy. That is, I have learned that any relational empathy and problem solving that are attempted between black and white students cannot presume an unledgered equality or absence of cultural memory on the part of black students. Rather, the historical sensitivity that exists on the part of many black students must be acknowledged as coming from a legacy that includes prejudice, discrimination, racism, stereotypes, underprivilege, powerlessness, and economic deprivation (of the sort mentioned by the black student who wrote the note to me explaining his absence from class).

I now return to a resolution of the confrontation in my class described in my Observation 4. In my immediacy in addressing the matter, I asked for other reactions to the portrayal in the skit. More African-American students spoke out, that to them the portrayal was offensive because it was extreme, stereotypical, and did not represent the majority of African Americans. I then framed the discussion in such a way as to assure African-American students that they had a right to be heard and to share the reasons for their reactions, believing that the class would genuinely listen and learn. At the same time, however, I reminded them of their responsibility to help keep the lines of communication open and to mutually participate in problem solving, while allowing for their historical sensitivity to be made known.

The test of what was learned during that discussion came a few days later, during the next graded assignment, a printed case for a take-home analysis. The case copy had been given to students prior to the confrontation in class, but its contents were remarkably similar to the incident that caused the confrontation in class. In their written analyses, the European-American students showed that they had learned something of African Americans' historical sensitivity, and they even accounted for it through historical reconstruction. African-American students showed that they wanted to express their feelings without closing the channels of interracial communication; they showed that they did not want to have dominance over the interaction, but merely a sense of fair play. I was pleased with this outcome.

Writing this essay has allowed me, for the first time, to think specifically of meeting the needs of African-American students in Communication classes. I had always thought of meeting the needs of students in general. As it turns out, my class (and other classes, I am sure) has the potential for meeting some of the needs of African-American students that I identified earlier: for a safe academic environment where they can have a voice, where they can make decisions with their peers (as in the small-group case analyses and in the skits), where they can discuss diversity and other issues that are important to them, and where they can make life-applications of the lessons learned. I do know that many African-American students enroll in more than one class with me. The student evaluations of my course in Intercultural/Interracial Communication tend to be good. I believe that the success of African-American students in Communication classrooms depends on their academic ability, of course; but also on our meeting their cultural and social needs shown in larger contexts.

References

Best, C., and V. Edwards. (December 1998). "Embracing Diversity: Diversity Peer Education Team Raises Awareness in Campus Community." *One Community* 6(1): 1.

Broome, B.J. (July 1991). "Building Shared Meaning: Implications of a Relational Approach to Empathy for Teaching Intercultural Communication." *Communication Education* 40(3): 235-249.

Carrell, L.J. (October 1997). "Diversity in the Communication Curriculum: Impact on Student Empathy." *Communication Education* 46(4): 234-243.

Daniel, J.L., and G. Smitherman. (February 1976). "How I Got Over: Communication Dynamics in the Black Community." *The Quarterly Journal of Speech* 62(1): 26-39.

Fields, C.D. (February 4, 1999). "Preparing Leaders for a New Century." *Black Issues in Higher Education* 15(25): 14-15.

Mansell, M. (April 1981). "Transcultural Experiences and Expressive Response." *Communication Education* 30(2): 91-108.

Neuliep, J. (July 1995). "A Comparison of Teacher Immediacy in African-American and Euro-American College Classrooms." *Communication Education* 44(3): 267-277.

Rosenfeld, L.B., and J.M. Richman. (October 1999). "Supportive Communication and School Outcomes, Part II: Academically 'At-Risk' Low Income High School Students." *Communication Education* 48(4): 294-306.

Pedagogies of Empowerment

A Framework for Promoting the Success of Students of Color

Mary E. Triece, Patricia S. Hill, Kathleen D. Clark, Yang Lin,
and Julia A. Spiker

> To commit ourselves to the work of transforming the academy so that it will
> be a place where cultural diversity informs every aspect of our learning, we
> must embrace struggle and sacrifice. . . . Our solidarity must be affirmed by
> shared belief in a spirit of intellectual openness that celebrates diversity,
> welcomes dissent, and rejoices in collective dedication to truth. (hooks
> 1994: 33)

Black feminist scholar bell hooks's words provide a useful starting point for conceptualizing our roles as Communication scholars and teachers. How might we transform our classrooms so that cultural diversity informs our teaching and learning? What teaching philosophies and activities might enable us to engage our students in diversity and open discussion as we strive to create more socially just classrooms and communities? These questions are particularly important as we consider ways to ensure the success of students of color in our Communication classes. Scholars have examined the experiences of students of color on college campuses, revealing ways that historical inequalities and patterns of racial exclusion continue to marginalize this group (Allen, Bobo, and Freuranges 1984; Cross 1985; Feagin 1992; Fleming 1984; Gibbs 1973; June, Curry, and Gear 1990; Styles-Hughes 1987; Taylor 1986; Willie and McCord 1973; Zweigenhaft and Cody 1993). Further, recent research maintains that while students of color continue to make progress in higher education, they still lag significantly behind European-American students in both the rate at which they enroll in college classes and their college completion rates (Chesler and Malani 1993).

What efforts might be employed to transform the inequalities that students of color continue to face on college campuses? This essay seeks to provide the underpinnings for a teaching process and learning environment based on *pedagogies of empowerment* that challenge the stereotypes and structures that have for so long impeded the advancement of students of color. We primarily teach the general-education Speech course (also referred to throughout the essay as the "Introductory Speech" course)[1] at a metropolitan, open-enrollment state university characterized by racial, ethnic, socioeconomic, and age diversity.[2] Each of our respective areas of research informs our teaching approach and viewpoints on pedagogies of empowerment. Yet, all of our contributions hold in common an emphasis on the importance of the concrete material experiences[3] that shape and inform students' needs and perspectives and that provide a foundation for motivating students to apply concepts beyond the classroom in struggles for race (as well as gender and class) equality.

Critical pedagogical philosophies inform the first two sections of this essay, which provide a theoretical overview for the notion of pedagogies of empowerment. We then explore classroom activities centering on self-reflection and cultural identity that further support pedagogies of empowerment. Finally, the essay concludes with a section on the roles that learning communities play in developing pedagogies of empowerment. Taken together, our ideas offer a coherent but multi-perspectival approach to the successful teaching of students of color.

Materialist Critical Perspective as Empowerment

Critical pedagogies have been developed and discussed by a number of scholars (see Carlson and Apple 1998; Giroux and McLaren 1994; Giroux et al. 1995; Luke and Gore 1992; Ng, Staton, and Scane 1995; Popkewitz and Fendler 1999). Though they might differ according to theoretical underpinnings or practical approach, critical pedagogies explore "the influences of educational knowledge . . . that perpetuate or legitimate an unjust status quo" and are concerned with "social injustice and how to transform inequitable, undemocratic, or oppressive institutions and social relations" (Burbules and Berk 1999: 46-47). Critical pedagogies have themselves been critically examined and challenged on a number of accounts. The concept of empowerment central to many critical pedagogical perspectives has been criticized as misleading and paternalistic (see Ellsworth 1992; Gore 1992). Other scholars have pointed to the potential for critical pedagogies to become paralyzed by an overemphasis on language and affirmations of happy pluralisms at the expense of attention to struggle, conflict, and the existence of material institutions and structures that require more than classroom tolerance to transform (McLaren 1994; McLaren and Gutierrez 1998; Mohanty 1994; Rezai-Rashti 1995). Similarly, multiculturalist discourses have been criticized for lack of attention to broad-based, entrenched material institutions that shape race, gender, and class relations and that have a stake in perpetuation of unequal relations.

This section discusses a pedagogy of empowerment underpinned by a materialist critical perspective that frames empowerment in collective terms and directs attention toward material institutions and practices that play a fundamental role in unequal race, gender, and class relations. In sum, a materialist critical perspective (1) *challenges mainstream integration* by emphasizing the importance of critique and the articulation of new ways to live and work; (2) *advances the importance of radical transformation* by encouraging application of communication concepts and skills in order to challenge dominant ideologies and institutions; (3) *recognizes inherent limitations* of critical pedagogies and acknowledges the classroom as a realm limited in its capacity to elicit meaningful (read: *material)* social transformation. As such, a materialist critical approach should be practiced in conjunction with other activities that directly engage economic production.

CHALLENGING MAINSTREAM INTEGRATION

A materialist critical approach employs a language of critique and a language of possibility (see Giroux 1983) in order to challenge what is referred to as "mainstream integration" or teaching basic communication skills with the aim of equipping students to participate in, or adjust to, the status quo. Through critique, both students and teachers deconstruct and demystify the values, narratives, beliefs, and behaviors that perpetuate racial discrimination (in addition to other social injustices). The concept of critique discussed here can be compared with the critical-thinking and critical-listening skills that many Communication educators and textbooks teach. Critical thinking encourages students to "seek reasons and evidence" and instills in students the disposition to do so (Burbules and Berk 1999: 48). In contrast, critique is contextualized and an overtly political analysis of a given message. It requires listeners to ask questions such as: Who benefits from this message? How? Whose interests are served by the values or beliefs espoused in a given message? What perspectives are ignored in this message? Why? Each of these questions encourages students to scrutinize and challenge the ways that racial discrimination is perpetuated through public discourses. In short, critique is critical thinking/listening with a counterhegemonic or oppositional bent. But more than that, critique as it is conceptualized here does not stop at altering mindsets; it seeks to "challeng[e] and transform the institutions, ideologies, and relations that engender distorted, oppressed thinking in the first place" (Burbules and Berk 1999: 52).

In addition to critique, a materialist critical pedagogy challenges mainstream integration through a language of possibility, the envisioning and articulating of new and more just ways of being, living, and working. Freire asserts that "To exist, humanly, is to *name* the world, to change it. Once named, the world in its turn reappears to the namers as a problem and requires of them a new *naming*" (1970: 76). As Communication scholars and teachers, we must begin the process of (re)naming based on the perspectives and experiences of people of color who have historically been left out of this process both in the classroom and in the broader community. Imagining anew, though, must be articulated in terms of a collective identity that recognizes differences — different voices, backgrounds, perspectives, needs — while not abandoning the imperative to speak collectively, as a unified voice, and to recognize common needs and concerns. This notion of a collectivity contrasts with liberal humanist concepts of personal voice, dialogue, and plurality, which are grounded in an individualist ethic (see Luke 1992); are disconnected from a history of conflict, struggle, and relations of inequality; and "require discursive rather than material intervention around issues of equality and reciprocity" (McLaren and Gutierrez 1998: 318). As McLaren and Gutierrez note:

> How we mark the boundaries of our ethnicities and racial identifications and representations does draw needed critical attention to the scribal power of dominant narratives and helps us both focus on and demobilize the neo-colonial system that energizes our collective values as a citizenry. Yet how we identify ourselves collectively, across differences as a totality, is equally important. (1998: 329)

Materialist critical pedagogy advances a language of possibility in terms of collectivity and locates concepts such as image and identity within a discussion of how broad-based material institutions benefit from and perpetuate discriminatory discourses in the first place.

RADICAL TRANSFORMATION AND THE LIMITATIONS OF MATERIALIST CRITICAL PEDAGOGY

Languages of critique and possibility offer many potentials for developing a pedagogical perspective. Yet, ideas must be enacted in the real world in order to make a real impact. As Communication teachers, we cannot (simply) teach our students how to organize, research, and deliver speeches, nor can we even stop at promoting radical critique in the classroom. We must foster in our students the motivation and desire to apply what they have learned in the Communication classroom to the world outside. Once armed with the critical-thinking and -speaking tools addressed above, students must learn to recognize and seize opportunities in their homes, workplaces, and communities to alter dominant practices that continue to discriminate according to race, ethnicity, gender, and class. Put differently, as teachers, we must be careful not to conflate critique and praxis. The former provides a basis for the latter. In the absence of application/action, critique — self-reflection, dialogue, whatever you want to call it — becomes mere intellectualism, and we fall into political paralysis. As Marx and Engels (1846) noted: "The philosophers have only interpreted the world, in various ways; the point is to change it" (123).

Furthermore, we must not remain blind to the limitations inherent in transformative attempts that come out of the college classroom. The radical potentials of critical pedagogies are often limited by the educational institution itself and its rootedness in a broader socioeconomic system based on labor exploitation (see Gore 1998: 276, 277). Institutions of higher learning reinforce status quo relations in the classroom and through research imperatives. In the classroom, teachers face the undeniable fact that they have a degree of power over students — to give grades, establish criteria, set class requirements. Further, the teaching approaches that are most often rewarded (implicitly or explicitly) are those that promote professionalism and equip students with skills for getting by in the world, rather than transforming it. A materialist critical pedagogy recognizes the limitations inherent in transformation that stem from the educational sphere, yet it also recognizes that what we teach and how we teach in our Communication classes matter and can form an important basis for collective action beyond the academy.

Standpoint Theory as Empowerment

Much like a materialist critical perspective, standpoint theory provides another philosophical underpinning for teachers striving to cultivate a classroom environment that promotes the success of students of color. Taken together, the two pedagogical perspectives offer a framework for pedagogies of empowerment that emphasize the centrality of material conditions in shaping the experiences and perspectives of marginalized groups, such as students of color.

Standpoint theory provides an interpretative framework for exploring the daily life experiences of persons situated in subordinate positions. It advocates using marginalized lives as a foundation for constructing knowledge about social relations of power (see Collins 1986, 1990; Harding 1986, 1987, 1991; Hartsock 1983, 1997; Smith 1987; Wood 1992). Marginalized groups — e.g., women, people of color — hold a unique "outsider within" position in society; that is, they are both outside of (marginalized by) and inside of (participate within) dominant society (Collins 1986). As a result, according to standpoint theory, marginalized groups are in a better position to produce knowledge and insights that are less distorted and less partial. Individuals in oppressed groups have less of a stake in the status quo and thus are more likely to offer provocative insights on social change that are often overlooked or censored.

Standpoint theory is of particular value in teaching students of color because it broadens the classroom content and discussion in order to more adequately represent diverse experiences. Further, it allows students to recognize and validate their own personal experiences as individuals who have historically been marginalized by dominant society. Applied to our Introductory Speech classes, standpoint theory encourages a reconceptualization of what constitutes knowledge and how it is conveyed in the classroom. Standpoint theory fosters a learning environment where students of color speak from their reality and thus reveal aspects of the social order that otherwise remain difficult to see (Collins 1986). Students are encouraged to work from their own experiences and to interrogate their experiences to explore how "what they know" reveals something about their social location. Asking students to share what they know with one another can illuminate how privilege and power operate to those who are least able to view the world outside dominant race, class, and gender ideologies. In order to encourage students to openly draw on their own experiences (and to be open to the experiences of others), a teaching approach informed by standpoint theory emphasizes experiential learning strategies, which link theory more meaningfully to direct experience and practice and empower students of color to think and speak critically.

EXPERIENTIAL EXERCISES

Students often question the relevance of enrolling in a Public Speaking course because they fail to see the connection between learning public speaking skills and applying these skills in real-life situations (Ford and Wolvin 1993; Mino 1988). Teaching from the perspective of standpoint theory encourages teachers to apply communication concepts beyond the classroom in order to reach students' personal, academic, and professional lives. This is accomplished through classroom exercises that actively engage students with one another, with the teacher, and with the course material. Firsthand involvement in their own learning encourages students to reflect upon their own social experiences as students of color.

To foster critical application of classroom concepts, teachers can employ the exercise "Each One Teach One." The title takes its name from an old West African proverb that advocates the importance of community, and is in the spirit of collaborative learning that is espoused in pedagogies of empowerment. Given that much scholarship on small groups validates the importance of group dynamics to both social and work life (see Fisher 1980; Pavitt and Curtis 1994; Tubbs 1988; Wall, Galanes, and Love 1987), "Each One Teach One" provides a valuable teaching tool for interrogating these dynamics and applying communication concepts to everyday life experiences.

In "Each One Teach One," students engage in a small-group learning exercise aimed at facilitating understanding of how public speaking concepts such as listening, language, and delivery can be applied to, and are inherent in, real-world communicative experiences. As a small group, students select a concept of public speaking and reflect on how that concept is used in their personal or professional lives. In round-robin fashion, students share cogent examples that describe for their classmates the utility or value of a variety of public speaking concepts in numerous personal and professional contexts. The cooperative aspect mirrors hooks's (1994) assumptions that a goal of an engaged classroom is to open up a space for everyone and to create exercises that encourage students to apply theoretical concepts to their own lives and their own standpoints as students of color.

The quality of the Introductory Speech course continues to be of primary importance to the field of Communication in general as this is the course where most college students become familiar with our field. A growing diversity in our classrooms urges a reexamination of classroom practices that have historically benefited students from one segment of society. Standpoint and materialist critical perspectives represent two pedagogies of empowerment that encourage teaching with a "vision of a better life" (Giroux and McLaren 1989: xii) in which accepted canons of knowledge can be challenged, and attention can be given to creating classroom space that best fulfills the needs of all students, but especially those of students of color who have been historically marginalized.

Teaching practices informed by standpoint theory acknowledge and explore how different standpoints affect communicative practices. The next two sections describe specific classroom activities that explore the relationship between standpoint and communication.

Self-Reflection as Empowerment

As a pedagogical tool of empowerment that can be employed to help students of color succeed in the Introductory Communication course, self-reflection holds much in common with standpoint theory. Self-reflection empowers students of color by (1) making connections between their life context (standpoint) and the context of the university classroom; (2) encouraging students to take their own voice/standpoint (thoughts, feelings, insights, beliefs) seriously; (3) developing their public speaking skills to accomplish purposes that are meaningful to them; (4) developing the ability to adapt successfully to a variety of audiences and situations without losing integrity with themselves.

Repeated self-reflection throughout the course enables students of color to discover and develop their authentic voices and the skills to use those voices in a variety of public contexts. Self-reflection as a pedagogical tool draws upon several strands of literature and research that emphasize three meta-communicative elements: an awareness of context, developing authentic voice, and self-reflective critique. The process emphasizes contextualization of student speeches and the discovering and development of authentic voice. Similar to the standpoint perspective elaborated above, the emphasis on context encourages students of color to draw on personally meaningful experiences, interests, and concerns when choosing and researching speech topics, since their speeches will not be disconnected from their life situations, or standpoints. This emphasis provides a way for students to discover and develop their authentic voice. Students of color also encounter self-reflective critique, which entails planning, acting, reflecting on the action, and using insights gained to inform the planning of subsequent action. As a part of self-reflective critique, learning the skills of cognitive restructuring helps students to understand the workings of their own brains/bodies and provides a powerful tool for engaging realistically with the public speaking situation.

Now let's explore each of these three meta-communicative elements in more depth.

CONTEXT

Examining the nature of the context allows us to have a fuller understanding of what a student is bringing into the classroom. Current educational philosophy argues strongly for the importance of grounding learning in the reality of the lives of students (see Kincheloe, Slattery, and Steinberg 2000; McDermott 1999) and using the classroom to learn skills that are transferable and meaningful to the rest of life. Part of the intention of Introductory Speech courses is to equip incoming freshmen with presentational skills so as to improve their chances of educational and professional success. However, students bring their lives with them to the classroom, and this provides a rich source of topics that are already meaningful to them. Students of color will necessarily bring aspects of their lives that are unique to their situations into this "public" context, which can help them bridge gaps of many kinds. Drawing on this wealth of the already-known increases students' confidence and interest in speech assignments, which permits a greater integration of public speaking and group skills. Additionally, this increases the comfort of students when we ask them to do assignments that could produce anxiety, including anxieties specific to students of color. With an understanding of the possibilities inherent in attention to context, attention to helping students of color find and use their voice continues the empowerment.

VOICE

Clark (1999) has focused on a concern for silenced voices and on cultivating one's authentic voice. Insights such as the "unarticulated self perishes" (Christ 1986) and "hearing into speech" (Morton 1985) suggest the importance of creating a space where each student's "voice" can be heard into existence, and each student can articulate her or his own experiences and meanings (see also Kincheloe, Slattery, and Steinberg 2000; McDermott 1999). Using the genuine interests and concerns of students of color as a source of speech topics and encouraging certain delivery skills help cultivate authentic voice. Maintaining eye contact and spending substantial portions of a speech with no lectern or table as a barrier between themselves and their audience cultivate a sense in students that they can truly connect with others about what matters to them most, and that others find their "voice" worth hearing.

Becoming aware of the role of one's context and voice can be achieved by many means, some mentioned elsewhere in this essay. One particular approach that has proven effective is regular self-reflection about many aspects of one's public speaking.

SELF-REFLECTIVE CRITIQUE

Drawing from cognitive psychology, personal reflection on the reality of what is happening versus distorted nonreality-based thinking is a proven method for dealing with anxiety (Burns 1999), including the common anxiety of speaking in public. Using self-reflective critiques about individual and group presentations throughout the course seems to successfully help students cognitively restructure their thinking about the public speaking situation, decrease anxiety, and gain a sense of control over themselves (Dwyer 1998; Foss and Foss 1994; Lucas 2001). Self-reflective critique can be used after each speech assignment in the form of sense-making triangulation (Dervin and Clark 1999) to reflect on different aspects of the situation. Sense-making triangulation is a methodology that asks a person to reflect on the situation, gap, bridge, and outcome of a step they are taking. Applying this methodology to speech assignments, students are asked to consider the following questions, after some time has passed (to allow the adrenaline to leave their bodies, and thus to facilitate more realistic thinking): (1) What did I want to accomplish in this speech? (2) What actually happened as I delivered the speech? (3) Did anything help? What? (4) Did anything *not* help? What? (5) What do I want to try next time? By using this triangulation, students begin to get a sense of how their own thinking can help or hinder them, and plan strategies to build on strengths and strengthen weaknesses.

Self-reflective critique is grounded in the notion that students' life experiences as members of marginalized groups play a central role in learning and cultivating speaking skills. As an empowering classroom tool, it encourages students to cultivate authentic voice and link daily experiences with classroom concepts. In addition to self-reflective critique, students of color can be empowered through classroom activities that encourage them to explore cultural identity.

Cultural Identity as Empowerment

As racial and ethnic diversity on college campuses grows, students are challenged with finding a means to maintain and strengthen their cultural identity while engaging successfully in the diverse environment. Introductory Speech courses provide an ideal environment in which students can examine the relationship between communication and cultural identity and can develop communication skills that will empower them as they live and work in a diverse world.

Research in intercultural communication has generated much knowledge of identity and cultural adaptation (see Chen and Starosta 1998; Gudykunst and Kim 1997; Martin and Nakayama 1997; Samovar and Porter 2000). Identity develops through communication with others (Collier 2000; Hecht, Collier, and Ribeau 1993), and our cultural identities influence our communication with others. Further, individuals might have multiple cultural identities that are defined through communication with others (Collier 2000). How much individuals want to maintain their own identity versus how much they want to become part of the new environment is one of the important issues that affects their adaptation to a culturally diverse environment (Martin and Nakayama 1997).

Students' identities are shaped by their racial and ethnic experiences as well as by their social interactions with family members, friends, schoolmates, and others. Through a specific speaking assignment — the "Who I Am" speech — students can explore issues surrounding cultural identity and race/ethnic diversity. The "Who I Am" speech allows students to use a first-person voice to speak about their cultural experience and helps them develop positive impressions toward their racially and ethnically diverse classmates. Because it represents such a valuable learning opportunity, teachers would do well to use the "Who I Am" speech as the first graded speaking assignment, rather than merely as an ice-breaker (which is often the case in the Introductory Speech course). Through this assignment, students learn how racial, ethnic, and cultural diversity shapes their own beliefs, attitudes, and behaviors as well as those of others. This recognition helps maintain and further develop an individual's cultural identity.

Research for the "Who I Am" speech has two objectives. First, because their direct experience and access to cultures other than their own might be limited, students are to explore not only their own cultural experience but also that of other cultural groups through a variety of sources. Knowledge of other cultures can help them understand their own culture and identify the significant aspects of their experiences and the important issues in their life. Second, with the teacher's guidance, students are to search and evaluate the information pertaining to their culture and the issues with which they are connected. Based on their own experience, students can examine the nature of the information, whether it is accurate or inaccurate and biased or unbiased. Students then will better understand the potential impact of communication (e.g., mass media) on their own life and other people's lives as well.

Additional benefits of the "Who I Am" speech come after the speeches are delivered. Teachers can select a few speeches and ask students to discuss them from their own perspectives/experiences. Students are to list the things they learned about a different culture and some things not covered that they want to know. They also document the unique features of the speaker's delivery style and writing. Several objectives can be accomplished through such discussion. First, teachers can emphasize how culture influences our communication with others; for example, the verbal and nonverbal language used in the speeches and the opinions expressed in them. Second, teachers can demonstrate how communication can help people better understand and respect the differences between cultures, and how miscommunication can yield negative effects such as prejudice and stereotyping. Third, and perhaps most important, critiquing speeches of cultural identity opens a direct dialogue between students with different cultural backgrounds. Communication is the means to overcome many barriers they face on culturally diverse campuses.

Through the "Who I Am" speech, students are exposed to the concepts of social diversity and multiculturalism; they learn about differences between race, ethnicity, and cultural groups; they come to understand the importance of communication in dealing with complex cultural issues; and more important, they prepare themselves for cultural diversity in the classroom and the broader community. In conjunction with self-reflective critique, the "Who I Am" speech empowers students by enabling them to cultivate their own voices grounded in their experiences as members of marginalized groups. These exercises — when framed by the critical teaching philosophies elaborated on in this essay — encourage students and teachers to explore how material experiences rooted in and shaped by race and ethnicity impact communication, including what one chooses to speak about, how one researches and delivers a speech, and how one's message is interpreted.

Learning Communities as Empowerment

Teaching philosophies and classroom activities are only effective to the extent that they reach students "where they are" and encourage active engagement that fosters a deeper, more meaningful learning experience. So it is imperative that we discover ways to engage our students, particularly students of color.

Research has demonstrated that students stay engaged when they participate in learning communities (Gabelnick et al. 1990), and engaged students succeed in the university setting and their retention rates increase. More specifically, students of color benefit from the learning community model, which fosters an appreciation for diversity in the campus setting. The block scheduling of classes characteristic of learning communities encourages students of various backgrounds to spend more time together, and within the classroom they continue the dialogue with other students as they work together on projects. In research, participants in learning communities express an appreciation for diversity — they were able to go beyond a stereotype and get to know an individual.

THE LEARNING COMMUNITY MODEL

The structure of the learning community model varies — some might be prepared in exhaustive detail, while others are loosely structured (Goodsell et al. 1992; Shapiro and Levine 1999). Learning communities do share two characteristics: Students are scheduled together in several courses, and the faculty attempt to provide an intellectual bridge between the various courses. The university coordinates the grouping of faculty and courses and the block scheduling of students. In preparation, the faculty members meet to coordinate goals and assignments; then during the semester they meet periodically to discuss students' progress and ways to achieve student success. Tinto, Love, and Russo (1994) discuss the use of learning communities to address students' needs. Let's close this essay with a case study from our own campus, the University of Akron, where we have seen the benefits of the model for students of color.

APPLICATION

The assistant dean of the University College coordinates the learning communities for the University. (Other administrative structures are possible, as discussed by Shapiro and Levine 1999.) Coordination duties include the scheduling of students in blocks so they attend the same three courses, and holding meetings with the faculty members to encourage discussion. Three courses — Freshman Orientation, English Composition, and Effective Oral Communication (an Introductory Speech course) — make up a typical learning community. Its faculty members coordinated course goals and assignments prior to the semester beginning. Then during the semester, they met to discuss each student's grade, attitude, and progress. By working together and by letting the students know they worked together, the faculty were able to maintain close contact with each student.

The success of the learning community lies in the continued dialogue between faculty, between students, and between faculty and students. Students of color benefit from such engaged dialogue because it creates a sense of community within our large, urban, commuter school — a community that stems from, and draws upon, the specific standpoints of students with various racial, ethnic, and socioeconomic backgrounds. The University is set in a metropolitan area of 2.8 million people. Within walking distance of downtown, it enrolls some 24,000 students. The University faces typical educational needs, which can be addressed by learning communities. As Goodsell et al. (1992) state:

> Learning communities directly confront multiple problems plaguing under-graduate education: the fragmentation of general-education classes, the isolation of students (especially on large campuses or commuter schools), the lack of meaningful connection building between classes, the need for greater intellectual interaction between students and faculty, and the lack of sustained opportunities for faculty development. (19)

The learning community model offers a practical reform to the modern-day splintering effects of education (Lieberman 1996, 2000) by working within the current financial restraints (Kadel and Keehner 1994) of the typical university and offering real benefits to students.

BENEFITS

Sharing similar schedules and the challenges of academic assignments forges bonds among learning community students. Students work together through group projects that might cross over traditional course boundaries. The learning community model encourages understanding and diversity. In our case, one student acknowledged that she developed friendships with students whom she typically would not have come in contact with, as a result of her learning community. She learned to appreciate diversity as a positive factor on the University campus.

Sonia Nieto (1999) addresses creating multicultural learning communities. Students' views toward the world become more global and they develop more-inclusive perspectives. This increased awareness encourages civic participation (King 1997). Another student involved in our learning community learned about student government in researching a speech for a Communication class. He subsequently ran for office in the Student Government Association.

Studies indicate that students of color lag behind European-American students in the rate at which they enroll in and complete college (Chesler and Malani 1993). When students participate in learning communities, however, grade-point averages and student retention rates increase. The retention rate for students involved in our Fall 1999 learning communities was 89 percent, compared with an overall University retention rate of 83 percent. One student stated that he learned to study and his GPA was 3.9 during the semester he participated in a learning community. Students gain self-confidence as a result of the camaraderie that carries over between classes. This self-confidence is evident in behavioral changes. Gabelnick et al. (1990) report that students "form study groups and pay close attention to subgroups in the community" (59). Students develop a "sense of responsible citizenship" insofar as they "feel a community obligation to complete their assignments, attend class, and share their ideas with one another" (59). These positive behavioral changes ultimately contribute to success.

The learning community model is based on block scheduling and faculty coordination to create an intellectual bridge. The University of Akron is one example of the successful incorporation of learning communities as part of a school's academic mission. In conjunction with critical teaching philosophies and specific classroom activities, learning communities assist in the development and success of students of color by creating an environment of empowering, engaged communication.

Conclusion

Communication classrooms hold the potential to create a learning environment that engages and empowers students who have historically been marginalized on college campuses. This essay explored pedagogies of empowerment, a teaching approach that builds on the insights that come out of diverse learning environments. A central premise underlying pedagogies of empowerment is that students' needs and perspectives are shaped, in part, by concrete material experiences, which must be recognized and engaged in order to promote student success. Critical teaching perspectives informed by materialist and standpoint theories establish an overall classroom philosophy that views both teaching and learning as the "practice of freedom" and that seeks to challenge dominant ideologies and institutions that continue to marginalize students of color. Through classroom activities that center on self-reflection and cultural identity, students gain further experience applying Communication concepts and skills to their lived experiences in order to gain insight into the ways that discrimination can be challenged, in the classroom and the broader community. Finally, the learning community model provides an institution-wide means for creating classroom communities that explore diversity and devote attention to the needs of students of color.

The teaching philosophies and classroom activities explored in this essay do not exhaust the possibilities for pedagogies of empowerment. Rather they provide a starting point from which future studies could expand. As Communication teachers committed to ensuring the success of students of color, we all must continue to develop teaching philosophies and classroom activities that speak to students' real-life experiences, which have been marked by exclusion, discrimination, and marginalization. We must continue to explore how to make the Communication classroom a place where dominant ideologies are challenged, diverse voices are heard, and perhaps most important where motivation is fostered to apply Communication concepts to the broader community in order to transform our students' world for the better.

Notes

1. The general-education Speech course is a hybrid course that examines group communication and public speaking.

2. The University of Akron has a population of 23,264 undergraduate and graduate students. Some 20% of the student population is minority or international students. Most students — about 90% — commute to campus. A substantial proportion are considered "nontraditional" — 41% are older than 25, and 37% of all students attend school part-time while holding part- or full-time jobs and meeting family responsibilities outside of school.

3. Throughout this essay, "material" and "materiality" are used to refer to a reality that exists outside of, but is understood through, human discourse. For instance, students of color are affected not only by racist language and ideologies but also by racist structures and institutions that continue to shape their lives in very concrete ways. It is our contention that recognition of material structures and institutions, and knowledge of their impact, can be used as a starting point for engaging students of color and for cultivating a classroom environment where these institutions can be challenged.

References

Allen, W.R., L. Bobo, and P. Freuranges. (1984). *Preliminary Report: 1982 Undergraduate Survey of Black Undergraduate Students Attending Predominantly White, State Supported Universities.* Ann Arbor, MI: Center of Afro-American and Asian Studies.

Burbules, N.C., and R. Berk. (1999). "Critical Thinking and Critical Pedagogy: Relations, Differences, and Limits." In *Critical Theories in Education: Changing Terrains of Knowledge and Politics*, edited by T.S. Popkewitz and L. Fendler, pp. 45-65. New York: Routledge.

Burns, D.D. (1999). *The Feeling Good Handbook*. Rev. ed. New York: Plume.

Carlson, D., and M.W. Apple. (1998). *Power/Knowledge/Pedagogy: The Meaning of Democratic Education in Unsettling Times*. Boulder, CO: Westview.

Chen, G.-M., and W.J. Starosta. (1998). *Foundations of Intercultural Communication*. Boston: Allyn and Bacon.

Chesler, M., and A. Malani. (1993). "Perceptions of Faculty Behavior by Students of Color." *The Michigan Journal of Political Science* 16: 54-79.

Christ, C.P. (1986). *Diving Deep and Surfacing: Women Writers on Spiritual Quest*. 3rd ed. Boston: Beacon.

Clark, K.D. (December 1999). "A Communication-as-Procedure Perspective on a Women's Spiritual Group: A Sense-Making and Ethnographic Exploration of a Communicative Proceduring in Feminist Small Group Process." *The Electronic Journal of Communication/ La Revue Electronique de Communication* 9 (2-4). [Online at http://www.cios.org/www/ejcrec2.htm]

Collier, M.J. (2000). "Understanding Cultural Identities in Intercultural Communication: A Ten-Step Inventory." In *Intercultural Communication: A Reader*, edited by L.A. Samovar and R.E. Porter, pp. 16-33. Belmont, CA: Wadsworth.

Collins, P.H. (1986). "Learning From the Outsider Within: The Sociological Significance of Black Feminist Thought." *Social Problems* 33: 14-32.

———. (1990). *Black Feminist Thought: Knowledge, Consciousness and the Politics of Empowerment*. New York: Routledge, Capman and Hall.

Cross, W.E. (1985). "Black Identity: Rediscovering the Distinction Between Personal Identity and Reference Group Orientation." In *Beginnings: The Social and Affective Development of Black Children*, edited by M.B. Spenser, G.K. Brookins, and W.R. Allen, pp. 131-155. Hillsdale, NJ: Erlbaum.

Dervin, B., and K.D. Clark. (December 1999). "Exemplars of the Use of the Sense-Making Methodology (Meta-Theory and Method): Introduction to the Sense-Making Issues of the Electronic Journal of Communication." *The Electronic Journal of Communication/ La Revue Electronique de Communication* 9 (2). [Online at http://www.cios.org/www/ejcrec2.htm]

Dwyer, K.K. (1998). *Conquer Your Speechfright: Learn How to Overcome the Nervousness of Public Speaking*. New York: Harcourt Brace.

Ellsworth, E. (1992). "Why Doesn't This Feel Empowering? Working Through the Repressive Myths of Critical Pedagogy." In *Feminisms and Critical Pedagogy*, edited by C.L. and J. Gore, pp. 90-119. New York: Routledge.

Feagin, J.R. (1992). "The Continuing Significance of Racism: Discrimination Against Black Students in White Colleges." *Journal of Black Studies* 22(4): 546-578.

Fisher, B.A. (1980). *Small Group Decision Making.* 2nd ed. New York: McGraw-Hill.

Fleming, J. (1984). *Blacks in College.* San Francisco: Jossey-Bass.

Ford, W.S., and A.D. Wolvin. (1993). "The Differential Impact of a Basic Communication Course on Perceived Communication Competencies in Class, Work, and Social Contexts." *Communication Education* 42(3): 215-223.

Foss, S.K., and K.A. Foss. (1994). *Inviting Transformation: Presentational Speaking for a Changing World.* Prospect Heights, IL: Waveland.

Freire, P. (1970). *Pedagogy of the Oppressed.* New York: Seabury.

Gabelnick, F., J. MacGregor, R.S. Matthews, and B.L. Smith. (1990). "Teaching in Learning Communities." In *Learning Communities: Creating Connections Among Students, Faculty, and Disciplines,* edited by R.E. Young, pp. 53-60. San Francisco: Jossey-Bass.

Gibbs, J.T. (1973). "Black Students/White University: Different Expectations." *Personal and Guidance Journal* 51: 463-469.

Giroux, H.A. (1983). *Theory and Resistance in Education.* South Hadley, MA: Bergin Garvey.

——— , C. Lankshear, P. McLaren, and M. Peters. (1995). *Counternarratives: Cultural Studies and Critical Pedagogies in Postmodern Spaces.* New York: Routledge.

Giroux, H.A., and P. McLaren. (1989). *Critical Pedagogy, the State, and Cultural Struggle.* Albany, NY: State University of New York.

——— , eds. (1994). *Between Borders: Pedagogy and the Politics of Cultural Studies.* New York: Routledge.

Goodsell, A.S., M. Maher, V. Tinto, B.L. Smith, and J. MacGregor. (1992). *Collaborative Learning: A Sourcebook for Higher Education.* University Park, PA: National Center on Postsecondary Teaching, Learning, and Assessment.

Gore, J. (1992). "What We Can Do For You! What Can 'We' Do For 'You'?: Struggling Over Empowerment in Critical and Feminist Pedagogy." In *Feminisms and Critical Pedagogy,* edited by C. Luke and J. Gore, pp. 54-71. New York: Routledge.

——— . (1998). "On the Limits to Empowerment Through Critical and Feminist Pedagogies." In *Power/Knowledge/Pedagogy: The Meaning of Democratic Education in Unsettling Times,* edited by D. Carlson and M.W. Apple, pp. 271-288. Boulder, CO: Westview.

Gudykunst, W.B., and Y.Y. Kim, eds. (1997). *Communicating With Strangers: An Approach to Intercultural Communication.* 3rd ed. New York: McGraw-Hill.

Harding, S. (1986). *The Science Question in Feminism.* Ithaca, NY: Cornell University Press.

————. (1987). "Conclusion: Epistemological Questions." In *Feminism and Methodology: Social Science Issues*, edited by S. Harding, pp. 181-190. Bloomington, IN: Indiana University Press.

————. (1991). *Whose Science? Whose Knowledge? Thinking From Women's Lives*. Ithaca, NY: Cornell University Press.

Hartsock, N. (1983). "The Feminist Standpoint: Developing the Ground for a Specifically Feminist Historical Materialism." In *Discovering Reality*, edited by S. Harding and M.B. Hinitikka, pp. 283-310. Amsterdam: D. Reidel.

————. (1997). "Comment on Hekman's 'Truth and Method: Feminist Standpoint Theory Revisited': Truth or Justice?" *Signs* 22(2): 367-374.

Hecht, M.L., M.J. Collier, and S.A. Ribeau. (1993). *African American Communication: Ethnic Identity and Cultural Interpretation*. Newbury Park, CA: Sage.

hooks, b. (1994). *Teaching to Transgress: Education as the Practice of Freedom*. New York: Routledge.

June, L.N., B.P. Curry, and C.L. Gear. (1990). "An 11-Year Analysis of Black Students' Expectations of Problems and Use of Services: Implications for Counseling Professionals." *Journal of Counseling Psychology* 37(2): 178-184.

Kadel, S., and J.A. Keehner. (1994). *Collaborative Learning: A Sourcebook for Higher Education, Volume II*. University Park, PA: National Center on Postsecondary Teaching, Learning, and Assessment.

Kincheloe, J.L., P. Slattery, and S.R. Steinberg. (2000). *Contextualizing Teaching: Introduction to Education and Educational Foundations*. New York: Addison Wesley Longman.

King, P.M. (1997). "Character and Civic Education: What Does It Take?" *The Educational Record* 78(3-4): 87-93.

Lieberman, A. (1996). "Creating Intentional Learning Communities." *Educational Leadership* 54(3): 51-55.

————. (2000). "Networks as Learning Communities: Shaping the Future of Teacher Development." *Journal of Teacher Education* 51(3): 221-227.

Lucas, S.E. (2001). *The Art of Public Speaking*. 7th ed. Boston/New York: McGraw-Hill.

Luke, C. (1992). "Feminist Politics in Radical Pedagogy." In *Feminisms and Critical Pedagogy*, edited by C. Luke and J. Gore, pp. 25-53. New York: Routledge.

————, and J. Gore, eds. (1992). *Feminisms and Critical Pedagogy*. New York: Routledge.

Martin, J.N., and T.K. Nakayama, eds. (1997). *Intercultural Communication in Contexts*. Mountain View, CA: Mayfield.

Marx, K., and F. Engels. (1986, orig. 1846). *The German Ideology*, introduction and edited by C.J. Arthur. New York: International Publishers.

McDermott, J.C., ed. (1999). *Beyond the Silence: Listening for Democracy*. Portsmouth, NH: Heineman.

McLaren, P. (1994). "Multiculturalism and the Postmodern Critique: Toward a Pedagogy of Resistance and Transformation." In *Between Borders: Pedagogy and the Politics of Cultural Studies*, edited by H.A. Giroux and P. McLaren, pp. 192-222. New York: Routledge.

———, and K. Gutierrez. (1998). "Global Politics and Local Antagonisms: Research and Practice as Dissent and Possibility." In *Power/Knowledge/Pedagogy: The Meaning of Democratic Education in Unsettling Times*, edited by D.Carlson and M.W. Apple, pp. 305-340. Boulder, CO: Westview.

Mino, M. (1988). "Making the Basic Public Speaking Course Relevant: Is It Preparing Students With Work-Related Public Speaking Skills?" *The Speech Communication Teacher* 3(1): 14.

Mohanty, C.T. (1994). "On Race and Voice: Challenges for Liberal Education in the 1990s." In *Between Borders: Pedagogy and the Politics of Cultural Studies*, edited by H.A. Giroux and P. McLaren, pp. 145-166. New York: Routledge.

Morton, N. (1985). *The Journey Is Home*. Boston: Beacon.

Ng, R., P. Staton, and J. Scane, eds. (1995). *Anti-Racism, Feminism, and Critical Approaches to Education*. Westport, CT: Bergin and Garvey.

Nieto, S. (1999). *The Light in Their Eyes: Creating Multicultural Learning Communities*. New York: Teachers College Press.

Pavitt, C., and E. Curtis. (1994). *Small Group Discussion: A Theoretical Approach*. Scottsdale, AZ: Gorsuch Scarisbrick.

Popkewitz, T.S., and L. Fendler, eds. (1999). *Critical Theories in Education: Changing Terrains of Knowledge and Politics*. New York: Routledge.

Rezai-Rashti, G. (1995). "Multicultural Education, Anti-Racist Education, and Critical Pedagogy: Reflections on Everyday Practice." In *Anti-Racism, Feminism, and Critical Approaches to Education*, edited by R. Ng, P. Staton, and J. Scane, pp. 3-19. Westport, CT: Bergin and Garvey.

Samovar, L.A., and R.E. Porter, eds. (2000). *Intercultural Communication: A Reader*. Belmont, CA: Wadsworth.

Shapiro, N.S., and J.H. Levine. (1999). *Creating Learning Communities: A Practical Guide to Winning Support, Organizing for Change, and Implementing Programs*. San Francisco: Jossey-Bass.

Smith, D. (1987). *The Everyday World as Problematic: A Feminist Sociology*. Boston: Northeastern University Press.

Styles-Hughes, M. (1987). "Black Students' Participation in Higher Education." *Journal of College Student Personnel* 41: 523-544.

Taylor, C.A. (1986). "Black Students on Predominantly White College Campuses in the 1980s." *Journal of College Student Personnel* 27: 196-201.

Tinto, V., A.G. Love, and P. Russo. (1994). *Building Learning Communities for New College Students: A Summary of Research Findings of the Collaborative Learning Project.* University Park, PA: National Center on Postsecondary Teaching, Learning, and Assessment.

Tubbs, S.L. (1988). *A Systems Approach to Small Group Interaction.* New York: Random House.

Wall, V.C., G.J. Galanes, and S.B. Love. (1987). "Small, Talk-Oriented Groups: Conflict, Conflict Management, Satisfaction and Decision Quality." *Small Group Behavior* 18: 31-55.

Willie, C., and A. McCord. (1973). *Black Students at White Colleges.* New York: Praeger.

Wood, J. (1992). "Gender and Moral Voice: Moving From Women's Nature to Standpoint Epistemology." *Women's Studies in Communication* 15: 1-24.

Zweigenhaft, R.L., and M.L. Cody. (1993). "The Self-Monitoring of Black Students on a Predominately White Campus." *The Journal of Social Psychology* 133(1): 5-10.

Reshaping Rhetorical Rivers

Climate, Communication, and Coherence in the
Basic Speech Course

Mark Lawrence McPhail, Ronald B. Scott, and Kathleen M. German

The three students stood a few feet apart in the locker room, two speaking and one overhearing their conversation, as they all changed clothes. One of the two students engaged in the casual conversation remarked how he was thinking about transferring from Miami University to another university elsewhere in Ohio.

"I was considering the University of Cincinnati because a lot of my friends go there. But I think that I'd rather go to Xavier University."

"How come?" said the other student.

"Well, last time I went to visit I walked around off campus, you know, in the neighborhood around the school, and it wasn't the kind of place I wanted to be. It's in a bad part of town, you know."

"Yeah, like the ghetto."

"Definitely the ghetto."

The conversation occurred between two young European-American men, who stood less than five feet from the third student, an African-American man. As the two white students walked by him, one heading to the same class he was about to attend, the black student wondered to himself whether they had any idea how uncomfortable their comments had made him feel, and how it was that the white student who had decided not to attend the University of Cincinnati had come to believe that it was in a "bad" part of town. Had he been accosted or followed? Had someone called him a bad name, or used a racial slur? Or had he simply seen nothing more than people different from himself, people whom he could only see through his "inner eyes," who were for all intents and purposes invisible to him as people. People who were just like this black student standing a few feet away, with whom he shared a classroom experience and, evidently, not much more.

We begin with this anecdote because we, like Mary Patterson McPherson, former president of Bryn Mawr College, believe that the students of color "most comfortable at whatever college they [attend] also [tend] to be the most successful academically" (in Bowen and Bok 1998: 82). McPherson's comments suggest that any attempt to address the academic success of students of color must ultimately deal with the issue of climate, and we agree. In this essay, we will amplify her observations to consider how the intellectual and institutional climates that students of color are likely to face in basic Communication courses have the potential to ensure — or injure — their chances of success.

Our focus is first on the social and institutional contexts that circumscribe how and what faculty teach and evaluate, and then on those specific curricular strategies that might transform the atmosphere and outcomes of the basic Public Speaking course. That is, while we wish to offer some insights into the importance of pedagogical and curricular strategies for creating inclusive and affirmative climates for student learning, we believe that it is equally important, if not more important, to carefully consider what impact beliefs and assumptions about identity and difference have on the ability to create such climates. If we are to successfully reshape Communication curricula in ways that will encourage conversations about inclusive teaching and learning and the importance of larger diversity issues across disciplines, then we must acknowledge the social exigencies and cultural impediments to education and communication that inhibit the success of students of color and continue to cripple the moral and intellectual development of large numbers of European-American students and faculty.

Initially, we shall consider one of the more important contemporary studies addressing the issue of climate generally, and reframe one of the observations made by its authors about racial difference and identity. Next, we will examine one particular university's efforts to address issues of inclusivity at an institutional level, and consider how those efforts suggest that an enlarged understanding of diversity is critical to transforming the cultural and intellectual climates within which students of color must function. Finally, we will discuss how we might recognize the Public Speaking class, one of the most essentially basic courses in Communication, as an arena within which students of different backgrounds and experiences might renegotiate their relationships with themselves and one another. Our purpose is to establish a theoretical framework for examining the institutional and attitudinal impediments to diversity efforts, then segue between theory and practice by examining an existing university program that cuts across the curriculum, and finally synthesize the theoretical and practical insights into a program of implementation that can reshape pedagogical practice and redefine what it means to be a good person who speaks well.

The challenge facing Communication scholars of conscience, we believe, is twofold: We must recognize how our discipline and the society in which it evolved are implicated in the creation of contexts that devalue diversity and undermine an appreciation of difference. And, we must be willing to embrace perspectives and positions within our field that, although not in the mainstream, offer opportunities for reshaping the intellectual tributaries of our discipline and redefining the stream of our collective moral consciousness.

Some Consequences of Reconsidering Race, Identity, and Difference

In *The Shape of the River: Long-Term Consequences of Considering Race in College and University Admissions*, William G. Bowen and Derek Bok (1998) comment on the effect of climate on students of color at several of America's academically selective universities. Their study, which examines personal histories as well as statistical data, suggests that climate plays an important role in determining the success of students of color in general and African-American students in particular:

> The academic performance of a number of black students seemed clearly affected by difficulties in adjusting to new environments. Feelings of in-security are by no means limited to any single group of students. Still, black students may feel them with special intensity (along with other minority students and some low-[socioeconomic status] white students). (82)

Because academic institutions reflect the beliefs and assumptions of a particular class, race, or gender, students whose identities and experiences fall outside those social and symbolic boundaries often suffer academically and face difficulties adjusting to unfamiliar intellectual and cultural contexts. To succeed, both academically and socially, black students, other students of color, and white students of low socioeconomic status are often forced to conform to dominant institutional and attitudinal norms.

Learning how to adjust to contexts and norms different from what they are used to — that is, "learning to cope with diversity" (1998: 222) — is an especially critical skill for African-American students to gain, assert Bowen and Bok:

> Because of their minority status, it has to be much harder for black Americans . . . to contemplate "doing well" in life if they are unable to work effectively with members of the white majority. They have no choice but to take seriously the importance of "getting along." (221-222)

From this, Bowen and Bok conclude that

> the educational value of learning to cope with diversity may well be even greater for black students than for white students — in spite of the fact that much of the discussion of diversity focuses on ways in which white students are presumed to learn from black classmates. (222)

While we agree with Bowen and Bok's assessment of the significance of climate and the importance of learning to cope with diversity for African-American students' success, we question any implication that the lessons of diversity might be more important for students of color than for white students. That is, if, as Bowen and Bok suggest, the focus has been on what white students can learn about diversity from their classmates' black identity, then it is clear to us that not enough thought has been given to *white* identity and its impact on the creation of climates in which diversity is valued. Why might this be? As Robert Terry argued almost 30 years ago, "to be white in America is to not have to think about it"

(1981: 120). Thus, any attempt to create a culture of inclusion in university and college classrooms must directly deal with the extent to which whiteness is seen as the norm as it impacts the beliefs and assumptions of European-American students and faculty.

Our reframing of Bowen and Bok's point in *The River* is influenced by a significant amount of contemporary research in Education and Communication. As Maurianne Adams observes,

> The general absence of conscious cultural identity among many Euro-American students . . . obscures the larger issue of cultural difference, reduces all cultural experience to a single dominant norm, and dismisses as frivolous the culture-consciousness of nontraditional students who want to stress and value their own ethnic roots. (1992: 6)

Adams also examines the impact that faculty have on creating and sustaining classroom climates that can disadvantage and disempower students of color: "The role of college faculty in consciously or unconsciously transmitting a dominant cultural system is especially important in addressing present challenges, since, in higher education, all roads lead back to faculty, who have control of matters of teaching, evaluation, and curriculum" (1992: 7).

Faculty play a particularly critical role in creating context for inclusivity and valuing diversity, explains Adams, and many have begun to recognize that creating a context for enhancing diversity demands that faculty address more than what students of color might or might not be capable of teaching white students. They must also address what white students have been taught to believe about themselves — and its consequences. "On many college campuses, efforts to preserve gains of the civil rights movement are yielding a growing white backlash," explains Christine Sleeter, "as white students fear that they are now the victims and targets of systematic racism" (1997: ix). This ideology of innocence, which has surfaced in classrooms across the country, undermines the possibility for white students to speak openly and honestly about race with black students in particular and with students of color in general.

Indeed, the "recovery of race" (Gresson 1995) that lately characterizes much of white discourse reflects the psychological anxieties brought about by an increasingly pluralistic and multicultural society in which European Americans must come face-to-face with difference on a daily basis. There are significant consequences for communication, especially those forms of communication that place a premium on self-reflexivity and affirmative interaction. Sleeter continues:

> Cross-racial dialogue about racism, which involves white people, however, is rare and difficult to develop and sustain. Dialogue requires that people be able to articulate some analysis of racism and one's own position in a racist
> . structure, one's own feeling and experiences, and the choices one has for acting differently. Most white people do not talk about racism, do not recognize the existence of institutional racism, and feel personally threatened by the mention of racism. (1997: x)

The lack of constructive communication about race between white people and people of color and the rhetoric of denial that characterizes European-American discourse on race have been addressed by Communication scholars interested in the ways in which language constructs *difference* and *identity* (see van Dijk 1987; McPhail 1994). Communication researchers also have examined the ways in which education itself influences racial understanding and misunderstanding in increasingly subtle and insidious ways.

Among them, Rosalee Clawson and Elizabeth Kegler (2000) have examined how race is "coded" in textbook discussions of poverty. Their examination of American Government textbooks reveals that portrayals of poverty are "much more likely to reinforce existing (erroneous and insidious) beliefs regarding black citizens in our society than to challenge prevailing stereotypes or undermine racism" (184). Because textbook portrayals of poverty have a potentially detrimental effect on students, who generally view such portrayals as "objective" accounts of "reality," Clawson and Kegler are very interested in the role of professors and publishing companies in perpetuating a distorted understanding of relationships between poverty and race. "In the world of textbook publishing, professors make the acquisition decisions. Is it the case that publishing companies are simply providing professors with textbooks that resonate with their predispositions?" (2000: 185). Or, they ask, is it possible that the racial coding of poverty might be perpetuated by the publishers themselves, which "may have an ideological interest in promoting visual depictions of the poor that reinforce existing inequities in our society" (185)? Given the extensiveness of this misinformation and miseducation and the failure of educational institutions themselves to interrogate the social and symbolic realities of racial privilege, it is not difficult to understand how students could uncritically conflate race and poverty, seeing the two as isomorphic: "Definitely the ghetto."

Indeed, as van Dijk's research reveals, educational institutions are deeply implicated in the perpetuation of racial privilege. He writes that "neither the content and style of educational discourse nor the organization of education exactly favors a point of view that might challenge the extant power relations in Europeanized societies" (1993: 238). The result, he suggests, is the creation and perpetuation of academic climates that undermine the success of students of color. "Lacking identification and recognition, and confronted with many subtle and blatant forms of everyday racism in textbooks, classrooms, or playgrounds, minority students face a challenge that has obvious repercussions on their performance" (238).

Although van Dijk contends that the defense of whiteness is directly related to the problems that students of color face in academic contexts and communities, he indicates also that the climate it creates undermines the capacity for white students to critically interrogate their own identities. Whereas students of color develop strategies for resistance to the negative messages they encounter on a regular basis, white students "are largely prevented from acquiring the fundamental knowledge and attitudes that prepare them for a more critical role in society" (240). Van Dijk's research, like that of a number of race-relations scholars, prompts us to critically reconsider the roles of race, identity, difference, and privilege in defining the exigencies and constraints facing Communication educators committed to creating more-inclusive classroom communities.

Reshaping What We Mean by "Race"

The current rhetorical situation of race relations in America is marked by an imperfect understanding of the role of *racial privilege and entitlement*, imperfect in that its material and economic consequences have been erased from the minds of most white Americans. "Whites, according to polls," explains Harlon L. Dalton, "do not view the current racial malaise as their responsibility" (1995: 7). Dalton argues that this denial, while perhaps understandable, is ultimately "wrongheaded," since it leads to a distortion of history, a retreat from reason, and the belief that African Americans are simply the victims of their own self-destructive behavior. He concludes that "unless one attributes the community's self-inflicted wounds to some character defect inherent in the race, we cannot simply dismiss the lively possibility that white indifference and 'benign neglect' have contributed to the problem" (8). Unfortunately, contemporary discourse on race would seem to indicate that most white Americans have done just that — opted for the "character defect" explanation.

Further compounding this misperception is the tendency for contemporary discussions of difference and diversity to reduce race to black and white and ignore the complex elements of social stratification and subordination that are factors in the lives of many Americans of color. Thus, while an understanding of the role of whiteness is necessary, it is by no means sufficient for the reshaping of our intellectual and cultural climates.

A reshaping of the very idea of *race* is also called for.

EXPANDING OUR UNDERSTANDING OF DIFFERENCE AND DIVERSITY

The 1968 Kerner commission report, in addressing issues of black/white racial discord in this country, warned: "Our nation is moving toward two societies, one black, one white — separate and unequal." Now, more than three decades later, that warning could be modified to acknowledge that the nation is moving toward a divide on not only black/white relations but also brown/white, black/brown, male/female, young/old, and on and on. In effect, today we are moving toward a nation — regardless of our growing need to function collectively — that is more segregated and separated on more dimensions than ever and less able to communicate across those lines. We see rifts between diverse groups only exacerbated by growing and destructive ignorance of "the other," in which rumor, myths, stereo-types, and miscommunication supplant informed, accurate understanding.

While conversations about diversity generally imply a broader understand-ing of the various differences that members of American society bring to the table of our common destiny, such conversations too often turn back to discussions of race in terms of black and white. This conversational turn continues to occur in spite of an enormous amount of data showing that America is becoming a multi-cultural population with global interests and connections. At the level of social and institutional policy, the need to reframe *race* in terms of diversity is critical. Soci-ologist William Julius Wilson (1999), in the conclusion of his recent work on racial inequality in American society, concurs: "Adequate political solutions to the global economic problems confronting the majority of Americans will not be found until white, black, Latino, Asian, and Native Americans begin thinking more about what they have in common and less about their differences" (117). Consequently, Wilson suggests that we must not only rethink, revitalize, and rearticulate our own founding principles but also come to grips with the potential human bonding and cultural growth that can occur if diversity is viewed as a pos-itive resource for intellectual growth, change, and nation building.

At the same time, he notes, the nation must acknowledge and realize that embracing diversity and achieving equity, as the past informs us, will be no easy matter: "Given the racial friction that has adversely affected intergroup relations, particularly in urban America, the formation of a multiracial reform coalition to pursue a mass-based economic agenda is likely to be difficult" (123). Although Wilson is primarily concerned with the larger economic and political conse-quences of social division and stratification, he also addresses the impact of "cul-tural racism" on the potential for building coalitions in educational institutions. The assumptions of cultural racism support the notion that minorities suffer dis-proportionately from poverty and inequality because of something inherent in the contents of their characters. Wilson explains that "cultural racism, not only in educational institutions but also in other public and private institutions of Ameri-can society, impedes the progress of blacks and other minorities, and ultimately reinforces individual cultural racist beliefs about their traits and capabilities" (18). The unfortunate result of cultural racism is that it undermines the possibility of constructive dialogue and coalition building: "Many white Americans are more likely to have an unfavorable impression of African Americans and therefore [are] less likely to join forces with them in a common endeavor" (18-19). While Wil-son's focus is on black and white Americans, his analysis of racial antagonism is clearly concerned with the need for contemporary dialogues about diversity to move beyond black/white conceptions of race.

In terms of its educational implications, Wilson's analysis suggests that mov-ing forward and establishing meaningful understanding and productive relations will require honest dialogues, difficult (though not hostile) confrontations, and a willingness to learn from others to explore issues and experiences across the boundaries that currently fragment the community. Thus, to appreciate diversity, each member of the community will need to engage in reflection and meaningful discussions about all forms of difference. Put another way, we must learn to communicate with one another across the divides, to move beyond debate and toward dialogue.

But by *dialogue* we mean more than simply discussion, we mean a consciously nonoppositional discursive strategy, "a communicative process that reflects social experience in order to understand the social and historical forces at work" (Adams 1997: 39) in our interactions with one another. Maurianne Adams describes *dialogue* in precisely these terms, and views it as a pedagogical strategy for educating individuals about social justice and diversity. Drawing upon the work of Freire and others, she acknowledges the capacity for such dialogue to enhance critical and self-reflexive understanding, and to provide students with the intellectual and empathic resources necessary "to name and discuss 'coded situations'" (39). Like Adams, Communication scholars also see the value of dialogue as a potentially transformative strategy for understanding and appreciating diversity. Sally Miller Gearhart's (1979) articulation of a "womanized" rhetoric and Mark McPhail's (1995) theory of "rhetorical coherence" both emphasize dialogue as a nonoppositional, nonconfrontational alternative to the persuasive emphases of traditional rhetoric. We shall return to this conception of *dialogue* below to illustrate how it offers a viable vehicle for understanding and appreciating diversity within the context of the basic course in Communication.

However, for any Communication program to contribute to improving campus climate for all students (including students of color), we must remember that success is possible only by focusing on the development of the complete student, with a particular emphasis on his or her individual identity. Quality education in today's environment facilitates such development by stimulating students to appreciate their own cultural backgrounds; the diversity of cultural backgrounds they will encounter on and off campus; and understanding other significant aspects of identity such as race, gender, sexual preference, physical ability, social class, religious beliefs, and different value hierarchies.

Such an approach to education and development reflects the process of what Aaron David Gresson (1995) describes as "enlargement," a strategy for self-recovery that is inclusive and integrative. Gresson explains that enlargement "cannot occur as sleight of hand" or be "gerrymandered into vitality and integrity" (214). It cannot, in short, simply be a quick fix; instead it must "be part of a global, species-specific maturation. But it requires that we collectively begin the systematic rebuilding of a healthier, more inclusive set of formative images" (214). Those images, Gresson suggests, demand that we see racial difference in relation to its many shades, and diversity in terms of its numerous nuances: "We must delimit these images enough to inspire identification and involvement, yet make them expansive enough to embrace the integrity of world communities" (214). Gresson's transformative vision, like those of Wilson, Adams, and Gearhart, acknowledges the need to understand diversity in terms of not only race but also class, gender, and other shades of difference. It is the same vision that informs our own university's attempt to affirm the value of diversity, through an institutionally initiated program called "Mosaic."

FROM THEORY TO PRACTICE AT MIAMI UNIVERSITY

Like many colleges and universities across the country, Miami University (Ohio) was faced with all of the challenges that accompany attempts to address issues of overall climate and diversity on campus. As a predominantly white campus challenged with improving diversity in terms of raw numbers and representation of minority populations, Miami was realizing that improving numbers without actually altering the campus climate would solve little. In fact, as a result of many long and impassioned discussions, many at Miami came to understand that regardless of the composition of the student/faculty body, students from diverse backgrounds would not remain or feel comfortable in the current environment, regardless of all recruiting and support efforts. At the same time, Miami recognized that its homogenous composition was not effectively preparing its students for an increasingly diverse world. The Mosaic program was the university's response.

Mosaic was consciously developed at Miami University to improve the educational environment, and to create a climate where each member of the academic community could engage others and learn from their individual experiences and knowledge in an atmosphere as open and hospitable to all as possible. The program emphasizes several goals and principles, with recommendations to bring about the changes necessary to improve the existing campus environment. Its objectives were to create an environment that:

- is safe and free from harassment and discrimination for all members of the community, and especially for members of underrepresented groups;

- would facilitate each student's ability and opportunity to learn about his or her own unique cultural identity; and

- would facilitate each student's learning and appreciation of national cultures different from his or her own.

In all respects, the recommendations were designed to make the environment on Miami University's campus open and receptive to difference and diversity, and to begin the process of communication across the divides.

Success of the Mosaic program has not yet been definitively measured, but an anecdote might indicate its potential to create change and reframe diversity issues. At a recent meeting of administrators in which the adoption of a diversity requirement was being discussed, one associate dean who had been actively involved in Mosaic was asked whether the program had been successful in its attempts to change student attitudes and beliefs. "I can't be sure about the effect it's had on the students," he remarked, "but I sure know that it has transformed me." His comments indicate to us that the Mosaic program has the potential to successfully address issues of climate and diversity on our campus.

Central to that success, we believe, was the realization that faculty could be trained through interactive, dialogical programs to recognize the factors that silence people, and trained to address those problems when they surfaced. This dialogic emphasis helped faculty reshape their own understandings of difference and identity and better understand the points of view of their students, and it offered insights into how they might conduct their own classes in ways that would create more comfortable learning atmospheres.

Many faculty discovered that diversity was less about the numbers of students and faculty of color on campus than it was about the ability of an individual to create an environment in which people could speak to one another without silencing anyone else. That discovery has critical implications for the discipline of Communication and our ability to successfully create similar environments in our basic classes. Explains Lori J. Carrell: "Increasing awareness of diversity has generated introspection, discussion, and change in many disciplines at many universities in this country. . . . The [C]ommunication discipline is no exception to this national trend" (1997: 234). Carrell's essay is one of the few systematic assessments of diversity initiatives in the Communication curriculum. While her main emphasis is on facilitating student empathy, her conclusions have implications for faculty as well. "Complete integration of multiculturalism into our discipline," she writes, "will involve infusing, adding, and changing our curriculum and pedagogy" (243).

So what might those infusions, additions, and changes look like in one of our discipline's most basic courses, in Public Speaking?

Reshaping Rhetoric

TRANSFORMING THE BASIC COURSE IN PUBLIC SPEAKING

The comments of that associate dean about the success of the Mosaic program invite us to consider how Communication curricula might be similarly transformative, not only for faculty but also for students. If the key to enabling inclusion is the creation of a classroom climate that celebrates diversity, then each of us must assess the assumptions upon which we base our teaching style and course design, recognizing limitations and barriers to cultivating an inclusive classroom. This is particularly important in introductory courses such as Interpersonal Communication and Public Speaking, because such courses are often students' first experience of the Communication discipline.

Yet, that assessment can be extremely difficult, even for educators committed to diversity and social justice. Maurianne Adams quotes bell hooks's observations that even teachers who have no trouble "embracing new ways of thinking may still be as resolutely attached to old ways of practicing teaching as their more conservative colleagues" (1997: 30). Nowhere are these attachments more pronounced, we would suggest, than in our basic courses. Yet, those courses offer singular opportunities for faculty to engage issues of inclusion and demonstrate the ways that communication sensitivity can transform ourselves and others. Such ideas of inclusion are deeply embedded in the history of our discipline. From its early rhetorical tradition to the emergence in this century of the discipline of Communication, ours is a hybrid of disciplines as we recognize our connections to Poetics, Philosophy, Psychology, Sociology, Political Science, Critical Studies. This position — at the intersection of many academic disciplines — offers us a unique opportunity to engage students in reflections on their own identities. The prospects for addressing inclusion are more apparent in the basic Interpersonal Communication course, because it centers on individuals engaged in dyadic interactions; but the Public Speaking course presents a challenge, because it has evolved through a relatively unchanged and unchallenged set of parameters for effective public address.

Paradoxically, these parameters arose from Greco-Roman cultures that recognized the inherent right of citizens to participate in their own governance, even as they suppressed a majority of the population by excluding them from the public forum. Perhaps our own tradition of public address education exhibits a similar internal paradox. That is, while valuing the act of public expression, conventional Public Address courses sanction unexamined assumptions about public advocacy. Our courses frequently adopt the models of Greece and Rome without further examination. This lack of reflection privileges Western, hierarchical models over other alternatives. In an increasingly interconnected world, it is important to expand the choices to equip our students to both understand and appreciate other approaches to public discourse.

While we might be tempted to simply reject "the tradition" as incapable of addressing contemporary issues of difference and diversity, we might also consider a more inclusive approach. Susan Jarratt, in *Re-Reading the Sophists: Classical Rhetoric Refigured*, resolves the choice that confronts us in this manner: "One possible course for the contemporary rhetorician would be to jettison those classical origins as unassimilable to a contemporary context. . . . But I propose that a more comprehensive view of 'the tradition' will provide rich antecedents for later rhetorical developments" (1991: xix). Jarratt notes that while her analysis "borrows from deconstruction the critique of binary structures" (xxiii), it is ultimately a reconstructive project, one whose "critical capacity for exposing the contradictions inherent in dominant discourse suggests its relevance for literacy teachers today who seek ways to draw out minority voices" (xxiv). Although Jarratt's primary audience is teachers of Composition, her re-reading of the Sophists has important implications for teachers of Public Speaking, whose own reshaping of rhetoric represents an important challenge to the dominant paradigm of our discipline: the practice of persuasion.

At other junctures in Communication's history, we've encountered similar challenges to the dominant paradigm, and often they have resulted in stretching the boundaries of acceptable public expression. When Abraham Lincoln addressed listeners in the cemetery at Gettysburg, his message was initially over-shadowed by rejection of his presentational style; and yet, although Lincoln violated the expansive oratorical style of his era, the power of his thoughts and words lives on. In similar ways, the messages of Sojourner Truth, Chief Seattle, Frederick Douglass, and Susan B. Anthony were rejected because of who they were or how they framed their ideas. In retrospect, our lives have been enriched because expanding the parameters of communication to include others has encouraged our receptiveness to those messages. The fundamental lesson taught by our own public address history is that valuable ideas often are disregarded because they do not fit the prevalent model of communication. If nothing else, history makes the case for a more varied, inclusive approach to public expression. Giving people more ways to communicate should, by the very nature of our discipline, be our goal in the educational process, but particularly at the foundational level of our introductory courses.

In designing the basic courses, however, we realize that we could unintentionally build in structural impediments to inclusiveness. As Adams explains: "So powerful and pervasive are the folkways of academe as reinforcers of traditional academic practice that is it understandably difficult for college faculty to see beyond their own acculturation and to imagine alternative possibilities for the classroom" (1992: 7). Adams's admonition reminds us that the development of a basic course that values diversity must consider the theoretical as well as practical dimensions of discourse and pedagogy. If, for example, we echo the words of our textbooks and call for a linear pattern of argumentation, then we implicitly send the message of privilege for that pattern. Realistically, other patterns have worked as effectively and the process of argumentation depends not on a single pattern but on arguments in many different guises that reflect the lived interactions of speakers and listeners with shared sociocultural assumptions within which the arguments operate. In creating a basic course that conveys the importance of valuing diversity, we must operationalize inclusion by addressing day-to-day issues.

Practically, this means choosing a textbook that offers alternatives, designing assignments to encourage exploration, addressing concerns about how the course will be conducted, and sometimes convincing students that it is important to explore multiple views. This process of guiding students, Baxter Magolda (1997) explains, "in exploring themselves, evaluating their ideas, and making judgments in the context of multiple views helps them to move forward in establishing values and beliefs that are separate from those in which they were acculturated" (18). By thinking about such choices, we're providing our students with opportunities to experience inclusion.

This emphasis on inclusion returns us to the concept of *dialogue* as it has emerged in contemporary rhetorical theory. While Gearhart's aforementioned emphasis on dialogue saw it, paradoxically, in opposition to *persuasion* (which she defined as "an act of violence") (1979: 195), recent conceptualizations of the rhetorical possibilities of dialogue have placed more stress on inclusivity in both theory and practice. Drawing on the work of Gearhart and various other proponents of dialogue, Sonja K. Foss and Cindy L. Griffin (1995) offer an "invitational rhetoric" as a communicative strategy that moves public discourse beyond persuasion. Foss and Griffin describe invitational rhetoric as "an invitation to understanding as a means to create a relationship rooted in equality, immanent value, and self-determination" (5). The theoretical emphasis of invitational rhetoric is on dialogue, which stresses inclusivity, empathy, and the withholding of judgment. "Invitational rhetoric," they write, "constitutes an invitation to the audience to enter the rhetor's world and to see it as the rhetor does" (5).

> In presenting a particular perspective, the invitational rhetor does not judge or denigrate others' perspectives, but is open to and tries to appreciate and validate those perspectives, even if they differ dramatically from the rhetor's own. Ideally, audience members accept the invitation offered by the rhetor by listening to and trying to understand the rhetor's perspective and then presenting their own. When this happens, rhetor and audience alike contribute to the thinking about an issue so that everyone involved gains a greater understanding of the issue in its subtlety, richness, and complexity. (1995: 5)

Foss and Griffin suggest that invitational rhetoric is not simply an ideal, but it has been realized in the discourses of various men and women from different populations and perspectives, all of whom emphasize nonoppositional approaches to communication. "Because of the nonhierarchical, nonjudgmental, nonadversarial framework established for the interaction, an understanding of the participants themselves occurs, an understanding that engenders appreciation, value, and a sense of equality" (5). Foss and Griffin's invitational rhetoric coheres theoretically with the concerns of educators committed to the teaching of diversity, and offers a viable communicative strategy for creating the types of inclusive and accepting climates that diversity scholars believe are necessary for transforming educational institutions and practices.

The practical manifestation of this theoretical coherence is seen in Sonja and Karen Foss's (1994) book *Inviting Transformation*. Foss and Foss offer their text as complementary to traditional Public Speaking textbooks, and focus on "presentational speaking" as a strategy for inviting transformation. They note that the conditions of "safety, value, freedom, and openness" (5) are essential to such transformation, and directly explain to students that because the two authors "have chosen to privilege the opportunity for transformation, the kind of speaking dealt with in this book may look very different from the kinds of speaking with which you are familiar" (7). The practice of invitational speaking, they suggest, is neither confrontational nor competitive, but is intended to create climates "in which others feel valued and free to hold their own perspectives" (7). The conditions and values they emphasize are reminiscent of those embraced by Miami University's Mosaic program. Foss and Foss are similarly concerned with the need to create an environment in which individuals feel safe and free to express themselves without condemnation or criticism. We believe that their book offers an excellent theoretical and practical model for the reshaping of rhetorical inquiry and expression as it is incorporated into the basic Public Speaking class. In fact, we anticipate designing a basic course in which invitational rhetoric will be the primary strategy through which students are introduced to the ideas of communicative diversity and reconceptualizing difference and identity.

This reconceptualization results in a Public Speaking course in which responsibilities for the communicative act have shifted. Instead of placing all focus on the speaker, presentational speaking moves some of the responsibility to the listener. Privilege has also shifted. Instead of placing emphasis on the speaker for generating ideas, the message becomes a co-construction of listeners. The speaker's role is now seen as the midwife of the message rather than its architect. The listener is elevated from an afterthought or one chapter in the standard Public Speaking textbook to an integral part of the transaction. In addition, the hierarchy of the communication process has flattened through recognition of the equal, participatory role of the listener. Shifting from the dominant emphasis on persuasion to an invitational approach in presentational speaking challenges the traditional privileging of the speaker that is evident in our unquestioned choices of seemingly innocuous parts of the communication process such as patterns of argument. It invites us to recognize that there are multiple opportunities within the Public Speaking course to alter our viewpoints and interrogate the Western model of argumentation (i.e., vocally/publicly articulated conclusions, external standards for evaluating evidence/supporting material rather than standards created by audience, and credibility/ethos dimensions of speakers based on qualities reflecting the patriarchal Eurocentric assumptions of our culture). An invitational rhetoric implicitly calls into question that dominant paradigm, and explicitly offers an alternative conceptualization of discourse that values and affirms diversity and creates a climate of inclusivity that could potentially begin the difficult process of transforming our educational and intellectual practices.

We believe that the transformation of our Public Speaking classrooms necessarily involves establishing an inclusive climate. However, we also recognize that it is clearly the instructor who initiates the process. As we examine the role of the speaker/listener throughout the course, we can call our students' attention to the value of individuals and how the community recognizes or is constrained. This is the fundamental assumption that we need to foreground in our execution of the course. Ultimately, we are responsible for modeling alternative perspectives, articulating them in our framing of the syllabus, the examples we choose to highlight, and in opening the speaking process. Fundamental to this process is the recognition of the inherent assumptions we make in speaking. These are prompted by our textbooks. Fundamentally, we privilege whiteness, Western perspectives, and the hierarchies inherent in our inherited traditions of communication. These stress the linear, assertive demonstrations of credibility: materiality over spirituality, assertion over cooperation, aggression over invitation.

We hope to have shown here how an emphasis on invitational rhetoric in the Public Speaking course might help all students better understand the role that these privileges play in our lives and relationships with one another. Such an understanding could lead to not only a reshaping of rhetoric but also a "re-sourcement" of our world and words. As Foss and Foss explain, re-sourcement "may create an open space, then, in which a wider variety of communicative options are possible. Opportunities for transformation may emerge that may have seemed virtually impossible to create at the start of an interaction" (1994: 13). Re-sourcement, like dialogue and invitational rhetoric, creates new possibilities for the reshaping of rivers, race, and rhetoric and is a reaffirmation of our ability to encourage our students to become, in the best tradition of our discipline, good persons who speak and act well.

Reshaping the Student

We began with an anecdotal account of an interaction whose type, we suspect, is all too common on college and university campuses. We began with it because it reveals the subtle and unconscious ways in which white students can create uncomfortable climates for students of color, in this case an African-American student. Although the story told a tale of black and white, we hope that you recognize that the issues we've tried to raise here reveal a much more diverse definition of difference, and that the complexity of the issues that face us all cannot begin to be understood through the soundbites of casual conversations.

Indeed, what is perhaps most important about the anecdote is what was left unsaid — that the black man in the locker room, in this particular instance, was a student in a course but *also* was a member of the faculty (in fact, one of the authors of this essay). But he was assumed to be a student by all in the locker room. And, as we said at the outset of this essay, it is such "beliefs and assumptions about identity and difference" that so impact our ability to create inclusive and affirmative climates for student learning.

The discomfort he felt most acutely was the kind that comes from fearing that we might not be able to reshape our students or institutions in ways that will facilitate an appreciation of diversity and social justice. It was the kind of fear expressed in the words of The Honorable Leon Higginbotham in the aftermath of the *Hopwood* decision, "I sometimes feel as if I am watching justice die" (in Bowen and Bok 1998: 286). The kind of fear that makes us sometimes wonder why we even try to facilitate a rethinking of identity, difference, and diversity.

But beyond the fear, we continue to search for hope, and hope to find new ways of defining and redefining identity, difference, and diversity. And in our searching we will undoubtedly find others also committed to transforming climates and transgressing boundaries, to reconstructing educational institutions and individual attitudes. The roots of this reconstruction can be grounded in our basic courses if we, as Communication scholars and teachers, are willing to rethink our pedagogical practices and their implications for enhancing diversity. In the case of the basic course in Public Speaking, the incorporation of dialogical and invitational approaches to rhetoric would move us in the right direction and would enhance the contribution that Communication education can make to understanding and valuing diversity. Ultimately, an invitational approach to Public Speaking might impart to our students a sense of rhetorical coherence, a "capacity to integrate diverse conceptions of reality" (McPhail 1995: 214), that might help them synthesize the disciplined study of traditional approaches to Public Speaking with a compassionate and nonadversarial appreciation of identity and difference. This would be a fitting achievement for a discipline long disparaged by the privileged epistemologies and "white mythologies" (Derrida 1974) of science and philosophy, and denigrated for nothing other than having been the product of an accidental birth in the cradle of Western culture, a strange bedpartner of freedom and democracy.

References

Adams, M. (1992). "Cultural Inclusion in the American College Classroom." *New Directions for Teaching and Learning* 49: 5-17.

———. (1997). "Pedagogical Frameworks for Social Justice Education." In *Teaching for Diversity and Social Justice: A Sourcebook*, edited by M. Adams, L.A. Bell, and P. Griffin, pp. 30-43. New York: Routledge.

Baxter Magolda, M.B. (November-December 1997) "Facilitating Meaningful Dialogues." *About Campus*, pp. 14-18.

Bowen, W., and D. Bok. (1998). *The Shape of the River: Long-Term Consequences of Considering Race in College and University Admissions*. Princeton, NJ: Princeton University Press.

Carrell, L.J. (1997). "Diversity in the Communication Curriculum: Impact on Student Empathy." *Communication Education* 46: 234-244.

Clawson, R.A., and E.R. Kegler. (July 2000). "The 'Race Coding' of Poverty in American Government College Textbooks." *The Howard Journal of Communications* 11(3): 179-188.

Dalton, H.L. (1995). *Racial Healing. Confronting the Fear Between Blacks & Whites*. New York: Doubleday.

Derrida, J. (1974). "White Mythology: Metaphor in the Text of Philosophy." *New Literary History* 6: 5-75.

Foss, S.K., and K. Foss. (1994). *Inviting Transformation: Presentational Speaking for a Changing World*. Prospect Heights, IL: Waveland Press.

Foss, S.K., and C.L. Griffin. (1995). "Beyond Persuasion: A Proposal for an Invitational Rhetoric." *Communication Monographs* 62: 2-18.

Gearhart, S.M. (1979). "The Womanization of Rhetoric." *Women's Studies International Quarterly* 2: 195-201.

Gresson, A.D. (1995). *The Recovery of Race in America*. Minneapolis: University of Minnesota Press.

Jarratt, S. (1991). *Re-Reading the Sophists: Classical Rhetoric Refigured*. Carbondale, IL: Southern Illinois University Press.

Kerner, O. (1968). *Report of the National Advisory Commission on Civil Disorders*. Washington, DC: Government Printing Office.

McPhail, M. (1994). *The Rhetoric of Racism*. Lanham, MD: University Press of America.

——— . (1995). *Zen in the Art of Rhetoric: An Inquiry Into Coherence*. Albany, NY: State University of New York Press.

Sleeter, C. (1997). "Foreword." In *Making Meaning of Whiteness: Exploring Racial Identity With White Teachers*, edited by A. McIntyre, pp. ix-xii. Albany, NY: State University of New York Press.

Terry, R. (1981). "The Negative Impact on White Values." In *Impacts of Racism on White Americans*, edited by B. Browser and R. Hunt, pp. 119-152. Beverly Hills, CA: Sage.

van Dijk, T.A. (1987). *Communicating Racism: Ethnic Prejudice in Thought and Talk*. Beverly Hills, CA: Sage.

——— . (1993). *Elite Discourse and Racism*. Beverly Hills, CA: Sage.

Wilson, W.J. (1999). *The Bridge Over the Racial Divide: Rising Inequality and Coalition Politics*. Berkeley, CA: University of California Press.

A Time for Inclusion

Strategies for Encouraging the Success of All Students

Linda G. Seward

> Knowledge is not exactly power. Knowledge is the power to know, to under-
> stand, but not necessarily the power to do or to change. . . . Knowledge
> is power only for those who can use it to change their conditions. (Shor
> 1992: 6)

Responses to an increasingly diverse America have run the gamut from
denying the existence of cultural differences among our citizens (see,
e.g., Kochman 1981) to explicitly addressing issues from multiple perspectives (see, e.g., DeVito 2001; Hecht, Collier, and Ribeau 1993; Samovar and
Porter 2000). While there are a variety of issues to consider when it comes
to the educational success of students of color, it makes sense to take our cue
from M.K. Asante. A leading proponent of Afrocentric studies, Asante has
been in the forefront among those who call for African Americans to be
included "as a *subject* of history, not as an object in someone else's experiences" (1992: 22). Although universities typically study nonwhite, nonmale
cultures in separate courses or in separate sections of existing courses, Communication classes can be exemplars of an integrative approach. Interpersonal Communication is particularly amenable to countering such intellectual
segregation or omission when it comes to diversity.

The reason that Interpersonal Communication is particularly appropriate as
a class in which to address diversity issues is that it focuses on concepts rather than
on groups. Thus, the course sidesteps the issue of bias in who is chosen and who
is avoided for study and discussion. With topics such as self-concept, perceptions,
language, family and nonverbal communication, Interpersonal Communication
presents not only a viable but a natural site for the infusion of multiculturalism. As
Downey and Torrecilha (1994) note, a concept-oriented course — as opposed to
one that examines "a group a week" — is preferable when addressing multicultural
topics, because it avoids the tendency of some students to exoticize and stereotype
"others."

Several years ago I developed a Multicultural Communication course for a
small Midwestern private religious university with an overwhelmingly white student body. Since 1987, the nonwhite student population has increased from 3 percent to its current level of 7 percent. Developing a diversity course for a decidedly nondiverse population posed new challenges to my teaching practices, as well
as prompted a great deal of self-reflection. Cognizant of the need for teacher-
scholars to identify and reflect upon their role in the collection and analysis of

data, I consciously reflected upon the implications of my own race (Anglo/Caucasian) and gender (female) for a course about diversity in the United States in such a campus environment (for discussions of researchers' influence on their subjects, see Bell 1993; Clifford and Marcus 1986; Geertz 1988; Orbe 2000; Pettigrew 1981).

While the class does, in fact, draw a high percentage of minority students, it is not unusual for one or two students to be the only members of a particular minority group. Given this set of circumstances, I was confronted with a dilemma: How could I foster a supportive environment for members of racial (and religious) minorities while encouraging dialogues that examined controversial issues from a variety of perspectives? This essay, then, is the result of classroom experiences, discussions with students, and personal reflection. It is offered less as a definitive piece than as a report from which suggestions and guidelines might be gleaned in the teaching of an Interpersonal Communication class.

Developing a Supportive Environment

Developing a supportive environment for students is crucial to laying the groundwork for student success. Infusing diversity into course content without sufficient forethought, however, can lead to polarization or can reinforce stereotypes. Unlike topics that are distant or "objective," diversity issues and concepts are received in a very personal way that can raise strong emotions in students. A common stumbling block to developing a supportive environment in which students feel comfortable discussing what are often socially taboo or "politically incorrect" topics is the common reaction of white students to glance furtively at classmates who are members of the group being discussed. Even though the minority students have not been asked to "speak for their race" — a problem reported by many students of color in conversations — the white students *de facto* view them as representatives. Two strategies can sidestep this common reaction.

The first strategy is to employ unexpected comparisons. For example, when discussing racial epithets or stereotyping, instead of selecting the expected black/white comparisons, I use Irish, Italian, and gender examples. Some students are visibly startled as they are confronted with this more inclusive perspective. They are aware that Irish and Italian Americans were targets of discrimination at various times in our history, and since many students at my institution (John Carroll University) reflect those heritages, they respond to the issue differently than if I used other groups as examples. Because we know that empathy is instrumental in motivating people to help others (Hoffman 2000), it makes sense to engender empathy with the examples we select in class.

In fact, selecting less obvious examples achieves three goals: It turns the "picture" to a different angle, resulting in a fresh view of a common topic; it permits the discussion to include all groups; and it allows for cross-group comparisons. No one group — or student — is made to feel stigmatized or singled out; neither is any group ignored as unimportant.

This technique also allows for discussions of similarities and differences in the treatment of various groups. As noted by Waters (1990), ethnic misunderstandings occur when people fail to recognize that while discrimination has been experienced by almost every group in America at some time, differences still exist in degree and current relevance. Waters points out, for example, that although early Irish immigrants faced fierce discrimination, the length and depth of that discrimination were not as great as what African Americans and Native Americans have encountered, nor as recent. Further, as she reminds us, legislation was not required to improve conditions for Irish immigrants and their children.

A second strategy that sidesteps the tendency to expect minority students to "represent their race" is to use supplementary readings and films as the focus of discussion, rather than just lecture. "What does this author argue?" is a good way to prompt students to explore the issues for themselves. Freire (1970) has advocated that removing the teacher as an authority figure from whom knowledge flows allows students to actively participate in the learning process. Presenting topics over which students are free to disagree allows them the opportunity to work through the issues and "own" the knowledge in a way that is not offered in the traditional lecture approach.

Discussion without research can prove counterproductive, however. Just as James (1997) realized that her views of whites were formed by family discussions and stories, so, too, do our students enter a discussion on race, religion, or gender with a full — rather than blank — slate. What students often lack, however, is judgment about generalizability or ability to see another side to the events as told at home, or both. An obvious remedy would be to have students share their own stories. Unfortunately, if students do not self-censor their stories, the result is that minority students must face reading or hearing about their classmates' negative reactions to their group, which hardly fosters a supportive classroom environment.

An alternative approach is to have students learn secondhand about events that affect others. In one assignment, I require students to read a weekly magazine whose audience is members of another race (or religion). Over a semester, all students are exposed to issues and stories not typically covered in what they would normally read. Another assignment that has proven quite powerful is to have students select a topic, such as police relations or housing, and then research stories of discrimination. Each of these approaches allows students to learn other people's stories without making anyone feel personally vulnerable.

Another way to supplement traditional texts is with assigned short readings that present diverse perspectives or new information, allowing students to apply interpersonal concepts beyond themselves or others like themselves. There are always current events that focus on issues of race and ethnicity (and gender). And while we know that people of different races and socioeconomic levels can differ in their views of society's institutions (police, courts, scientists, etc.), the Interpersonal Communication course presents an opportunity to explore *why* those differences exist. As Gudykunst and Matsumoto (1996) pointed out regarding cross-cultural interactions, understanding dimensions of cultural variability is what helps us understand *why* various ways of communicating are found in different cultures.

For students in an Interpersonal Communication course, the short editorial article "Black; White; Other" (by J. Marks, *Natural History*, December 1994), for example, provides an accessible summary of attempts to construct "race" as an objective biological category. While race is no longer accepted as an objective construct by academics or scientists, important controversies still remain about its conceptualization (see Angier 2000; Davis, Nakayama, and Martin 2000; Montagu 1997). Longer readings can provide valuable background information to white students, who might be blissfully unaware of the differences in treatment for members of various groups in the United States.

Because a key tenet of an effective communicator is the ability to adjust to one's audience, material that students can relate to only enhances the learning process. In "Walking While Black, Suspicious Minds and the Color-Blind" author P. Butler (*CommonQuest*, Winter 1998) recounts his experiences with police as he walked home after his car broke down just a few blocks from his house. Given college students' own often antagonistic relationships with the police, the story resonates with their feelings of alienation from the power structure. The use in sports of certain words or images for team names and logos provides yet another avenue to relate to students' lives on issues of diversity.

Giroux and Simon (1989) use the example of the film *Dirty Dancing* to explain their support for developing a "critical pedagogy of the popular," in which students are exposed to material that allows them to understand and give meaning to their lives. Films that can be used in an Interpersonal Communication course to introduce diversity concepts without placing a spotlight on students include *Double Happiness*, a film about a Chinese-Canadian woman living in the West who tries to both please and resist her Chinese parents; *Smoke Signals*, which focuses on the reconciliation between a father and a son; and *School Daze*, an early Spike Lee film that takes place over one weekend on a college campus. Each of these films touches on topics covered in Interpersonal Communication classes and addresses common issues that college students confront.

Having students consider how their own life might be different if they had been born a different race (or gender, or sexual orientation) can fit course sections that focus on empathy and taking an "other" orientation in conversations. A colleague, for example, has developed an assignment in which students select an identity different from their own, conduct an in-depth interview with a member of that other group, and then write how their own autobiography would be different had they been born into that group.

Caveats and Concerns

DEFINITION

A common problem found in articles and books on racial issues is the tendency to confuse the race factor with that of socioeconomic level — intentionally or not. Making that distinction clear to students is important, as most are uncritical in their acceptance of textbooks. Kochman's (1981) often-cited and otherwise useful book *Black and White Styles in Conflict* is a text, for example, that must be employed with caution. From its title, the book purports to discuss blacks and whites, but Kochman's own definitions clearly include a socioeconomic dimension. Thus, his definition of *white* focuses on "mainstream" and "middle class," while his definition of *black* focuses on African Americans who live in the "inner city" and "in the ghetto" (1981: 12-13). Instructors who use this source as their only presentation of blacks as a group risk perpetuating a stereotype of African Americans as poor, uneducated, and unemployed. Even researchers who acknowledge the disparity in Kochman's definitions continue to produce research that equates "black" with "poor" (see Hanna 1984).

The Communication discipline is not alone in perpetuating this phenomenon. If a student reads Kochman's book and then goes to an introductory American Government course, for example, the stereotype of African Americans as poor underachievers will be reinforced by images in texts there as well. According to a study by Clawson and Kegler (2000), textbook images convey a host of erroneous messages, including the inaccurate implication that African Americans make up 50 percent of poor people, rather than the 27 percent recorded in the 1996 Census.

African Americans are not the only group subject to such stereotyping. Sauceda (1982) pointedly rejects attempts by researchers to use poor, rural, Catholic populations as the basis from which to generalize descriptions of Chicano culture. He rejects these descriptions as nonrepresentative, and argues that "Chicano" exists as a category due to "racist intolerance and stereotypic classifications imposed by the mainstream American society" (191); he offers his own definition as "one's psychological identification with, and subjective belief of acceptance into, the presumed identity of the group" (189).

Sauceda's challenge aside, we find that — intentionally or not — other researchers continue the practice. In Aoki's (2000) article on Mexican Americans in Biola, California, he clearly describes a rural farm community that is poor. One of the informants in the study, a new resident to the area of East-Indian descent, described Mexican Americans in Biola as living from paycheck to paycheck without any thought of the future. While Aoki is clear that he is describing a specific community, students still might commit the error of generalizing his descriptions, assuming that what is true of those poor Mexican Americans in Biola is true of all Mexican Americans.

How do we counter the reinforcing of stereotypes? One way is to select readings written by members of the group being studied. Possible sources can range from short magazine pieces to books. Good examples include these: Gaiter's "The Revolt of the Black Bourgeoisie" (*New York Times Magazine*, June 26, 1994), in which he rejects the identification of "black" with inner-city, Ebonic speakers; Gonzalez, Houston, and Chen's *Our Voices: Essays in Culture, Ethnicity, and Communication* (Roxbury, 1997), in which each chapter is written by a member of the group being described; and Young Bear and Theisz's *Standing in the Light: A Lakota Way of Seeing* (University of Nebraska Press, 1994), which provides an excellent supplement to a traditional text in examining such concepts as listening, self-concept, and verbal communication.

While relying on authors who are members of the minority groups eliminates the imposition of an "outgroup" perspective, it does not eliminate differences. Three readings in *Our Voices* present very different perspectives on a people traditionally categorized as one, monolithic group (see Gangotena's "The Rhetoric of *La Familia* Among Mexican Americans"; Lozano's "The Cultural Experience of Space and Body"; and Tanno's "Names, Narratives, and the Evolution of Ethnic Identity"). These essays, combined with Sauceda's, provide an excellent pedagogical opportunity to discuss diversity *within* a group. A commercial film to underscore that point is *Thunderheart*. Native American characters in the film demonstrate a range of educational and social views, and it can be used to discuss Banks's typology of stages used to describe a person's view of themselves in relation to their group (1981: 129-139).[1]

SELECTIVE PERCEPTION

Certainly, the use of readings or films can lower discomfort levels of students of color when diversity issues are addressed, by removing the students as the point of reference. It also can provide them the opportunity to *choose* to participate. My experience has been that students of color remain silent initially; but after several readings, they invariably will contribute their own stories. This progression, and that their information is offered without prompting, adds great power to the course materials.

But, despite these benefits, be forewarned that students do not always perceive readings or films in the way the instructor intended. Summerfield (1993) argues that patently biased and ethnocentric films can be used pedagogically as long as each film is preceded by a carefully thought-out "warmup" to explain why the films are being shown. It is true that historical films in particular can be useful in illustrating the hateful ideas and images of a specific time period. But I would contend that for some students, no amount of "responsible handling of the material" (Summerfield 1993: 68) will be sufficient to counter their racist and ethnocentric views. In fact, materials the instructor intends to illustrate a problem could actually compound the situation, by reinforcing stereotypes or racist beliefs. A colleague in our History Department showed the famous but racist film *Birth of a Nation* in an upper-level undergraduate History of Film course. At the end of the screening, he was rather taken aback when a student remarked that "It represents a refreshing point of view that we don't get to see very often." In one of my classes, I showed a 20-minute news investigation of racial bias that used hidden cameras. To me, the film clearly revealed important differences in how people are treated on the basis of their skin color; however, one of my students dismissed it as a manufactured tool of the media to further a liberal agenda. Thus, it is critical to give sufficient forethought to the selection of films and readings. Used properly, they can add an important dimension of inclusiveness to the Interpersonal Communication course; used poorly, they can inadvertently reinforce prejudices.

EXCLUDING WHITES

In designing a more inclusive approach to Interpersonal Communication, it is easy to make the error of excluding whites. But it is an error that can prove detrimental on two levels.

First, it establishes an unstated — and therefore unexamined — assumption that whites represent "the norm." That is the effect anytime our textbooks bracket a group by chapter or box within a chapter; it reinforces the view that the bracketed group is "the other" in society whereas whites can to be assumed to represent the basis of comparison or the desired reality. Further, by including readings or films on whites, the group becomes just one among the subjects of the course — not greater, not lesser, just one more part. Not excluding whites is particularly important in countering false dichotomies and their damaging "we versus them" mentality, and in encouraging the realization that whites are *one* component of a multifaceted society.

Second, excluding whites from the discussion alienates white students in the class in the same way that students of color are alienated when they are not included as subjects. As mentioned earlier, research by Waters (1990) opens ways for students to consider the similarities and differences between their own experiences (and their ancestors') and their classmates' experiences. It is particularly important to bring white students into the process to consider topics such as white privilege and institutionalized racism (McIntosh 1989). If we want our Interpersonal Communication courses to improve the ability of individuals to communicate with people of a wide range of backgrounds, then it is imperative that we include discussions of power.

RESPONDING TO OFFENSIVE REMARKS

"It's okay to tell jokes about Jews as long as you don't tell them to a Jew." . . . "Poor blacks don't value good education, so it doesn't matter if their schools are good." . . . "If we would just stop talking about race, we wouldn't have any problems." . . . "Italian men are controlling and have violent tempers."

Early in my teaching career, a student made the statement that "There are two kinds of blacks. . . ." I responded immediately, forcefully contradicting her view; but in so doing, I also undercut any true discussion of that view. Even as the words passed my lips, I knew I had erred. By responding as an *individual*, I had abrogated my responsibilities as a teacher. Learning how to respond to racist (or sexist, or homophobic, or anti-Semitic) remarks, in fact, has proven the greatest challenge in my efforts to be inclusive at my overwhelmingly white university. At my institution, such comments are expressed not only because white students are in the majority but also because of how these students define racism. They associate "racism" only with extreme antisocial actions; that is, anything short of Klan membership is merely "freedom of speech." Even if students don't express such ideas during class, their papers reveal the pervasiveness of such thoughts.

Over the years, students have made an amazing array of statements. Learning to respond in a way that invites investigation was a challenge for me that required great thought and took several missteps. But the lesson has been a most valuable one. Now when a student makes an offensive statement, I realize that the response need not come from me. Not only is it better for students to think through the issue themselves, the strategy invites all of the students to join the process of discovery. They will, after all, leave my class and discuss these issues on their own. And I have found that I can trust the abilities of my students to, in fact, bring out the relevant issues.

My argument is similar to that made by Barge (1989) with regards to small-group leadership: If we invest in a *process* rather than a *person* to be responsible for all the tasks, we make use of everyone's contributions. As their instructor, it is my responsibility to train students in steps of analysis and to moderate — that is, to ask questions, when needed, that guide students in their analysis. Under this approach, students learn to explore unstated assumptions and implications, as well as to articulate and defend their positions. In short, they learn to develop critical-thinking skills useful throughout their lives.

Conclusion

As an undergraduate in a physics course, I remember vividly my reaction to reading a textbook that used the pronoun "she" as frequently as it did "he." That acknowledgment of my gender was a startling experience. Years later, the words of W.E.B. DuBois would resonate when he wrote of "a veil" in which African

Americans had "no true self-consciousness" because they were only allowed to see themselves "through the revelation of the other world" (1993: 9). In our attempts to prepare students for life in an increasingly multicultural world, it behooves us to reflect upon pedagogical issues of style and content, particularly as they affect the performance and understanding of our students. Just as some history books better reflect the diverse nature of our culture's development (e.g., Takaki 1993), so, too, must we follow a policy of inclusion in our Communication courses.

Today we find ourselves trying to balance a variety of needs and demands. How we respond has repercussions beyond the classroom into society itself. If our goal is to improve society, then knowledge is one step in that direction. We also reap a side benefit when we pursue a policy of inclusiveness: increased self-knowledge. As Hall notes in his book *Beyond Culture*,

> The great gift that the members of the human race have for each other is not exotic experiences but an opportunity to achieve awareness of the structure of their *own* system, which can be accomplished only by interacting with others who do not share that system. (1977: 44)

Note

1. The major Native-American characters are played by Native-American actors — among them Val Kilmer.

References

Angier, N. (August 22, 2000). "Race No More Than Skin Deep, DNA Indicates." *Plain Dealer*, pp. 1A, 8A.

Aoki, E. (July 2000). "Mexican American Ethnicity in Biola, CA: An Ethnographic Account of Hard Work, Family and Religion." *The Howard Journal of Communications* 11(3): 207-227.

Asante, M.K. (September 1992). "Learning About Africa." *The Executive Educator* 14(9): 21-23.

Banks, J.A. (1981). *Multiethnic Education: Theory and Practice*. Boston: Allyn and Bacon.

Barge, J.K. (Fall 1989). "Leadership as Medium: A Leaderless Group Discussion Model." *Communication Quarterly* 37(4): 237-247.

Bell, D. (1993). "Introduction 1, The Context." In *Gendered Fields, Women, Men and Ethnography*, edited by D. Bell, P. Caplan, and W.J. Karim, pp. 1-18. New York: Routledge.

Clawson, R.A., and E.R. Kegler. (July 2000). "The 'Race Coding' of Poverty in American Government College Textbooks." *The Howard Journal of Communications* 11(3): 179-188.

Clifford, J., and G.E. Marcus, eds. (1986). *Writing Culture, The Poetics and Politics of Ethnography*. Berkeley, CA: University of California Press.

Davis, O.I., T.K. Nakayama, and J.N. Martin. (September 2000). "Current and Future Directions in Ethnicity and Methodology." *International Journal of Intercultural Relations* 24(5): 525-539.

DeVito, J.A. (2001). *The Interpersonal Communication Book*. 9th ed. New York: Longman.

Downey, D.J., and R.S. Torrecilha. (July 1994). "Sociology of Race and Ethnicity: Strategies for Comparative Multicultural Courses." *Teaching Sociology* 22(3): 237-247.

DuBois, W.E.B. (1993, orig. 1903). "Of Our Spiritual Strivings." In *The Souls of Black Folk*. New York: Knopf.

Freire, Paulo. (1970). *Pedagogy of the Oppressed*. New York: Seabury.

Geertz, C. (1988). *Works and Lives, The Anthropologist as Author*. Stanford, CA: Stanford University Press.

Giroux, H., and R. Simon. (April 1989). "Popular Culture and Critical Pedagogy: Reconstructing the Discourse of Ideology and Pleasure." *Curriculum and Teaching* 4(1): 51-68.

Gudykunst, W.B., and Y. Matsumoto. (1996). "Cross-Cultural Variability of Communication in Personal Relationships." In *Communication in Personal Relationships Across Cultures*, edited by W.B. Gudykunst, S. Ting-Toomey, and T. Nishida, pp. 19-56. Thousand Oaks, CA: Sage.

Hall, E.T. (1977). *Beyond Culture*. Garden City, NY: Anchor.

Hanna, J.L. (1984). "Black/White Nonverbal Differences, Dance, and Dissonance: Implications for Desegregation." In *Nonverbal Behavior: Perspectives, Applications, Insights*, edited by I.A. Wolfgang, pp. 373-409. Lewiston, NY: C.J. Hogrefe.

Hecht, M.L., M.J. Collier, and S.A. Ribeau. (1993). *African American Communication, Ethnic Identity and Cultural Interpretation*. Newbury Park, CA: Sage.

Hoffman, M.L. (2000). *Empathy and Moral Development, Implications for Caring and Justice*. New York: Cambridge University Press.

James, N.C. (1997). "When Miss America Was Always White." In *Our Voices: Essays in Culture, Ethnicity, and Communication*, 2nd ed., edited by A. Gonzalez, M. Houston, and V. Chen, pp. 46-51. Los Angeles: Roxbury.

Kochman, T. (1981). *Black and White Styles in Conflict*. Chicago: University of Chicago Press.

McIntosh, P. (July/August 1989). "White Privilege: Unpacking the Invisible Knapsack." *Peace and Freedom*, pp. 10-12.

Montagu, A. (1997). *Man's Most Dangerous Myth: The Fallacy of Race*. 6th ed. Walnut Creek, CA: Alta Mira.

Orbe, M.P. (September 2000). "Centralizing Diverse Racial/Ethnic Voices in Scholarly Research: The Value of Phenomenological Inquiry." *International Journal of Intercultural Relations* 24(5): 603-621.

Pettigrew, J. (1981). "Reminiscences of Fieldwork Among the Sikhs." In *Doing Feminist Research*, edited by Helen Roberts, pp. 62-82. Boston: Routledge and Kegan Paul.

Samovar, L.A., and R.E. Porter, eds. (2000). *Intercultural Communication: A Reader.* 9th ed. Belmont, CA: Wadsworth.

Sauceda, J.S. (1982). "Chicano/a Ethnicity: A Concept in Search of a Content." In *Intercultural Communication: A Reader*, 3rd ed., edited by L.A. Samovar and R.E. Porter, pp. 185-198. Belmont, CA: Wadsworth.

Shor, I. (1992). *Empowering Education: Critical Teaching for Social Change*. Chicago: University of Chicago Press.

Summerfield, E. (1993). *Crossing Cultures Through Film*. Yarmouth, ME: Intercultural Press.

Takaki, R. (1993). *A Different Mirror: A History of Multicultural America*. Boston: Little, Brown.

Waters, M.C. (1990). *Ethnic Options: Choosing Identities in America*. Berkeley, CA: University of California Press.

Native-American First-Year Experiences

Sacrificing Cultures

Nanci M. Burk

Communication scholars recognize the necessity to continually assess basic Communication course curriculum and how we can most effectively use pedagogical strategies to teach communication theories and skills. Generally, we acknowledge the need to incorporate intercultural perspectives. Many basic course textbooks include critical components that integrate cultural influences within human communication concepts (e.g., verbal and nonverbal cultural cues). Braithwaite (1997) asserts that "the pervasiveness of culture means that all contexts for communication have a cultural component" (219).

Although we might pay respect to cultural influences on communication concepts, how frequently do we recognize that pedagogical techniques, activities, and textbooks themselves emerge from a specific cultural perspective? Braithwaite contends that "it is important to make explicit the cultural assumptions underlying educational communication practices. By doing so, we increase our awareness of how to apply what we teach to increasingly diverse populations" (1997: 219).

Community colleges especially reflect the changing face of America, including our multiple ethnicities, ages, educational backgrounds, and socioeconomic statuses. Native-American students are one ethnic group in that diversity. The Maricopa County Community College District, in Arizona, of which my campus, Glendale Community College, is a part, enrolls a significant number of Native-American students, who are required to take the basic Communication course. But is that curriculum culturally relevant to their lived experiences? Many Native-American students can find their academic success at risk if they do not assimilate to cultural expectations imposed by non-Native professors. Much of the research tends to focus on Native-American students' health risks, such as alcoholism, suicide, and drugs abuse (see Lowery 1998; Ma et al. 1998; Woods et al. 1997). But little to no Communication-specific research exists regarding Native-American students, save Bolls, Tan, and Austin (1997) and Braithwaite's (1997) notable work. I offer this essay as an invitation to further research by Communication scholars to investigate how educators might assist Native-American students in succeeding academically in higher education.

National Trends

According to Chenoweth (1998), "Native Americans, who have traditionally had very low rates of participation in higher education, have [over five years] increased the number of associate and baccalaureate degrees earned — by 7.3 and 7.2 percent, respectively" (20). This increase in earned degrees could be due to many factors, including accessibility of community colleges that grant associate's degrees. Community colleges offer locations convenient to the community, flexible class schedules, affordable courses, and a smaller ratio of students to faculty. These traits tend to appeal to underrepresented student populations, in that students perceive they are viewed more as individuals and less as institutional statistics. The percentage of Native-American students in the Maricopa District is minor, but these students have significant cultural contributions to offer.

In the Maricopa District in 1999, the percentage of Native-American students on 10 campuses was 2.7 overall. The percentages of Native-American students on specific campuses varies: At Phoenix College, for example, Native-American students make up 3.8 percent of students enrolled; at Scottsdale Community College, they make up 5 percent of the student population, the highest Native-American student population in the District. (Scottsdale's campus is adjacent to the Salt River Pima-Maricopa Indian Community, a reservation.) According to Roger McKinney, academic adviser and director of American Indian Programs at Scottsdale, the national dropout rate annually for Native-American students is three out of every four (personal communication, March 14, 2000). In contrast, Scottsdale has a dropout rate for Native American students of only 8 percent, an excellent retention rate.

One of the most successful retention programs for Native-American students in the United States is the Navajo Community College system (a.k.a. Diné College), with campuses in northern Arizona and New Mexico. As of spring 1994, Diné College graduated 88 percent of its Native-American students (Braithwaite 1997). That community college system uniquely focuses on incorporating Native-American (including tribes other than Navajo) cultural perspectives with traditionally Anglo pedagogical practices. This distinctive harmony of cultural teachings and college curriculum blends to produce significantly higher retention rates for Native Americans there than for those attending Anglo colleges and universities (Braithwaite 1997). Identifying ways in which basic Communication course instructors can make the curriculum more relevant to Native-American students can certainly contribute to a more holistic college experience and could increase retention rates.

Family Support and Academic Achievement

According to Machamer and Gruber (1998), "the links between students' family relationships and their educational attitudes and behaviors indicate that the family variables have an important influence on Native education" (359). My own teaching experiences with Native-American students in the basic Communication course lend merit to this theory. In Spring 1999, an Alaskan Native-American student named April irregularly attended my introductory course (her second semester in college). When in the classroom, she demonstrated positive immediacy behaviors (made sufficient eye contact, smiled frequently), but she rarely answered questions posed to her regarding course material. I knew she was capable of answering the questions, based on conversations with her following class. She was able to relate course concepts to situations involving family members' difficulties, thus demonstrating her comprehension of communication terms. In my experience, April's classroom behaviors were not unique among Native-American students. While she spoke candidly with me outside of class in private, her in-class behaviors were consistent with many other Native-American students' behaviors. Those specific behaviors might earn a student the label "at-risk."

April had many concerns that threatened her academic success. Constant family crisis, whether perceived or real, consumed her thoughts and dictated her behaviors (i.e., missing class, failing to turn in assignments). She lived alone (for the first time in her life) and spoke with her family several times a week. Her mother had chronic, debilitating illnesses, her father suffered from heart problems, and her older sister did not work and lived at home with a toddler. April felt responsible to help financially. She worked a minimum-wage job in order to send money home while enrolled in 15 hours of classes. She confided to me regularly about her perceived responsibilities to her family. She felt guilty for having the opportunity to go to college (which her family encouraged) while the family struggled at home emotionally and financially. She was a first-generation college student, with financial grants (from her tribe), and had ample campus support available to her.

Although April's family verbally supported and encouraged her to stay in school, they did not understand the commitment required to succeed in a college environment. By calling April often to update her on the family's daily crises, her family kept her (from an Anglo perspective) negatively connected to the constant difficulties. She lacked the total family support that she needed to continue and succeed in obtaining an education. From a Western pedagogical perspective, April was a classic example of an at-risk student, easily fitting into several of the factors identified in the research — low socioeconomic status, ethnic or minority membership, unstable family, physical or emotional handicapping conditions, lack of school readiness (e.g., Blount and Wells 1992; Frost 1994). But from the family's cultural perspective, her family's continual calls were their way of including April in communal needs for their collective identity. The calls were her security, connected to self-definition, and self-identity through the tribal collective.

After that semester, April left school and returned to her family home in Alaska. As in many collectivist cultures, family needs are considered paramount and attended to before individual needs. In April's situation, her identity with her family was predominant to her identity as a student. "The reality of a culture is experienced by those who live in it" (Philipsen 1987: 245).

Home-related problems, lack of parental support, and the influence of family support on scholastic confidence account for approximately 40 percent of dropout rates for Native-American students (Machamer and Gruber 1998). While educators cannot change the impact that family support, or lack thereof, has on student retention, there are areas we can examine to help retain Native-American students and help them achieve academic success. One method that basic Communication course instructors could consider is to provide a means for giving their Native-American students "voice" in the classroom.

Storytelling Methodology

The primary goal of using storytelling as a pedagogical tool is to give students "voice" in the classroom to explore their self-efficacy, demonstrate cultural pride, and share lived experiences. It is also an effective approach to help students connect lived experiences to communication concepts. I have used this pedagogical methodology effectively as part of the curriculum in both Interpersonal Communication and the hybrid courses. Communication concepts such as self-concept, perception, proximity, inference, selective retention, critical-listening skills, and the like can be demonstrated and discussed as a rationale for this methodology.

Storytelling is a method that comes naturally to most students. Virtually every human culture has used storytelling to convey experiences, provide information, and entertain. Native-Americans' oral traditions reveal rich perspectives of their world, that depict cultural and humorous events as well as explicate their traditions (Bugeja 1993). Kremer (1998) views storytelling as a means to "affirm an ancient way of being present to knowing" (2).

For many, storytelling yields great insight and a deeper understanding of the world around us. "Stories are told in a society to reflect and reinforce a shared sense of values" (Spagnoli 1995: 221). Through the use of this teaching method, Native-American students can come to a better understanding of specific communication concepts by linking them to personal experiences through oral reflection. Oral sharing of experiences and events is a natural part of our everyday lives, which helps us conceptualize our life experiences (Langellier 1989; Stahl 1983).

From a Western perspective, reflecting upon and analyzing a personal situation by sharing a story seems an effective device for relating lived experiences to communication concepts. An example of this is an activity I was using in my Interpersonal Communication and hybrid courses called "Conflict Storytelling." I would ask students to reflect on a minor conflict between themselves and a close friend or family member, then write a story as if they were being videotaped during the conflict, without incorporating any emotions into the story. The instructions explained that they will "share the story aloud in class, and they are to just tell the facts" (Burk 1997: 9). The intention for the "Conflict" exercise was to provide an opportunity for students to relate communication concepts (conflict styles, inference, passive perception, etc.) to lived experiences, and to analyze their conflict options in a relevant situation. Sharing personal information, from a Western pedagogical perspective, is appropriate for self-analysis: an individualistic, cultural expectation.

Caution is warranted, however, when developing storytelling activities. From a collectivist/Native-American perspective, such an assignment could be viewed as invasive and inappropriate. Rachel, a Native-American student enrolled in my Interpersonal Communication course, missed class on the day that students were to share this assignment aloud in class. Upon reflection, I realized that Rachel had been absent on a variety of occasions when assignments regarding personal experience were due and shared aloud. Otherwise, she was a quiet student who came prepared and turned in satisfactory work on time. Later, I inquired about why she had been absent and missed the opportunity to share a personal experience with her classmates. She explained that it would be as difficult for her to do the exercise as it would be for her to walk in the street in her underwear. For Rachel, to discuss personal information with classmates or an instructor publicly was inconceivable and inappropriate. She had chosen to sacrifice grade points rather than bring individual attention to herself or to expose her family's personal conflicts.

I have since redesigned the "Conflict Storytelling" assignment so that there is less emphasis on the individual, and more emphasis on recognizing conflict styles. Observing conflict in a video or similar depersonalized genres can refocus the nature of this type of activity simply. In the instance documented above, the student lacked not only a "voice" in the classroom but also control of her own academic success. Rachel was culturally unable (which might be viewed as unwilling) to complete the exercise as assigned. It was the instructor's perspective and expectations that placed the student at risk.

Teacher Expectations

In order for Native-American students to achieve success in the classroom, Anglo educators must recognize the pervasive, dominant cultural perspective that dictates their expectations of students. There are many behavioral expectations that are defined by the dominant culture. In the basic course, Communication teachers expect students to participate verbally, often by analyzing textbook concepts.

This pedagogical strategy violates the Native-American cultural expectation that prohibits students from speaking for others (Machamer and Gruber 1998). Native cultures oppose much of what the basic course requires in regard to self-analysis, which is individualistic in nature. Much of what Anglo or non-Native teachers impose on students is culturally specific to Western individualism. Interpersonal Communication textbooks, assignments, and pedagogical strategies "focus on the 'self' and the interpersonal dyadic 'relationship'" (Braithwaite 1997: 231). Compounding the situation, behaviors that are viewed as appropriate within many Native cultures include "shying away from speaking aloud in class, avoiding eye contact, and avoiding asking questions from authority figures" (Machamer and Gruber 1998: 359). It is understandable why Anglo faculty might see such students as nonparticipative, unprepared, resistant, or possibly slower to process complex communication concepts.

Assignments that require students to support oral presentations or speeches with concrete evidence disallow one of the most important and traditional resources treasured in Native-American cultures — their oral history. In those cultures, stories passed down from elders are perceived as ways to link with their collective identities. In Anglo classrooms, when "oral history and personal accounts are considered supplemental and not primary source material, Native students may perceive this judgment as disrespectful of their cultural values" (Braithwaite 1997: 231). "By understanding the basis of Native-American students' attitudes and how teacher communicative behavior affects these attitudes, attempts can be made to alter expectations" (Bolls, Tan, and Austin 1997: 201).

Immediacy behaviors on which Communication educators often pride themselves could be the very behaviors Native-American students perceive as disrespectful or displaying a lack of understanding. In their 1997 study, Bolls, Tan, and Austin (1997) found that Native-American students perceived that their teachers displayed less respect and understanding toward them than toward Caucasian students. Whether teachers' behaviors toward Native-American students differed from behaviors toward Caucasian students in perception or in reality, the lesson is the same. Native-American perceptions of basic course requirements and teacher behaviors should be considered when investigating how Communication scholars can help to retain Native-American students.

Conclusion

It is clear that the basic Communication course has made positive strides toward incorporating culture and diversity into the language of the textbooks, and thus into discussions by Communication educators in classrooms with students. It is also obvious that we can further discussions and understanding of diverse cultures by using pedagogical methodologies such as storytelling to view the world as others view it. We are too frequently bound by our own culture. Seeking the counsel of others, such as Native Americans, who have unique perspectives when we are writing basic course texts and developing and designing instructional tools and techniques to be more inclusive of nondominant cultures will enrich and benefit not only students but also educators.

Some 60 to 70 percent of Native Americans in Arizona live in urban areas, seeking education and better jobs with better benefits to realize their dreams and provide for their families. Although many have left their reservations, that is no indication that they wish to leave their heritage, culture, traditions, or collective identities. In becoming more aware of Native-American cultures, Communication scholars will, I hope, be inspired to embrace and incorporate diverse perspectives into basic course curriculum, influencing how we teach our culturally diverse student populations.

References

Blount, H.P., and M.G. Wells. (1992). "Battering Children Educationally." *Contemporary Education* 64: 21-24.

Bolls, P., A. Tan, and E. Austin. (July 1997). "An Exploratory Comparison of Native American and Caucasian Students' Attitudes Toward Communicative Behavior and Toward School." *Communication Education* 46: 198-203.

Braithwaite, C.A. (1997). "Sa'ah Naaghái Bik'eh Hózhóón: An Ethnography of Navajo Educational Communication Practices." *Communication Education* 46: 219-233.

Bugeja, M.J. (December 1993). "Listen to Your Elders: Few Cultures Have an Oral Tradition as Rich as Native Americans' — And All Poets Can Learn From It." *Writer's Digest* 73: 12-17.

Burk, N. (1997). "Using Personal Narratives as a Pedagogical Tool: Empowering Students Through Stories." Paper presented at the Annual Meeting of the National Communication Association, Chicago, Illinois.

Chenoweth, K. (1998). "The Surging Degree Wave." *Black Issues in Higher Education* 15: 20-24.

Frost, L.E. (1994). "'At-Risk' Statutes: Defining Deviance and Suppressing Difference in the Public Schools." *Journal of Law and Education* 23: 123-165.

Kremer, J. (1998). "Narrative Explorations of Culture, Roots, and Ancestry." *ReVision* 21: 2.

Langellier, K. (1989). "Personal Narratives: Perspectives on Theory and Research." *Text and Performance Quarterly* 9: 243-276.

Lowery, C. (May 1998). "American Indian Perspectives on Addiction and Recovery." *Health and Social Work* 23: 127-136.

Ma, G., J. Toubbeh, J. Cline, and A. Chisholm. (April 1998). "Native American Adolescents' Views of Fetal Alcohol Syndrome Prevention in Schools." *Journal of School Health* 68: 131-137.

Machamer, A.M., and E. Gruber. (1998). "Secondary School, Family, and Educational Risk: Comparing American Indian Adolescents and Their Peers." *The Journal of Educational Research* 91: 357-370.

Philipsen, G. (1987). "The Prospect for Cultural Communication." In *Communication Theory: Eastern and Western Perspectives*, edited by D.L. Kincaid, pp. 245-254. San Diego: Academic Press.

Spagnoli, C. (1995). "Storytelling: A Bridge to Korea." *The Social Studies* 86: 221.

Stahl, S. (1983). "Personal Experience Stories." In *Handbook of American Folklore*, edited by R. Dorson, pp. 268-276. Bloomington, IN: Indiana University Press.

Woods, E., Y. Lin, A. Middleman, P. Beckford, L. Chase, and R. DuRant. (June 1997). "The Associations of Suicide Attempts in Adolescents." *Pediatrics* 99: 791-797.

Holistic Teaching Strategies in the Public Speaking Classroom

Victoria O. Orrego, Patricia Kearney, and Timothy G. Plax

Given the large influx of African-American, Hispanic, Asian-American, Native-American, and international students into the classroom, scholars and teachers alike have argued for a comprehensive instructional approach that recognizes the cognitive assets and learning preferences of both white and non-white students (see Abi-Nader 1993; Anderson 1988; Milhouse 1995). For example, Anderson (1988) points out that culturally diverse students differ in learning styles, relying on multiple functions of learning including thinking, feeling, perceiving, and behaving. She claims that the cognitive learning styles of African-American, Mexican-American, and Puerto Rican-American students are based on holistic and visual thinking, where imagery and metaphors dominate speech and writing processes; the use of theoretical and abstract models is not as central to their learning as is instruction that focuses on direct experience and application. Consequently, an integrative instructional approach that reflects broader-level learning styles should benefit all students represented in today's multicultural classroom.

Communication classrooms are ideal contexts for engaging students in conversations and activities that use their diverse learning perspectives. No other discipline provides as many instructional opportunities for illustrating how cultural background impacts and enhances the communication process. When Communication instruction is inclusive, diverse, and involving, minority students are more likely to find the learning experience positive. Such inclusive teaching reduces students' anxiety while heightening validation and support for their individual and cultural identities. Minority students, then, can benefit from taking Communication classes from instructors who are knowledgeable of and responsive to students' diverse learning needs, styles, and preferences.

In this essay, we discuss a number of inclusive teaching strategies that we use in one foundational communication skills course, Public Speaking. These strategies promote positive learning experiences and academic success for minority students — particularly for those who are new to the college environment. Moreover, these strategies encourage minority student enrollment in subsequent Communication classes. We provide one illustrative example, but these strategies are not limited to Public Speaking classes; they can function effectively in a variety of Communication courses.

In line with current research focusing on multicultural education (see, e.g., Beebe and Biggers 1986; Bennett 1986; Gudykunst, Ting-Toomey, and Wiseman 1991; Harrison and Hopkins 1967; Milhouse 1995), we advocate incorporating a combination of cognitive, affective, and behavioral teaching/learning goals in Public Speaking classes. These goals obviously will dictate the selection of course content and methods used. We organize the discussion that follows around these three separate but interrelated goals. In our curriculum, we also infuse multiculturalism by discussing general cultural factors that influence communication and by presenting the material in a holistic manner. We conclude the essay by recognizing the unique communication challenges teachers face in their attempts to infuse cultural issues in their instruction of diverse student groups, and we offer recommendations for meeting those challenges.

Learning and Teaching Goals

All too often, teachers enter the Communication classroom preoccupied with teaching cognitive learning outcomes — almost to the exclusion of other, equally important outcomes of affective and behavioral learning (Beebe and Biggers 1986). Emphasizing the unique challenges of teaching university-wide Intercultural Communication courses, Gudykunst, Ting-Toomey, and Wiseman (1991) recommend that instructors balance their teaching goals to include all three: cognitive, affective, and behavioral teaching. *Cognitive* goals focus on understanding communication differences and similarities, as well as understanding the process of communication. Simply put, cognitive goals emphasize the acquisition of knowledge. *Affective* goals are designed to motivate students by positively influencing their attitudes toward the course content. In Public Speaking, affective goals might emphasize the reduction of students' public speaking anxiety, while simultaneously increasing their affect toward the class. *Behavioral* goals emphasize skill development necessary for making effective presentations. While incorporating all three learning outcomes could be critical for teaching culturally diverse classes and Intercultural Communication, such practices are also a prerequisite to good teaching more generally.

COGNITIVE GOALS

In our teaching of Public Speaking, we extended our initial goal of teaching principles and skills of public speaking to include a multicultural perspective. Our primary cognitive goal remained: to teach students basic processes, theories, and concepts of public speaking. We wanted students to be able to develop and construct (research, outline, and organize) a variety of speeches, including informative, persuasive, and specialized. Our extended cognitive goal involved teaching students the effects of culture on public speaking. We considered, then, the impact of cultural diversity in every aspect of the speech preparation process, including selection of speech topics, organizational structure, and types of evidence, persuasive appeals, and audience analysis. We stressed that to ignore or give only token attention to the impact of cultural diversity on public speaking is to be an ineffective public speaker. We also discussed how cultural background affects the speaker's level of apprehension, use of body language — including eye contact and gestures — and use of words and phrases, repetition, and other rhetorical devices that affect delivery. Finally, we considered how audience expectations and responses might be tied to cultural affiliation. Providing students with this type of information is empowering because it legitimizes alternative forms of communicating.

Finding an appropriate Public Speaking text that met these multiple cognitive goals was almost impossible. Until recently, textbooks on public speaking ignored or made only token reference to cultural issues, so we wrote our own. We became experts in the literature on intercultural and interethnic communication. We applied the research and thinking in the area to each and every facet of public speaking that we could. And then, with the help of our friends, we tested our instruction of the content in hundreds of Public Speaking classes across the country. Today, our book is in its second edition: *Public Speaking in a Diverse Society* (by P. Kearney and T.G. Plax; Mayfield, 1999). Now there are a number of other books that integrate and embrace issues of diversity in the teaching of public speaking. These texts make meeting our extended cognitive goal much easier.

AFFECTIVE GOALS

Perhaps no other Communication course requires attention to the affective domain more so than Public Speaking. Recognizing that a number of students enter Public Speaking classrooms highly apprehensive about delivering a speech, a teacher must work hard at sensitively alleviating their anxieties and fears. Affective goals are designed to influence students' affinity, or liking, toward the course content and practices. Unlike cognitive goals, instruction in the affective domain is rarely strategically planned. However, students are likely to learn cognitively and practice what they learn when they are predisposed to like the content (Kearney and McCroskey 1980). Consequently, teachers need to plan their instruction to include affective outcomes.

Students in our classes learn how to reduce and successfully manage their apprehension about communicating in public contexts. In class, we discuss communication apprehension and how common it is. We distinguish among apprehensive people, apprehensive situations, and apprehensive cultural groups. Specific to culture, we help students recognize the influence of culture on a person's communication apprehension (see Klopf 1984; McCroskey and Richmond 1990; McCroskey, Fayer, and Richmond 1985; Ralston, Ambler, and Scudder 1991). Similarly, we consider the English-as-a-second-language (ESL) speaker, who frequently becomes anxious and reluctant to engage in interactions with native English speakers — even when he or she apparently speaks English very well. Often anxieties of the ESL speaker derive from unrealistic expectations that spoken English should somehow be perfect. We help students understand that, in actuality, audiences appreciate a speaker's attempts to communicate in a second language, and they are more likely to make a special effort to listen attentively. This targeted discussion of ESL students also serves as a reminder to other students of their responsibility as audience members to be supportive and positive to their peers.

We provide highly apprehensive students with strategies and tools for managing their anxieties and fears throughout the public speaking process: during preparation, at the time of performance, and in follow-up evaluations of their presentations. In addition to teaching the usual anxiety-reduction methods (e.g., systematic desensitization, cognitive restructuring, visualization, skills training), we begin speech performance days with student declarations of positive self-statements, predicting and affirming their success as public speakers. Initially, their affirmations are tepid at best, but with coaching the students become increasingly self-confident — at times, even pronouncing positive overstatements! Finally, we spend time helping them understand how the process of impression formation and self-presentation can be used to enhance their credibility and make them feel more confident as speakers.

Students also learn about audience and speaker characteristics that are influenced by cultural or ethnic affiliation. They learn to be mindful of their own tendencies to be ethnocentric, and to avoid being stereotypic in their responses to one another. A great way to stimulate discussion around these issues and their role in the public speaking process is to show students a video that accompanies our Public Speaking text. The video begins with a focus group of culturally diverse students talking about how their respective cultural backgrounds affect their communicative interactions. We use the video as a springboard for discussing the inaccuracies of stereotypes. This is a crucial time to involve students by having them share their opinions of the video as well as their own life experiences. Handled sensitively, these discussions help to establish supportive and safe environments where students feel comfortable talking and eventually presenting speeches.

BEHAVIORAL GOALS

Behavioral goals focus on obtaining the necessary skills to effectively deliver speeches to culturally and ethnically diverse audiences. During the course, each student presents at least three major (e.g., a five-minute extemporaneous informative speech) and several short speeches, where each speech builds upon the previous one. This incremental method is based on the idea that a complex behavioral activity (such as public speaking) is best learned in small units of instruction. When complex skills are developed gradually, opportunities for success and reinforcement are enhanced. We give students specific, behavioral criteria prior to each presentation, and they get teacher (and peer) feedback on what they did well and where they still need to improve.

An additional behavioral goal is to develop their own individual style of communicating with an audience. Important to promoting the success and self-image of students of color or minority status is recognition of how their culture, ethnicity, gender, or race contributes to their unique communication style. Communication ("rhetorical") style refers to the overall qualitative way a speaker communicates, using verbal and nonverbal messages. Everyone has a style of communicating, but not everyone knows what that style is or how to use it to his or her advantage. We examine dramatic, animated, humorous, and open styles of relating to audiences (see Norton 1983); we also recognize gender-based communication styles (see Wood 1993), and we provide representative examples from our textbook of both sexes that conform to or violate traditional sex-role stereotypes. Our behavioral goal is for students to develop their own delivery styles, but a related affective goal is for them to appreciate their own and others' uniqueness as communicators.

By identifying, defining, and strategically working toward attaining cognitive, affective, and behavioral goals, teachers stand a better chance of maximizing their effectiveness in the classroom. Teaching Public Speaking requires that we emphasize cognitive communication principles, theories, and processes. Reducing students' anxieties and motivating them to learn are equally important affective goals. Planning for the incremental development of presentation skills by engaging students in a variety of public speaking assignments fulfills important behavioral goals. Taken together, students are likely to learn the course content, deliver a well-executed speech, and be sufficiently motivated to participate actively in their own learning.

The next section addresses important cultural topics that can be infused into the teaching of the Public Speaking course. These topics have implications for all three goals of instruction.

Cultural Topics

By integrating the research and thinking on intercultural communication with what we know about public speaking, instructors can provide students with the tools to better adapt in a culturally diverse society. In our class, we begin by laying the foundation for the proposition that speakers and audiences interact in different ways depending on their unique cultural backgrounds. To assume that all speakers and audiences should act and respond in the same manner ignores our rich cultural mix. In looking at the effects of cultural diversity on public speaking, we focus on the six largest cultural groups living in the United States: Euro Americans, African Americans, Latinos/Latinas, Asian Americans, Native Americans, and Middle Eastern Americans.

In our discussion, we rely on what Gudykunst, Ting-Toomey, and Wiseman (1991) refer to as a *culture-general approach*. This approach focuses on "general factors that influence communication between people from different cultures and/or ethnic groups" (274). The understanding of how culture and ethnicity influence public communication helps students improve their own communication styles across a wide variety of situations. In our teaching of Public Speaking, we begin by introducing the impact of culture on communication more generally, issues of cultural exclusion and inclusion, and the universal tendency to be ethnocentric. We also talk about current demographics and the historical origins of diversity in the United States. We describe the six cultural groups in terms of their unique communication styles. Moreover, we identify the four major features that distinguish these cultures from one another (individualism-collectivism, high/low context, high/low power distance, and masculinity-femininity). So as not to stray too far from our primary cognitive goal of teaching public speaking, we limit our instruction to those communication factors that make a difference in how people relate between cultures.

It is important to note that our information is based on research using aggregate data and is not expected to apply to everyone within a given cultural group. The most interesting discussions arise from this caveat. None of us is easily categorized or stereotyped — we all like to think that we are unique. In the classroom, we pose the question how does assimilation of different cultures over time function to impact individual communication styles? We have students identify similarities as well as differences among cultures. They are encouraged to describe their personal experiences and how those experiences reinforce or contradict what we know from current intercultural research. Finally, implications for racism and prejudice naturally evolve from these discussions.

When describing the cultural styles of speaking, it's a good idea to not always use Euro Americans or majority groups as your basis for comparison. We do not want students to get the wrong idea that somehow the Euro-American culture is the standard. Moreover, other cultural groups might offer an easier way to make distinctions. For instance, try comparing the Asian-American communication style with the African-American. Given these two disparate styles of communicating, students will more readily see the communication differences than they would if comparisons were made between more similar cultural groups, such as Asian Americans and Native Americans.

Infusing a multicultural approach to instruction into our classrooms encourages inclusivity. Students learn firsthand that their cultural communicative styles are valued and accounted for in Public Speaking. For these reasons, students of color are more likely to feel that they are an important part of the learning experience. Moreover, students will perceive the classroom as a safe place for all students to speak out and be heard. In this way, they can assist the instructor by providing relevant examples to their classmates about alternative preferences for verbal and nonverbal behaviors important to their effectiveness as speakers.

Managing Challenges of Diversity in the Classroom

Teaching a Public Speaking course with a focus on cultural diversity differs from teaching a course without that emphasis. Although exciting, teaching issues such as diversity can be challenging: There is always the potential for disagreement, anxiety, and uneasiness among students. Talking about diversity is unexpected in a course on Public Speaking. You might find some students eager to learn, yet uncertain how to contribute to discussions that might reveal their own unfamiliarity with or intolerance of other cultures and ethnic or racial groups. Other students can be somewhat resistant to learning about and accepting new ways of relating to other people. Still others might use the course as an opportunity to present their own political agendas. Having taught this course many times and directed others in the teaching of it, we recognize that discussions about ethnocentrism, prejudice, different cultural styles of communicating, and other related topics introduce both uncertainty and anxiety. At the same time, we found these discussions both stimulating and worthwhile — and so did our students.

As teachers of this course, it is our responsibility to manage classroom discussion in such a way that a free exchange of ideas results. Students should recognize and respect one another's contributions — even when they disagree with those contributions. In this final section of our essay, we face head-on two distinctive challenges that are likely to surface in your teaching of diversity in the Public Speaking course. The first has to do with being prepared for students who communicate in class in ways that reflect their cultural backgrounds. The second challenge is managing students' intensity when a controversial issue arises.

When faced with a classroom of culturally diverse students, be prepared for students who communicate in ways that differ from one another (and you). Recognizing and respecting those differences is a good way to start. Begin by talking about your own cultural background. Discuss how, when, and where your cultural affiliations are important or unimportant to you and how they influence the ways you interact with others. Discuss your own flexibility as a communicator and the importance of being able to move in and out of different cultural and social environments. Next, invite students to participate in the discussion with similar disclosures. With a little encouragement and a lot of reinforcement, students will greatly appreciate the opportunity to talk about how they share (or fail to share) the communication characteristics of their culture.

Encouraging student input requires that you also be ready for what you hear. Allowing students to say what they really think and feel can be fraught with danger. Sometimes students' comments will offend or hurt, but knowing their true feelings can be beneficial. Practice being nondefensive when students make hurtful or prejudicial remarks. If you truly want students to engage in open and free exchanges about diversity, then you must be ready for comments that will personally distress you (or others in class). Correct inappropriate behavior; show your disapproval or disagreement, but withhold your anger.

At times you might encounter students who employ biased or sexist language. When they do, give such students a gentle reminder; help them substitute appropriate language for inappropriate language. There's no need to use the occasion to preach. Often, biased language slips out unwittingly; give each student the benefit of the doubt with a simple reminder: "You mean to say ____, don't you?" Then, encourage the student to proceed with the point. In this way, student input is encouraged, but monitored.

Introducing issues of cultural diversity can be further complicated by one's own cultural background. Should you and your students share the same ethnicity or race, you are likely to be perceived as highly credible on issues of diversity. If your backgrounds differ, however, students could make the assumption that you are incapable of understanding and relating the information accurately and without prejudice. We suggest that teachers of any cultural affiliation can identify with their students by being informed about different cultural learning styles, preferences, and communication behaviors. Showing respect and giving recognition to alternate ways of communicating are additional strategies that are likely to minimize student suspicion. Responding with tolerance, openness, and composure shows caring and concern; responding with displeasure or anger can communicate a lack of understanding and an intolerance for cultural differences. Finally, do not underestimate what you can learn from your students. Discussions regarding cultural communication differences are enhanced by students' own experiences and input. As teachers, we need to listen well and learn from our students.

We would also reiterate some important points stressed by Gudykunst, Ting-Toomey, and Wiseman (1991). First, consider the language that you use. It is important to use inclusive language that is nonracist and nonethnocentric. Additionally, be prepared to confront racial stereotypes that occur in lecture and class activities. It is important to note that "we cannot communicate without stereotyping" (277). What we must be willing to do, then, is to openly discuss the inaccuracy of those stereotypes and their detrimental effects. While it can be awkward or uncomfortable to confront these challenges as they occur, your message must be clear: We will not tolerate negative bias, sexist or racist language, or exclusion. As instructors, we should put ourselves in a position to heighten cultural awareness, not skew it.

Important to teaching any content area is how we relate to students. More than any other known teacher attribute, nonverbal immediacy positively influences student learning — cognitively, affectively, and behaviorally (Christensen and Menzel 1998; Christophel 1990; Frymier 1994; Rodriguez, Plax, and Kearney 1996). *Nonverbal immediacy* refers to those behaviors that signal physical and/or psychological closeness. Such immediacy behaviors include eye contact, head nods, smiles, gestural activity, forward body lean, movement, and other approach-oriented behaviors. Taken holistically, these behaviors communicate closeness and liking (Andersen 1979). A number of studies reveal that teacher immediacy begets positive student outcomes (Christophel 1990; Frymier 1994; Waldeck, Kearney, and Plax 2001). That is, students are more likely to approach a teacher whom they feel will respond favorably toward them. They are also more likely to participate in class discussions if they feel that their opinions count and are welcomed. The effects of teacher immediacy are not confined to the classroom either. Students will more readily seek out-of-class assistance from highly immediate teachers (Fusani 1994). And, they are more likely to be motivated to learn (Gorham and Christophel 1990, 1992). With immediate teachers, students will feel that they are important and worth acknowledging.

In sum, we have identified a number of special challenges that Communication instructors teaching diversity could encounter in the multicultural classroom. Fortunately, we know a number of strategies that teachers can use to manage these challenges. Most important, how a teacher communicates with students impacts students' perceptions of self-worth, degree of involvement, motivation, and learning. We want to stress that students, no matter what their cultural affiliation, appreciate an instructor who is responsive to their needs and demonstrates genuine liking, concern, and respect.

Conclusion

Our purpose in writing this essay was to describe teaching strategies that effectively promote learning and academic success for students of color. We ourselves are fortunate to work in college campuses of high cultural diversity, providing us with the opportunity to implement and evaluate the effectiveness of a variety of instructional tools. We discussed our approach within the context of the Public Speaking course. However, we do not mean to exclude other Communication courses; our strategies can be easily adapted to fit the specific course requirements and needs. We suggest that by integrating teaching/learning goals, employing a context-general approach toward multiculturalism, and recognizing and managing the unique challenges of teaching diverse students, any teacher can become better equipped to meet the individual needs of *all* of his or her students.

References

Abi-Nader, J. (1993). "Meeting the Needs of Multicultural Classrooms: Family Values and the Motivation of Minority Students." In *Diversity and Teaching: Teacher Education Yearbook 1*, edited by M.J. O'Hair and S.J. Odell, pp. 212-228. Fort Worth, TX: Harcourt Brace and Jovanovich.

Andersen, J.F. (1979). "Teacher Immediacy as a Predictor of Teaching Effectiveness." In *Communication Yearbook 3*, edited by D. Nimmo, pp. 543-559. New Brunswick, NJ: Transaction Books.

Anderson, J.A. (1988). "Cognitive Styles and Multicultural Populations." *Journal of Teacher Education* 39: 2-9.

Beebe, S.A., and T. Biggers. (1986). "The Status of the Introductory Intercultural Communication Course." *Communication Education* 35: 56-60.

Bennett, J.M. (1986). "Modes of Cross-Cultural Training." *International Journal of Intercultural Relations* 10: 235-254.

Christensen, L.J., and K.E. Menzel. (1998). "The Linear Relationship Between Student Reports of Teacher Immediacy Behaviors and Perceptions of State Motivation, and of Cognitive, Affective, and Behavioral Learning." *Communication Education* 47: 82-90.

Christophel, D.M. (1990). "The Relationships Among Teacher Immediacy Behaviors, Student Motivation, and Learning." *Communication Education* 39: 323-340.

Frymier, A.B. (1994). "A Model of Immediacy in the Classroom." *Communication Quarterly* 42: 133-144.

Fusani, D.S. (1994). "'Extra Class' Communication: Frequency, Immediacy, Self-Disclosure, and Satisfaction in Student-Faculty Interaction Outside the Classroom." *Journal of Applied Communication Research* 22: 232-255.

Gorham, J., and D.M. Christophel. (1990). "The Relationship of Teachers' Use of Humor in the Classroom to Immediacy and Student Learning." *Communication Education* 39: 46-62.

———. (1992). "Students' Perceptions of Teacher Behaviors as Motivating and Demotivating Factors in College Classes." *Communication Quarterly* 40: 239-252.

Gudykunst, W.B., S. Ting-Toomey, and R.L. Wiseman. (1991). "Taming the Beast: Designing a Course in Intercultural Communication." *Communication Education* 40: 272-285.

Harrison, R., and R.L. Hopkins. (1967). "The Design of Cultural Training. An Alternative to the University Model." *Journal of Applied Behavioral Science* 3: 431-460.

Kearney, P., and J.C. McCroskey. (1980). "Relationships Among Teacher Communication Style, Trait and State Communication Apprehension and Teacher Effectiveness." In *Communication Yearbook 4*, edited by D. Nimmo, pp. 533-551. New Brunswick, NJ: Transaction Books.

Klopf, D.W. (1984). "Cross-Cultural Apprehension Research: A Summary of Pacific Basin Studies." In *Avoiding Communication: Shyness, Reticence, and Communication Apprehension*, edited by J.A. Daly and J.C. McCroskey, pp. 157-269. Beverly Hills, CA: Sage.

McCroskey, J.C., and V.P. Richmond. (1990). "Willingness to Communicate: Differing Cultural Perspectives." *The Southern Communication Journal* 56: 72-77.

McCroskey, J.C., J.M. Fayer, and V.P. Richmond. (1985). "Don't Speak to Me in English: Communication Apprehension in Puerto Rico." *Communication Quarterly* 33: 185-192.

Milhouse, V.H. (1995). "Instructional Strategies and Pedagogy for Culturally Diverse Classrooms." *The Howard Journal of Communications* 6: 173-187.

Norton, R. (1983). *Communicator Style: Theory, Applications, and Measures.* Beverly Hills, CA: Sage.

Ralston, S.M., R. Ambler, and J.N. Scudder. (1991). "Reconsidering the Impact of Racial Differences in the College Public Speaking Classroom on Minority Student Communication Anxiety." *Communication Reports* 4: 43-50.

Rodriguez, J.I., T.G. Plax, and P. Kearney. (1996). "Clarifying the Relationship Between Teacher Nonverbal Immediacy and Student Cognitive Learning: Affective Learning as the Central Causal Mediator." *Communication Education* 45: 293-305.

Waldeck, J.H., P. Kearney, and T.G. Plax. (2001). "Teacher E-Mail Message Strategies and Students' Willingness to Communicate Online." *Journal of Applied Communication Research* 29: 54-70.

Wood, J.T. (1993). "Gender and Moral Voice: Moving From Women's Nature to Standpoint Epistemology." *Women's Studies in Communication* 16: 1-24.

Exploring Cultural Contracts in the Classroom and Curriculum

Implications of Identity Negotiation and Effects in Communication Curricula

Ronald L. Jackson II, Carlos D.J. Morrison, and Celnisha L. Dangerfield

> The first prerequisite to becoming a better practitioner in a multicultural classroom is having the attitudinal openness to improving your classroom practices. . . . This means that in order to be effective in a classroom of diverse students, we must reject the traditional model of college teaching — that the student must conform to the norms of the professor. Simply put, you cannot expect your students to clone your preferred way of learning.
> (Lou 1994: 33)

There they were, at the premier regional forensics tournament on the East Coast. Our individual events team had practiced all year long, preparing for their persuasive, informative, after-dinner, and dramatic-duo events. They were sharp, cogent, well-trained undergraduates who were eager to win. And they did, taking first, second, and fourth places in their respective events. They were proud, and so should they be. . . . But let's reflect afresh on that competition. What had they been taught? What had their instructor trained them to do? Essentially, to win at all costs. They learned to look stiff and planned and move almost robotically. Anyone who has trained students long enough and has judged forensics tournaments knows that after a while almost everyone begins to gesture alike and even sound alike. Conformity gets rewarded. Overexpressiveness, free-form gestures, and unique style are dangerous and often costly, so coaches follow a formula that works: Copy the one who is winning all the tournaments. It sounds a lot like *assimilation*, and it was. But it was easier than fighting the forensics association for being discriminatory.

This story is worth sharing because it is analogous to the institutionalized constraints of the academy. Many professors throughout the Communication discipline have classrooms filled with brilliant students each term. These same students are conceptually molded to embrace culture-absent or privileged European-centered paradigms. Curricular homogeneity, poor textbook coverage of cultural perspectives, and culture-insensitive pedagogy each fails to promote the success of students of color in Communication, as well as in other disciplines (Freire, Clarke, and Aronowitz 1998; Giroux 1997; Jackson 2000b). As a matter of fact, they inhibit it. When there is an absence of culturally inclusive teaching materials and research, or professors of color in the classroom, the discipline of Communication is sending a powerfully clear message to culturally marginalized students that they are not welcome, that their experience is not significant enough to consider.

But, we believe, if diversity is infused at every level of the curriculum and its administration, from textbooks and curriculum design to faculty hiring and student recruitment and retention efforts, the end result will be a conducive atmosphere for students of color to succeed and perhaps to become interested in pursuing a career in academe.

In this conceptual-theoretic essay, then, we seek as authors to demonstrate and argue for incorporation of cultural diversity in the Communication curriculum as a way to promote the recruitment, retention, and success of students of color within that discipline. Using as our model Peggy McIntosh's (1994) 26 daily ways of experiencing privilege, we will present a list of 21 ways that white students experience privilege in the Communication classroom and curriculum. We will explore how some identities are embraced (via "cultural contracts"), while others are disregarded in the design of the texts and curriculum for the basic Public Speaking course; and we offer an example of the kinds of curricular content that must be in basic Public Speaking texts and classrooms. It seems clear that without cultural inclusivity, curricular homogeneity will remain a constant in the disciplinary equation, with the effect of gradually filtering out would-be academicians who cannot imagine how they fit (Courts 1997; Davidson 1996; Giroux 1997; Jackson 1997).

Perhaps our greatest challenge is to consider these three components of promoting the success of students of color: understanding the cultural contract paradigm as an approach to diversity; attending to pedagogical and curricular strategies and concerns for empowering students of color within the basic Public Speaking course; and understanding the classroom as a "space" of privilege or resistance.

Cultural Contract Paradigms

A *cultural contract* is defined as an agreement between two or more interactants who have different interpretations of culture and who have decided to coordinate ("sign a contract") or via negotiations choose to resist coordination of a relationship with each other depending on whether the relationship is deemed valuable to both. Two points of clarity: First, this definition allows for the possibility of *intra*-cultural contracts. One example of this is a contract between two white persons, one of whom is perceived by the other as "being too liberal"; this could be considered a potential breach of a "ready-to-sign" cultural contract with whiteness as a socially constructed position of privilege. Second, this definition does not assume that the relationship is mutually satisfying, as some previous research did (Hecht and Ribeau 1984); instead, the relationship must only be deemed important. It is critical to mention this, since it is quite possible that a person can be *forced* to sign a cultural contract. For example, in some classrooms, it is an implicit agreement between teacher and student not to upset the balance of the class or the authority of the teacher with ideas that oppose those of the teacher. In a classroom driven by such a pedagogical philosophy, a student who breaks the contract is penalized, sometimes verbally and sometimes in other ways.

Hendrix (1998) addresses this penalty avoidance concern in her study of student perceptions of how race influences the credibility of professors. With a sample of 28 white respondents, Hendrix designed a triangulated study using semi-structured interviews, nonparticipant observation, and open-ended surveys. She discovered that race is a factor that tends to influence how some students evaluate their professor's teaching and credibility. That is, those students thought less of the professor who made race an issue in class, altering their collective "ready-to-sign" contract (to always hold the professor credible) in the classroom by implicitly demanding that the professor not devote much time, if any at all, to issues of race. Understandably, racial issues can promote discomfort among white students if they are led to feel responsible for racial injustice or racism. However, we contend that it is more than pedagogical approach; it is that the topic of race itself is volatile. But students must understand these issues if they are to truly communicate with cultural others. Though a decision to remain silent about race and culture in the classroom might not be the preferred choice for professors of color, students from marginalized groups, and cultural experts, silence is deemed valuable at times merely for the sake of survival. This kind of contract to be silent about race is too often signed in advance, and precludes in-depth discussions of race in a national climate heavily concerned with it. (These contracts are called "cultural" rather than "relational" contracts, because it is assumed that human beings can only relate using the apparatus of their cultures, e.g., language.)

Before proceeding any further, it is important that we explain what the different cultural contract types are. *Ready-to-sign* cultural contracts are prenegotiated, and no further negotiation is allowed. "Signing," or relational coordination, might or might not be the goal for the parties to such contracts. White students or professors, for example, have either directly or indirectly chosen to contract with themselves regarding what it means to be white in this society. White students or professors might not even be aware that their whiteness is a marker of normality and privilege that offers them the opportunity not to think about their whiteness as a racial position (Jackson 1999a, 1999b). Cultural contracts with whiteness are often defined by an interest in maintaining privilege, as in the case of curricular homogeneity; sometimes such contracts are defined by a resistance to retaining privilege. (Why in this example must they have contracted with themselves? Because there is no such thing as *not* having a contract. To say one has no cultural contract is to say that one has neither a culture of one's own nor any understanding of how to function in the culture where he or she lives.)

Quasi-completed cultural contracts are partly prenegotiated and partly open for negotiation. These interactants are not ready to "co-create" a contract (this type is discussed below) and they do not necessarily rule out maintaining their own worldviews. These persons straddle the fence in terms of their commitment to reorder privilege. The quasi-completed contract is perhaps the least durable and most popular contract in the discipline of Communication. It is easily observed in the "additive approach" to curriculum change. As explained by Courts (1997), the additive approach is enacted when, for instance, a textbook author tacks on a section or paragraph on race and gender rather than addressing the book's treatment, scope, or depth on the issues.

Finally, *co-created* cultural contracts are fully negotiable, with the only limits being personal preferences or requirements. Such a contract is often perceived as the optimal means of relational coordination across cultures, since the relationship between interactants is fully negotiable and open to differences. If a cultural contract is co-created, that means there is an acknowledgment and valuation of cultural differences. The co-created contract is the ideal context for students of color to thrive. Their cultural perspectives would be reflected, and the theoretic paradigms and curricular heterogeneity would benefit all students as they prepare to enter a multicultural workforce.

Unfortunately, too often we treat those multicultural intellectual legacies and cultural ancestries as secondary or as sensitivity-training components of the curriculum, rather than as fully legitimate lines of inquiry or rigorous explorations of indigenous and lived experiences. So we hear Communication scholars debate the significance of introductory-level Intercultural Communication courses: Should they be required? What is their utility? But in the process of asking these questions, we forget that we are preparing the next generation of professionals for that multicultural workforce. Instead, the questions really should be: Why are we questioning the significance of culture in the curriculum? What do we want our students to be able to do in that workforce? And are we preparing them to do it?

Pedagogical and Curricular Concerns

Postmodern curriculum theorists (e.g., Giroux 1991, 1997; hooks 1994; Kincheloe 1993; Lather 1991; Slattery 1994) suggest that power plays a vital role in the classroom and curriculum. It sustains privilege in vivid and tragic ways to the extent that people of color are uninvited to participate in what the academy represents unless they forfeit their desire to have their identities affirmed by the academy via institutionalized practices and/or curricular reform. Giroux (1997) articulates it best:

> In general terms, [radical educators] have argued that schools are "reproductive" in that they provide different classes and social groups with forms of knowledge, skills, and culture that not only legitimate the dominant culture

but also track students into a labor force differentiated by gender, racial, and class considerations. (119)

Giroux further contends that the "radical pedagogy" school of intellectuals seems to prematurely dismiss the possibilities of real change. He suggests that sometimes the overzealous insurgency of that school leaves no room for the possibilities after the discussion of ideological subordination is completed. Like Giroux, we recognize some clear weaknesses and assert that the extant traditional pedagogical paradigms are limited and oppressive, and therefore must be radically reformed to embrace global change. When working within the confines of a system to produce change, one must first identify the microbes that are infecting the system. That is the goal of critical pedagogy, a seed of cultural studies that polices the boundaries of authority, learning, and curricular practice in order to maintain institutional integrity. All of these boundaries have a profound effect on how knowledge is disseminated and consumed in the classroom and throughout the academy. It is within these boundaries that cultural workers must attend ethically to cultural particularities and asymmetrical relations.

There is much to be said about the possibilities of change, especially in the wake of the Oakland school board's Ebonics controversy. A referendum that was the representation of collective efforts to make schooling practical was mocked, scorned, and derided (Ogbu 1999; Rodriguez 2000). Meanwhile, the parents of that school district helplessly observed the enactment of politics inexplicably linked to their children's futures. This well-meaning gesture had been designed to restore agency to the children as true participants in their own educational experience. Instead, it was read as a debate about linguistic inferiority, racial tolerance, and lower class values being imposed on the middle and upper classes. The students were lost in the shuffle in much the same way they are in the discipline of Communication. Democracy was interrupted and homogeneity continues to live in the space of privilege (Aronowitz and Giroux 1991). There are ways to empower students of color to succeed. The possibilities are endless if properly guided.

Strategies for Empowering Students of Color

Below we present a few ways in which students of color can be empowered in the basic Public Speaking course; some can apply to any course.

- Choose a text that either incorporates or is wholly designed to address a diversity of perspectives concerning race, culture, ethnicity, gender, sexual orientation, physical disability, age, health.

- Use ancillary materials such as recorded discussions, live presentations, and/or class exercises in the form of simulation and gaming. These should be reflective of diverse cultural experiences and learning styles. Kincheloe (1993) recommends using the holographic mind to connect to holographic realities such that multiple dimensions or layers of reality can emerge from the classroom experience. This involves synthesizing linear and curvilinear thinking as often evoked in Afrocentric research (Jackson 1995, 2000a). Linear thinking alone leads to linear behavior and theory development. Mainstreaming a more diunital model to learning facilitates innovation and eventual paradigm shifts that are so vital to disciplinary progress.

■ Be innovative with assignments and have students make direct contact with the immediate community, using theoretic perspectives or a set of tools that allows them to apply what they are learning in the course. Do this so that they are encouraged to learn about diverse cultural experiences.

■ Invite guest speakers who can talk about their lived cultural experiences.

■ Use students from previous semesters to give you feedback on the class and how you might incorporate a more culturally diverse perspective. They can serve as auditors and perhaps be given a one credit-hour independent study or internship so that they can receive something in exchange for their time.

■ Have a friend or colleague of a different cultural background visit your class and evaluate you and your pedagogical approach. The key is accepting criticism and being honest about your limitations.

■ Consider how your own approach to learning is culturally biased. Do you have students in your class from cultures where speakers typically make indirect eye contact with audiences; will those students reside in the United States after graduation? Moderate your range of acceptable speech behaviors so your speaking advice does not ignore cultural differences, yet still prepares students for future success.

■ Don't be afraid to do periodic checks with students about the level of inclusiveness they perceive. For example, you might create and distribute a small survey that asks students to identify weaknesses in the course and discuss the perceived cultural and curricular diversity represented in the course.

■ Assign at least one speech that is nontraditional. For example, maybe the assignment would be for the speaker to sit down while in front of the class, or to serve as instructor to teach a lesson from the textbook or the student's own culture. Perhaps have the student serve as an external expert for a day. This strategy, especially, can lessen the communication anxiety that intercedes classroom performance (Ralston, Ambler, and Scudder 1991).

- Be conscientious about accommodating varied styles of learning and communicating. Vary your lectures so that some are visual, tactile, auditory, or experiential (i.e., hands-on) or are a synthesis of these.

- Establish teams of students early in the term. Give the class opportunities to bond through in-class games and exercises. This also facilitates development of new relationships and offers students who are reticent a sense of inclusion.

- After at least one speech, require students to give feedback; for another, require the speaker to include the names of two or more classmates in the speech, not preplanned. This way, they are engaging audiences and speakers.

Understanding the Classroom Climate as a Space of Privilege or Resistance

As academics, we romanticize about freedom, justice, independence, and integrity. These important touchstones of the academy must be upheld in the classroom and curriculum, otherwise these attainable ideas are mere fantasies in our imagination (Giroux and McLaren 1993). Allowing privilege to be perpetuated in the classroom politicizes and suppresses the possibilities for growth. But in rejecting the impulse to maintain privilege, you can make the classroom become a climate conducive for students of color to succeed (Jackson 1997). As critical theorists, we are well aware of how privilege sometimes creeps into our consciousness, so for this essay we have identified at least 21 daily ways that whites experience privilege in the classroom. We only talk about white privilege here because it is that brand of privilege that promotes a climate that is not conducive for the success of students of color.

1. Course content will most likely reflect a white perspective paradigmatically (Freire and Ramos 2000).

2. Course content will most likely reflect a white perspective of history or classics (Epstein 2000).

3. Course content will most likely make white students feel normal and included (Giroux and McLaren 1993).

4. The instructor will most likely be white (Kincheloe 1993; Lather 1991).

5. The instructor will most likely use examples, stories, and/or jokes most relevant to whites (Lou 1994).

6. White students rarely have to worry that their grade has anything to do with their race or perspective on race (Hendrix 1998).

7. Most textbook authors will most likely be white and writing from a white perspective (Aronowitz and Giroux 1991).

8. Most of the students in the classroom will most likely be white or have similar backgrounds.

9. The tests will most likely be structured to reflect a strong white cultural bias (Hernstein and Murray 1996).

10. White students often do not feel the need to learn about other cultures, and not doing so will have no bearing on their future success (Jackson 1999a, 1999b).

11. White students typically have no need to behaviorally or linguistically codeswitch in the classroom (Jackson 1999a, 1999b).

12. White students at a predominantly white or black university can be assured that they will not be singled out to be used as an example in class and then asked to represent the entire race or culture with their one response (Jackson 1999a).

13. White students are rarely asked to think about their privilege (Jackson 1999b).

14. White students can be assured that they will not be ingratiated with a compliment such as "You are so articulate" or "You are not like the others."

15. White professors at predominantly white universities do not have to be concerned about whether their race is a factor in end-of-the-semester student evaluations. This is especially related to course content and physical appearance of the professor (Hendrix 1998).

16. Whites typically experience little to no race-related performance anxiety, so there is little chance of self-talk such as "I have to perform well because I am a white man" (Kincheloe 1993).

17. Virtually all multimedia excerpts (i.e., radio, print, television, film) used by the instructor or classmates will be reflective of or relevant to whites.

18. Whites find it fairly easy to form or join study groups with peers, due to their minimized differences and constant reaffirmation of white identity as being okay.

19. White students feel empowered to question the syllabus and overall class structure.

20. White professors do not have to worry about their credibility being almost automatically called into question due to race (Hendrix 1998).

21. The teaching and learning styles used in the class will most likely reflect a style most comfortable for whites (Lou 1994).

Implications for Empowering Students of Color

Davidson (1996) recommends that discussions of empowering students of color not be taken lightly; and suggests that not all oppositional identities lead to academic failure, some remain resilient and intact despite the challenges. This is much like the Ralston, Ambler, and Scudder (1991) study in which African Americans were predicted to have more communication anxiety than white students. To the researchers' surprise, African-American students performed as well and sometimes better than did the white students and had less anxiety. This finding evidences a strong resilience to dominance, a factor that is common among African-American identity scales and studies.

Davidson (1996) admits that identities are politicized in the classroom; and while theories, approaches, and strategies have been employed to alleviate this problem, it is only gradually diminishing. For example, she explores ways in which students have empowered themselves and consequently have countered the identity politics by resisting social categories, changing academic institutions, and shifting transcultural realities. These three self-empowerment decisions reflect all three of the cultural contract types — ready-to-sign, quasi-completed, and co-created contracts, respectively.

As communicologists, we have the wherewithal to understand interactional dynamics in the classroom and curriculum. Although we are situated at the periphery of the national conversation, this volume and this chapter offer substantive critiques and strategies capable of enlivening the ongoing debate and shift how scholars and students see cultural diversity. Diversity is an identity issue. It suggests that one's self-definition is distinguishable from others' — and that enhances, rather than subtracts from, the overall mission of a university as a community of citizens decidedly committed to progress and the preservation of integrity. Whitson (1991), among others, criticizes Hirsch's (1987) work on cultural literacy, claiming it appeals to popular audiences but fails to promote social competence, the cloak under which race and gender anxiety lie. Whitson's analysis represents a progressive educational advocacy. Critical pedagogy scholars such as bell hooks, Henry Giroux, Joe Kincheloe, Patrick Courts, and Patrick Slattery have successfully vied for a position in the debate on multicultural curriculum development and reform, postmodern literacy and instructional practices, and radical pedagogy. They have taken the lead as they theorize about oppressive pedagogies (see Freire and Ramos 2000; Freire, Clarke, and Aronowitz 1998), border pedagogies (see Giroux 1991, 1997), politeracies (see Courts 1997), and postformalism (see Kincheloe 1993). Now, we must formally institute new progressive changes in the Communication curriculum and classroom.

Note

A version of the cultural contracts theory introduced here was presented at the April 2000 Eastern Communication Association Conference, in Pittsburgh, Pennsylvania.

References

Aronowitz, S., and H. Giroux. (1991). *Postmodern Education: Politics, Culture, and Social Criticism*. Minneapolis, MN: University of Minnesota.

Courts, P. (1997). *Multicultural Literacies: Dialect, Discourse, and Diversity*. New York: Peter Lang.

Davidson, A.L. (1996). *Making and Molding Identity in Schools: Student Narratives on Race, Gender and Academic Engagement*. Albany, NY: State University of New York Press.

Epstein, T. (2000). "Adolescents' Perspectives on Racial Diversity in U.S. History: Case Studies From an Urban Classroom." *American Educational Research Journal* 1: 185-214.

Freire, P., and M.B. Ramos. (2000). *Pedagogy of the Oppressed*. New York: Continuum.

Freire, P., S. Clarke, and S. Aronowitz. (1998). *Pedagogy of Freedom: Ethics, Democracy, and Civic Courage*. Wesport, CT: Rowman & Littlefield.

Giroux, H. (1991). *Border Crossings: Cultural Workers and the Politics of Education*. New York: Routledge.

——— . (1997). *Pedagogy and the Politics of Hope: Theory, Culture and Schooling*. Boulder, CO: Westview Press.

——— , and P. McLaren. (1993). *Between Borders: Pedagogy and the Politics of Cultural Studies*. New York: Routledge.

Hecht, M., and S. Ribeau. (1984). "Ethnic Communication: A Comparative Analysis of Satisfying Communication." *International Journal of Intercultural Relations* 8: 135-151.

Hendrix, K.G. (1998). "Student Perceptions of the Influence of Race on Professor Credibility." *Journal of Black Studies* 28(6): 738-763.

Hernstein, R., and C. Murray. (1996). *The Bell Curve: Intelligence and Class Structure in American Life*. New York: Free Press.

Hirsch, E.D. (1987). *Cultural Literacy: What Every American Needs to Know*. Boston: Houghton-Mifflin.

hooks, b. (1994). *Teaching to Transgress*. New York: Routledge.

Jackson, R.L. (1995). "Toward an Afrocentric Methodology for the Critical Assessment of Rhetoric." In *African American Rhetoric: A Reader*, edited by L.A. Niles, pp. 148-157. Dubuque, IA: Kendall-Hunt.

————. (1997). "For Those of Us Who Must Move Forward: Diversity Scholarship, Moving Into the New Millennium." In *NCA Summer Diversity Conference Proceedings*, pp. 67-81. Annandale, VA: National Communication Association.

————. (1999a). *The Negotiation of Cultural Identity*. Westport, CT: Praeger.

————. (1999b). "White Space, White Privilege: Mapping Discursive Inquiry Into the Self." *Quarterly Journal of Speech* 55(1): 1-17.

————. (2000a). "Africalogical Theory Building: Positioning the Discourse." In *International and Intercultural Communication Annual: Vol. 22. Rhetoric in Intercultural Contexts*, edited by A. Gonzalez, pp. 31-41. Newbury Park, CA: Sage.

————. (2000b). "So Real Illusions of Black Intellectualism: Exploring Race, Roles, and Gender in the Academy." *Communication Theory* 10(1): 48-63.

Kincheloe, J. (1993). *Toward a Critical Politics of Teacher Thinking: Mapping the Postmodern*.Westport, CT: Bergin & Garvey.

Lather, P. (1991). *Getting Smart: Feminist Research and Pedagogy With/in the Postmodern*. New York: Routledge.

Lou, R. (1994). "Teaching All Students Equally." In *Teaching From a Multicultural Perspective*, edited by H. Roberts et al., pp. 28-41. Thousand Oaks, CA: Sage.

McIntosh, P. (1994). "White Privilege and Male Privilege: A Personal Account of Coming to See Correspondences Through Work in Women's Studies." In *Race, Class, and Gender: An Anthology*, edited by M. Andersen and P.H. Collins, pp. 76-87. Belmont, CA: Wadsworth.

Ogbu, J. (1999). "Beyond Language: Ebonics, Proper English, and Identity in a Black American Speech Community." *American Educational Research Journal* 36(2): 147-184.

Ralston, S., R. Ambler, and J. Scudder. (1991). "Reconsidering the Impact of Racial Differences in the College Public Speaking Classroom on Minority Student Communication Anxiety." *Communication Reports* 4(1): 43-54.

Rodriguez, A. (2000). *Diversity as Liberation (II): Introducing a New Understanding of Diversity*. Cresskill, NJ: Hampton Press.

Slattery, P. (1994). *Curriculum Development in the Postmodern Era*. New York: Garland.

Whitson, A.J. (1991). *Constitution and Curriculum*. London: Falmer.

Part Two
Instructional Practices

Teaching Assistant Workshop

Race, Ethnicity, and Nationality in the Classroom

Katherine G. Hendrix and Aparna S. Bulusu

Workshop

The general purpose of the workshop would be to provide Communication graduate teaching assistants (GTAs) with a realistic view of the duties and responsibilities associated with joining the professoriate, whether temporarily as a graduate assistant or long term as a professor. The workshop also is an opportunity to discuss the intersection of race, ethnicity, and nationality in the classroom. Its sessions will introduce GTAs to the academic experiences of their undergraduate students and their graduate assistant peers who are students of color. In addition, its readings will facilitate a discussion of the classroom from the vantage point of being a white teaching assistant in a predominantly white environment.

Rationale

Unless graduate students have taken coursework in education, it is highly unlikely that they are familiar with the research that has investigated the experiences of students of color in predominantly white educational environments. GTAs are even less likely to have been exposed to experiences of teachers and professors of color, considering the absence of such research in Communication's instructional literature. In contrast to those of color, white educators typically enter the classroom from the privileged position of being a member of the "mainstream" culture; and while they might acknowledge the presence of the "other" in their classrooms, white educators rarely acknowledge how their own race influences communication dynamics (see readings by Hendrix 1998; Hendrix, Bulusu, and Johnson 1999; McIntosh 1988; Weinstein and Obear 1992).

To rectify this, the workshop should go beyond merely instructing GTAs on teaching specific content and general pedagogical principles; its instructors also should acknowledge and prepare GTAs for the influence in the classroom of gender, age, class, disability, race, ethnicity, and nationality. (Only those sessions dealing with the last three factors are described below.)

Session One: The Teaching Profession

The first workshop session provides GTAs with information about the responsibilities and expectations associated with selecting the professoriate as a career. This unit familiarizes GTAs with service, teaching, and research requirements for tenure, and it introduces the "scholarship of teaching" concept. GTAs also are exposed to some of the stresses associated with making the transition from graduate assistant to tenure-track assistant professor.

Readings

E.L. Boyer, (1990), *Scholarship Reconsidered: Priorities of the Professoriate* (Princeton, NJ: Carnegie Foundation for the Advancement of Teaching).

R.J. Menges, (1996), "Experiences of Newly Hired Faculty," in *To Improve the Academy, Vol. 15*, edited by L. Richlin, pp. 169-182 (Stillwater, OK: New Forums Press and the Professional and Organizational Development Network in Higher Education).

Guiding Question for Session Two

"What's missing?" After discussing the readings on what constitutes scholarship and the typical expectations for assistant professors, GTAs are asked about the absence of comments regarding diversity in the academy.

Transition Article

D. Smith, (1989), *The Challenge of Diversity: Involvement or Alienation in the Academy*, ASHE-ERIC Higher Education Reports, No. 5 (Washington, DC: George Washington University).

Session Two: The Undergraduate Experience for Students of Color

The second session of the workshop asks GTAs to consider the experiences of their students of color, beyond how they are performing in class. Specifically discussed is what are common experiences associated with being a "minority" in the college classroom, on campus, or both.

Readings

A. Aguirre, Jr., and R.O. Martinez, (1993), *Chicanos in Higher Education*, ASHE-ERIC Higher Education Reports, No. 3 (Washington, DC: George Washington University).

J.R. Feagin, H. Vera, and N. Imani, (1996), *The Agony of Education: Black Students at White Colleges and Universities* (New York: Routledge).

J. Hsia, (1988), "Asian-Americans Fight the Myth of Super Student," *Educational Record* 68: 94-97.

Guiding Questions for Session Three

What about you? Who are you? How does this affect your interactions with students, and theirs with you? After considering the experiences of being a "minority" undergraduate within a predominantly white setting, GTAs explore how their identity and predispositions influence interactions with others they perceive as different from themselves.

Transition Article

G. Weinstein and K. Obear, (1992), "Bias Issues in the Classroom: Encounters With the Teaching Self," in *New Directions for Teaching and Learning: Promoting Diversity in College Classrooms*, edited by M. Adams, pp. 39-50 (San Francisco: Jossey-Bass).

Session Three: What About You? Broad Overview

The third session allows for a general discussion among GTAs from all backgrounds. During this session GTAs can explore their departmental roles, personal characteristics, beliefs, and communication strategies for interacting with undergraduates, graduate colleagues, and professors.

Readings

R. Hardiman and B.W. Jackson, (1992), "Racial Identity Development: Understanding Racial Dynamics in College Classrooms and on Campus," in *New Directions for Teaching and Learning: Promoting Diversity in College Classrooms*, edited by M. Adams, pp. 21-37 (San Francisco: Jossey-Bass).

K.G. Hendrix, A. Bulusu, and O. Johnson, (November 1999), "The 'Other' GTA: You Know, Graduate Teaching Assistants of Color," paper presented at the meeting of the National Communication Association, Chicago, Illinois.

G. Luna and D. Cullen, (1998), "Do Graduate Students Need Mentoring?" *The College Student Journal* 32: 322-330.

D. Rubin, (1992), "Nonlanguage Factors Affecting Undergraduates' Judgments of Nonnative English Speaking Teaching Assistants," *Research in Higher Education* 33: 511-531.

B.R. Sandler, (July 1988), "The Chilly Climate for Women on Campus," *USA Today*, pp. 50-53.

J. Sprague and J.D. Nyquist, (1989), "TA Supervision," in *New Directions for Teaching and Learning: Teaching Assistant Training in the 1990s*, edited by J.D. Nyquist, R.D. Abbott, and D.H. Wulff (San Francisco: Jossey-Bass).

Guiding Question for Session Four

How does your presence "color" the classroom? This question allows GTAs to be more specific regarding the impact of their race, ethnicity, and nationality on their teaching.

Transition Articles

P. McIntosh, (1988), "White Privilege and Male Privilege: A Personal Account of Coming to See Correspondences Through Work in Women's Studies," Working Paper No. 189 (Wellesley, MA: Wellesley College).

M.L. Reyes and J.J. Halcon, (1988), "Racism in Academia: The Old Wolf Revisited," *Harvard Educational Review* 58: 299-314.

Session Four:
What About You? The Racially Diverse Classroom

The fourth workshop session will provide GTAs with an opportunity to speak more about how their personal backgrounds and demographics influence how they experience academia; specifically, how they are perceived as they teach and how they perceive others.

Readings

A. Aguirre, Jr., and R.O. Martinez, (1993), *Chicanos in Higher Education*, ASHE-ERIC Higher Education Reports, No. 3, pp. 53-68 (Washington, DC: George Washington University).

K.G. Hendrix, (1998), "Black and White Male Professor Perceptions of the Influence of Race on Classroom Dynamics and Credibility," *The Negro Educational Review* 49: 37-52.

T. Nakayama and R. Krizek, (1995), "Whiteness: A Strategic Rhetoric," *Quarterly Journal of Speech* 81: 291-309.

T.K. Nakayama and J.N. Martin, eds., (1999), *Whiteness: The Communication of Social Identity* (Thousand Oaks, CA: Sage).

A.M. Salomone, (1999), "International Teaching Assistants: Some Unique Problems," *The Journal of Graduate Teaching Assistant Development* 6: 13-24.

S. Townes, (November 1998), "Shut Those Thick Lips: Silence as an Incarcerating Condition for Minority Students," paper presented at the meeting of the National Communication Association, New York.

Conclusion

This four-part workshop is designed to provide GTAs with an opportunity to talk about something more fundamental than course content; that is, how who they are impacts their teaching. GTAs should complete the workshop more aware of what it means to be a professor and recognizing how their race, ethnicity, and nationality influence how they are perceived, as well as how they perceive others within their department setting — particularly in the classes the GTAs teach.

Public Speaking in a Second Language

Dale Cyphert

Rationale

For a great many students of color, issues of difference and identity do not begin or end with color. Instead, they *hear* themselves as members of a language community that is not represented, studied, or even acknowledged in the study of communication. From their first experience with Public Speaking, students whose own communication reflects nondominant discourse practices are subjected to a double burden. Not only must they meet the expectations of the dominant Western rhetoric of the university, but they must also reconcile their own language practices with the models of "competent" communication that are presented in the classroom.

A full curriculum in Communication Studies would eventually address issues of cross-cultural communication, subaltern discourse practices, and normative rhetorical hegemony; a student of color who discovers critical rhetoric or transcultural postcolonial critique might certainly find that the field of Communication can offer a relevant and supportive professional environment. Nevertheless, the typical introduction to the study of communication remains a required course in Public Speaking. Here, the student of color, who might also be an international or immigrant student, faces the immediate reality of cultural expectations regarding the "proper" use of message structure, relationship markers, evidence, persuasiveness, and other rhetorical strategies of the Western tradition. Such students find themselves making speeches in a dialect or second (or third or fourth) language to audiences who understand nothing of the students' cultures, languages, or communication practices.

Students of color have suffered significant damage in Speech classes that attempt to "discipline language" (Cantu 1979: 7), an experience that virtually guarantees those students will never seek entry into the discipline. Based on my experience as an instructor in a large, diverse, urban community college in California, plus additional research I conducted on the communication apprehension issues involved with second-language and cross-cultural public speaking (see Cyphert 1997), I have concluded that one effective way to mitigate the cultural and linguistic burden placed on students of color is to introduce the issues of rhetorical culture and linguistic dissimilarity as part of the basic Public Speaking curriculum.

Learning Objectives

This unit of instruction introduces the situation of speaking in a second language as a normal part of the rhetorical environment in a diverse society. The objectives of the unit are threefold: to develop speaking skill among second-language speakers, to develop tolerance on the part of dominant-culture audiences for accented and dialectic speech, and to have all students see the practical application of cross-cultural communication in the context of responsible public speaking.

Presentation of Material

Recent textbook editions have begun to incorporate discussions of culture and language as elements of audience analysis or civic responsibility, but Public Speaking texts typically do not address the speech skills that are unique to cross-linguistic situations. Some texts note variations in speech organization, communication styles, and cultural practices; but speakers are rather vaguely urged to "adapt language choices appropriately for each situation, audience, and setting" (Self and Carlson-Liu 1988: 40-41); "familiarize [themselves] with and use [their] audience's language codes" (Kearney and Plax 1996: 171); or "avoid" ethnocentrisim and unintended obscene gestures (Lucas 1995: 20-23). As a result, to attend to the topic of speaking in a second language probably will require giving students supplemental instructions.

In order to present cross-cultural communication as the normal condition, cross-linguistic speaking should be discussed as a rhetorical situation that could be faced by anyone. In fact, students who are studying foreign languages will appreciate the advice for using their language skills in formal presentations,[1] and those who anticipate any kind of business career can assume that they will be called upon to speak to diverse audiences. The instructional unit should be framed not as an attempt to accommodate cross-linguistic speakers, but as an opportunity for all students to become familiar with the special skills being practiced by their bicultural peers.

Instructional Content

COPING WITH LANGUAGE/COMMUNICATION APPREHENSION

Communication apprehension is a common student concern, and a topic usually covered in the Public Speaking curriculum. But speakers of a second language are subject to additional anxiety, the result of lack of communicative control and constant self-monitoring that occurs while speaking (Horwitz, Horwitz, and Cope 1986: 127). Performance anxiety can be exacerbated for international students whose performance might reflect on family, determine their ability to remain in the United States, or impact career success in the home country (Churchman 1986: 5). Alienation of the student of color from the dominant classroom audiences can create additional anxiety (Churchman 1986: 4). The perception of non-standard language as a "difficulty" is a legitimate concern in the United States, where it has been demonstrated that accent alone causes Anglo listeners to assess speakers more negatively (Cross et al. 1990; Cukor-Avila and Markley 2000; Powell and Avila 1986).

Although language itself might seem to be the primary communication barrier in a formal speech situation, simply gaining fluency might not address issues that are more important to speaker success. Research suggests that some students whose language is not as fluent as they think it "should" be will try to maintain their own positive self-image by attributing their communication difficulties to a lack of motivation or general ability, thus reducing their willingness to improve those factors (Hines and Barraclough 1995: 246). Furthermore, the self-assessment of fluency is not always related to objective measures of language use (Cyphert 1997). The student who speaks understandably but feels he or she "should" be speaking without any trace of an accent will be more apprehensive about speaking in public, and thus will face more preparation and delivery difficulties, than will the barely fluent student who feels he or she has "acceptable" mastery of the language.

Instructors can provide basic information on the physiology of stress and anxiety and on methods to reduce symptoms of communication apprehension. They also can mitigate some language-related sources of anxiety by addressing elements of language control, familiarity with the audience, and expectations of language mastery. That is, they can suggest that students:

- *Have an expert (an instructor, a native speaker, or the campus writing center) correct grammar in a speech draft.* Although this means the student will prepare a manuscript, the resulting sense of mastery over syntax can outweigh some of the disadvantages of that speech format.

- *Practice the speech with an audience of standard-English speaking American friends, roommates, or classmates, not just with cultural cohorts.* Increased familiarity with problem words and ideas, and with the target audience's probable reactions, will reduce anxiety as well as allow the speaker to anticipate and make plans to mitigate comprehension problems.

- *"Memorize" grammar constructions and vocabulary (but not the speech).* Even in an extemporaneous speech, key sentences and words can be planned and practiced ahead of time. Speakers can memorize sentence constructions, interchanging a variety of verbs, nouns, or objects in an extemporaneous way.

- *Discuss topics that are relatively new or unfamiliar.* Some second-language students find they are less apprehensive when they are speaking about a topic in which they have less emotional investment. Some also find that they are able to use the second language more comfortably when they have learned about the topic in the second language.

■ *Discuss a home country, culture, or area of expertise.* By selecting a topic on which the speaker is an expert, credibility is enhanced and anxiety thereby lessened. Further, an appropriate topic can foreground language and culture issues, allowing the student to mitigate comprehension issues in a straightforward and assertive way.

■ *Differentiate accent issues (which cannot be easily changed) from comprehensibility issues (which can be mitigated).* Second-language speakers are sometimes surprised to hear that audiences can find accents and unusual speech patterns charming, aesthetically pleasing, or dramatic. Students should concentrate their energy on ensuring comprehension, rather than on demonstrating a native-like command of the second language.

PRESENTATION TO A SECOND-LANGUAGE AUDIENCE

Audiences are not unwilling to work at comprehension, but they are alienated by situations they perceive as incomprehensible. A speaker who takes positive steps to mitigate language difficulties can invite the audience to participate in a satisfying exchange. Both second-language speakers and dominant-language audiences should see the speaking event as one of mutual responsibility. The speaker should take steps to ensure that he or she is comprehended, and the audience should be forthcoming about requesting clarification of pronunciations or concepts. Students can be instructed to:

■ *Write difficult or unfamiliar words on the blackboard before the speech begins.* As the speech progresses, the audience should be asked to raise a hand or otherwise signal that a word is not being understood. Those words can also be written on the board to help the audience comprehend the speaker.

■ *Use overheads and outlines so the audience can more easily follow accented speech.* When the speaker moves from one point to the next, the outline can be used as a visible signpost to help the audience anticipate and thus more easily comprehend the next point to be made.

■ *Allow "extra" time in the introduction for the audience to adjust to an accent.* It takes several minutes for the ear to adjust to a very unfamiliar accent. The speaker should offer some early material (perhaps a self-introduction or a formalized welcome) that is very easy to anticipate, very easy to comprehend, or nonessential to the main content of the speech in order for the audience to "tune" its ear to the speaker's accent.

■ *Offer the audience methods for stopping the speech to get clarification when necessary for understanding.* If the audience is given permission to ask for clarification, it will begin to take its listening responsibility more seriously and become actively engaged in a dialogic communication process.

■ *Provide explicit introductory preview and signposting transitions to clarify any unexpected organization style or communication conventions.* Some difficulties of cross-linguistic speaking are less a function of language comprehension than genre expectations. If the speaker knows that a rhetorical format or device might catch an audience by surprise, that feature can be explicitly noted and explained.

■ *Similarly, teach the audience how to respond to or interpret unfamiliar rhetorical conventions.* This way, the audience gains familiarity with the speaker's culture, while taking responsibility in the dialogue. For example, a speaker might preview a narrative format as such, and explain how the audience ought to provide its own interpretation. Or, the speaker might explain that "flowery" language is a sign of respect or enthusiasm.

■ *Speak slowly and clearly.* This is often wise for native speakers as well, but second-language speakers sometimes equate language fluency with speed. They need to realize that all speeches should be delivered more slowly than a "normal" conversational rate.

■ *Use gestures, facial expressions, and a "conversational" style to make perfect pronunciation less important.* An audience will be far more tolerant and responsive to the confident, happy speaker, and more likely to work harder to comprehend the speaker's intent.

■ *Accommodate or remediate volume and intonation expectations of the audience.* Speakers whose native language uses tonal ranges very different from those the audience expects can find themselves expressing unintended emotional messages.

Activities and Exercises

If the Public Speaking course enrolls students of subaltern cultures, every assignment becomes an opportunity to learn and practice the skills of cross-linguistic speaking. In most classrooms, only a few students will be second-language speakers, but the rest can be asked to play the proactive role of an engaged audience. Speakers should be encouraged to include feedback opportunities throughout the speech, and the audience should be given appropriate mechanisms to slow down or stop the speaker to ask for clarification. It is possible, in some contexts, to assign all students the task of addressing a speech to an audience of another culture or language. I have had excellent results with an assignment to tape-record an out-of-class speech, which also frees up valuable in-class time for other activities.

When grading speeches, it is important that any assessment of clear or effective delivery be made in terms of comprehension and effect, rather than adherence to arbitrary Western standards of pronunciation, syntax, vocabulary, intonation, or style. Students who mitigate the effect of a strong accent, or create a comfortable zone of dialogic exploration, or exploit the credibility of language proficiency should be rewarded for their creative and effective response to the rhetorical situation. Similarly, holding students responsible for learning and using specific organizational structures is entirely appropriate; but instructors will level the field by offering all students an opportunity to learn and use an unfamiliar genre when they require students to explore a variety of cultural paradigms (e.g., both an analytical speech and a persuasive narrative).

Note

1. Formal public speaking offers unique advantages in foreign language instruction: The activity builds self-esteem and confidence in the target language (Lore-Lawson 1993); it forces the integration of numerous skills, and requires the use of such intangibles as poise, confidence, and organized self-expression (Smallwood 1976).

References

Cantu, N.E. (April 1979). "My 'Excuse-Me Tongue,' Or, A Chicana in the English Classroom." Paper presented at the Conference on College Composition and Communication, Minneapolis, Minnesota.

Churchman, E.C. (1986). "Developing a Public Speaking Course for Non-Native Speakers of English: Problems and Approaches." Bowling Green, OH: Bowling Green State University, Department of Interpersonal and Public Communication.

Cross, H., G. Kenney, J. Mell, and W. Zimmermann. (1990). *Employer Hiring Practices: Differential Treatment of Hispanic and Anglo Job Seekers.* Washington, DC: Urban Institute Press.

Cukor-Avila, P., and D. Markley. (2000). "Employers Show Bias Against Accents, Study Says." University of North Texas News Service. <www.unt.edu/news>, accessed January 9, 2001.

Cyphert, D. (1997). "Public Speaking in a Second Language: An Investigation of Student Apprehensions." Paper presented at the Annual Convention of the National Communication Association, Chicago, Illinois.

Hines, S.C., and R.A. Barraclough. (1995). "Communicating in a Foreign Language: Its Effects on Perceived Motivation, Knowledge, and Communication Ability." *Communication Research Reports* 12(2): 241-247.

Horwitz, E.K., M.B. Horwitz, and J. Cope. (1986). "Foreign Language Classroom Anxiety." *Modern Language Journal* 70(2): 125-132.

Kearney, P., and T.G. Plax. (1996). *Public Speaking in a Diverse Society*. Mountain View, CA: Mayfield.

Lore-Lawson, J. (1993). "Self-Esteem in the Foreign Language Classroom." Paper presented at the Central States Conference/Iowa Foreign Language Association, Des Moines, Iowa.

Lucas, S.E. (1995). *The Art of Public Speaking*. 5th ed. New York: McGraw-Hill.

Powell, R.G., and D.R. Avila. (1986). "Ethnicity, Communication Competency and Classroom Success: A Question of Assessment." *The Western Journal of Speech Communication* 50: 269-278.

Self, L.S., and C.S. Carlson-Liu. (1988). *Oral Communications Skills: A Multicultural Approach*. Dubuque, IA: Kendall/Hunt.

Smallwood, B.A. (1976). "Public Speaking in the ESL Classroom." *TESOL Newsletter* 10(3): 44.

Exploring Personal Prejudices

An Activity to Develop Interpersonal Communication Competence

Cynthia Berryman-Fink

Course

Interpersonal Communication

Learning Objectives

As a result of this activity, students will be able to understand theories of perceptual processes, attribution, and symbolic interaction; demonstrate skills of provisional language, self-disclosure, empathy, feedback, indexing generalizations, supportive listening, probing, conflict management, and behavioral flexibility; practice interpersonal skills in an authentic discussion of personal attitudes; and demonstrate an appreciation for diversity.

Description of the Activity

This exercise solicits students' personal prejudices, and provides class time to discuss prejudices regarding race and ethnicity as well as gender, class, sexual orientation, and many other aspects of identity. Through the ongoing discussion of their own actual stereotypes and prejudices, with focused questioning by the instructor, students come to vividly understand how stereotypical perceptions of people are formed, how attributions can be faulty, and how language reveals attitudes. The activity provides ample opportunity to practice a variety of interpersonal communication skills.

Process

1. **Present background information.** Prior to the exercise, the instructor presents information about the nature of prejudice. Interpersonal Communication textbooks that do not treat the subject of prejudice can be supplemented with short readings from Intercultural Communication texts. For example, Chen and Starosta (1998: 32-58) cover such topics as the nature of perception, cultural influences on perception, stereotypes, prejudice, the origins and impact of stereotypes and prejudices, cultural values, and models of cultural values orientation. Gordon Allport's classic book *The Nature of Prejudice* (1979) lends itself to a mini-lecture. Relevant concepts include Allport's continuum of prejudice (antilocution, avoid-

ance, discrimination, physical attack, extermination) and the delineation of behaviors used by targets of prejudice (including obsessive concern, denial of membership, withdrawal, strengthening in-group ties, aggression against their own group, prejudice against other groups, militancy, enhanced striving).

2. Solicit students' prejudices. Students are assigned a homework activity in which they compose a list of all the prejudices they hold. They do not put their name on this sheet, and they type the list to preclude their handwriting being recognized. It is imperative that students feel safe in doing this exercise and that all responses are completely anonymous. The instructor should be prepared to deal with a wide range of prejudices — including racial ("African-Americans who are always angry," interracial couples, Asian students, Mexicans); gender ("extreme feminists," "women who put careers before children," "men who are supported by wives," teenage girls, women drivers, white males); class ("white trash," people on welfare, the poor, the upper class, "rednecks," "homeless people who beg," the wealthy); ethnicity (Appalachians, people from India, people from the Middle East, Cubans, Japanese); religion (Catholics, Jews, Southern Baptists, "religious fundamentalists," Mormons); appearance (fat people, people with tattoos or body piercings, "wiggers," "people who wear designer clothes"); sexual orientation (bisexuals, gays, lesbians, "heterosexuals who have too many children," "people who flaunt their sexuality"); political (Republicans, Democrats, Liberals, Conservatives); age ("old people"); hobbies (athletes, cheerleaders, fraternity members, sorority members, hunters); occupations (lawyers, police); lifestyle (vegetarians, smokers, drug users, "yuppies," gang members); behavior ("cheap people," "loud people," "dumb people"); and more (illegal aliens, handicapped people, "engineering students," "people living in the U.S. who do not speak English," mini-van drivers, homophobes, Nazis, freshmen, white supremacists).

3. Reveal prejudices and create discussion guidelines. The instructor compiles the individual lists, and the result is displayed for the class on Powerpoint slides or overhead transparencies. Students scan this master list without discussion, although typically they have difficulty containing their reactions. The instructor explains that periodically throughout the term, the class will have the opportunity to discuss these prejudices, but they must come to some collective guidelines for *how* that ongoing discussion will take place. Here, the instructor assists the students in setting rules for how communication will occur. Discussion guidelines typically include caveats such as the following: You have the option of owning the items you wrote. Avoid name-calling. Attack the issue, not the person. Do not interrupt a speaker. Ask questions. Listen to others. Respect differences of opinion. Try to empathize with others. Self-disclose only if you feel comfortable doing so. Manage anger.

4. Begin open-ended discussion of prejudices. The instructor next asks for students' reactions and commentary on the list of prejudices. Students' behavior can range from extreme tentativeness and reluctance to begin the discussion, to impatience and eagerness to address particular items. Often students will express shock that particular items are even listed, and demand explanations of why people hold those prejudices. Sometimes, students will admit they wrote an item, and attempt to explain why they hold that attitude; other students will not own items, but will speak about why people in general might have that prejudice. Over time, students become increasingly willing to describe their own experiences.

5. Use discussion probes. Discussions will rarely lack energy, but probing techniques can be used to direct the discussion toward course concepts and theoretical material. Sample questions include: What affects our perception of others? On what factors are attributions of people based? How does the wording of certain items or particular comments reveal attitudes? How can language offend others? How does your own cultural background influence your attitudes toward others? How prevalent is [specific item off the list] on this campus? In this city? In society? How might that particular prejudice be manifested in behavior? Can someone hold no prejudices? How might you react if someone attributed [specific prejudice off the list] to you? Why do we hold prejudices? Do prejudices have any value? How do we overcome prejudices? What are the best ways to communicate with someone who holds attitudes about identity issues vastly different from yours?

6. Apply course concepts. Because the class revisits this exercise regularly throughout the term, it can be a catalyst for teaching many different interpersonal communication concepts and skills. For example, the instructor can teach skills and then ask students to try to use such skills when participating in the discussion of prejudices. Examples of such skills from the prejudice discussions can be used to illustrate course concepts. If the prejudice discussion begins to deteriorate toward defensiveness or dysfunction, the class should be reminded of the benefits of using the interpersonal communication competencies they are acquiring in the course.

Cautions

1. Use with a heterogeneous student population. The exercise presumes a somewhat heterogeneous group of students. It should be effective as long as there is some diversity along racial, gender, ethnic, religious, political, and lifestyle lines.

2. Be prepared for unpredictability. To succeed with this activity, the instructor must be skilled at facilitating discussion and comfortable with the unpredictability and emotionality that can arise when the topic is prejudices. The exercise deals in affective and behavioral learning as well as content learning.

3. Be available outside of class. Students must be able to interact with the instructor outside of class or through email, as in-class discussion sometimes sparks questions or concerns.

4. Allow enough time. Sufficient time must be devoted to the activity so students are able to communicate fully and reach some resolution on issues. After soliciting and presenting such a list of prejudices, the instructor would be remiss to not allow students ample opportunity to express themselves, to question others, and to reconcile differences. While this activity can take 20 to 30 percent of overall class time throughout the term, it is time well-spent, because the activity can provide an understanding of the majority of Interpersonal Communication course concepts.

Assessment

A variety of measures to assess learning outcomes of this exercise can be used. A pretest/posttest measure of attitudes toward diversity or of open-mindedness would reveal changes in students over time. The instructor could rate student effectiveness in demonstrating various interpersonal communication competencies over time in the course. A focus-group discussion at the completion of the activity would solicit students' perceptions of their learning from the exercise. Finally, open-ended course evaluations allow students to comment on their learning from this activity.

Relevant Background

Most students, but especially those whose voices are often marginalized in traditional classrooms, seem to benefit from this exercise. Students who have been the targets of racial, gender, religious, ethnic, or other forms of prejudice express gratitude that their experiences are validated. They appreciate that classmates are able to discuss with interpersonal sensitivity the actual prejudice they experience.

Students are enlightened by seeing the wide range of possible prejudices. Some students who have never before been the target of prejudice find themselves in that role for the first time. Because the range of prejudices is so broad, students realize that they can be both the sender and the receiver of prejudiced remarks.

Though class discussion can be painful at times, the activity becomes a bonding experience where students learn to listen to and empathize with one another. They learn about themselves, about managing differences, and about communicating interpersonally with a diverse group.

References

Allport, G.W. (1979, orig. 1954). *The Nature of Prejudice*. Reading, MA: Addison-Wesley.

Chen, G.-M., and W.J. Starosta. (1998). *Foundations of Intercultural Communication*. Boston: Allyn and Bacon.

Learning About "Others," Learning About Ourselves

The Basic Communication Course

Heather E. Harris

Courses

This activity is structured mainly for introductory courses (Public Speaking, Intercultural Communication, Interpersonal Communication) because these courses usually have the necessary presentation time built into their format. Additionally, because students are usually required to take basic courses as prerequisites to subsequent courses, the basic courses are ideal for laying the foundation for co-cultural and co-ethnic understanding through the provision of fundamental and practical tools.

Definition of Terms

The term *co-culture* refers to the culture of the organizational members. Co-culturalism presumes the validity of all voices in an organizational setting. Furthermore, co-culturalism exists through the fostering of deep understanding, respect, and appreciation of others. An individual's *ethnicity* refers to the particular group that she or he chooses to identify with, regardless of the individual's cultural background. Ethnicity is a socially defined phenomenon by which groups of people consciously distinguish themselves from others; both the out group and the in group agree with the categorization.

Learning Objectives

This "Learning" activity is a pedagogical tool to reinforce culture and ethnicity as central to communication processes. As a result of the activity, students will be positioned to take the next step after affirmative action to affirming practices through their exposure to and exploration of the multiple communicative dynamics that stem from this country's co-cultures and co-ethnicities. They will have basic tools to facilitate their negotiation of intercultural and interethnic communicative meanings. These learned affirming practices have the potential to result in positive intercultural and interethnic encounters beyond the classroom.

Description of the Activity

Groups of students choose a culture of interest — e.g., Chinese, Barbadian, French Canadian, Lakota, the San. The aim is deep communicative analysis and understanding of the selected culture. The instructor tells the students that it will be necessary for them to go beyond the campus library to places such as embassies or cultural centers for their research. And that they are also expected to conduct at least two in-depth interviews with individuals from the culture being explored. Moreover, students are encouraged to be creative in their presentation of the selected culture by using the language, music, food , dress, or activities specific to it.

To guide students through the process, the instructor has them answer the following questions during the course of their final presentation: What is "communication"? What is "culture"? What is the worldview of this culture (guiding philosophies)? What are the dominant values (e.g., individualistic, collectivist)? What are the verbal and nonverbal communication styles? How do these communication styles differ for women and for men? And finally, how are these communication practices similar to and different from the group members' own cultures?

Process

1. Students are introduced to the activity during discussion of the syllabus during the first class.

2. During the second week of classes, they are randomly assigned to groups. The number of groups depends on the availability of presentation time.

3. By week four, each group should have selected a culture to explore.

4. The groups spend the semester meeting in preparation for the final presentation. (At commuter colleges, students should use online tools such as Blackboard™ to communicate. Blackboard™ also enables the instructor to keep track of participation by each group member.) Any student who does not participate in the group's work receives a group project grade of zero; this seems to reduce anxiety and resistance to group participation on the part of the other students.

5. One week before the final presentations, groups hand in their draft outlines (no fewer than 10 references, of which no more than 30 percent may be Internet sources).

6. Each group presentation typically lasts 25-30 minutes, depending on the size of the group. It might include video, food, music, art, Powerpoint, costumes — whatever the students decided was required to make a thorough and informative presentation of another co-culture's voice.

7. About 10 minutes are allotted for questions and additional student insights at the end of each presentation.

Cautions

Some students will want to define themselves simply as "American." However, this strategy defeats the purpose of the activity. Unless all students, especially those not considered "students of color," are encouraged to explore their own cultural backgrounds and the underlying basic assumptions that accompany them, little progress can be made toward understanding "others" — because the students have little understanding of themselves.

Assessment

This activity in co-cultural and co-ethnic communicative dynamics does more than provide a safe environment for students to build confidence as they increase their understanding and skills in the practice of diversity. It could also be considered a first step toward integrating diversity in the school. A feat that Garcia (1999) states has yet to be accomplished in most academic environments in the United States.

During the question period, students often report to have not only uncovered insights about the members of the culture being explored but also deepened their understanding of their own underlying cultural and ethnic basic assumptions and perhaps why those assumptions originated. The activity does more than affirm "students of color"; it benefits all students because it takes them beyond "color" to the cultures and ethnicities of others, as well as their own. It jettisons their familiar realities, exposing them to realities that their fear, comfort zone, lack of interest, or perceptions of inferiority or superiority might never have let them consider.

Students gain deep understanding from learning about the communicative dynamics stemming from culture and ethnicity because they are encouraged to dig beneath the surface of communication to the culturally and ethnically complex depths. Ultimately, this activity strives to prepare culturally and ethnically enlightened students as well as effective communicators.

Relevant Background

Fernandez (1991) claims that by mid-century, half of the population of the United States will be African-American, Asian-American, Latino-American, and Native-American. While that mix of cultures might be more apparent today — due to the obvious physical differences among students of different races — American schools have always reflected co-cultural and co-ethnic presence, even when that presence could not be (or was not) identified. Today's melange of cultures and ethnicities need not be viewed as a negative element to the classroom experience. On the contrary, the recognition of differences as well as similarities creates fertile ground for the understanding of "others" at a deep communicative level.

It is imperative that before they enter the workforce of the 21st century, students formally learn to negotiate the complex communicative meanings of those often perceived as "others." The United States is "poised to capture the gains of its long, albeit often troubled, experience with a multicultural population" (Norton and Fox 1997: 2). How much of a gain we capture will depend on our commitment to not just seeing one another but understanding one another.

References

Fernandez, J. (1991). *Managing a Diverse Workforce: Regaining the Competitive Edge.* Lexington, MA: Lexington Books.

Garcia, A. (May/June 1999). "Multiculturalism: An 'As If' Phenomenon." *International Journal of Qualitative Studies in Education (QSE)* 12: 299-310.

Norton, J., and R. Fox. (1997). *"The Change Equation": Capitalizing on Diversity for Effective Organizational Change.* Washington, DC: American Psychological Association.

Embracing Diversity Through Music in the Interpersonal Communication Classroom

Diane M. Monahan

Course

Music is a universal tool for expressing feelings about the self, relationships, and specific relational episodes, and its use in the Interpersonal Communication classroom can make course concepts come alive in song. Songs not only demonstrate various elements and concepts, but songs allow students to express themselves.

Learning Objective

This assignment provides a way for students to demonstrate their understanding of interpersonal communication concepts by applying them to the analysis of a song. As a result of this activity, students will see how songs are embedded with interpersonal concepts, and they gain a better understanding of relational communication. In addition, students learn to recognize how music is culturally based. The assignment can reveal cultural differences in interpersonal communication through music, and is a subtle way of embracing diversity in the classroom.

Description of the Activity

In this activity, students select a song that they feel reflects some aspect of themselves as relational beings. This assignment allows students to demonstrate their knowledge in a comfortable and familiar manner. Students have enjoyed this assignment in the past, and many say they appreciate the opportunity to express their opinions and perceptions. They also have commented on how the activity is a novel way to assess their learning.

In their final presentation, students play and then analyze the song for the entire class. Students feel as though they are substantively contributing to class discussion with their song selections, and the quality of those discussions is amazing. The activity particularly encourages conversations of diversity.

Process

In this activity, each student:

1. Selects an appropriate song to analyze. The song must represent interpersonal communication and be appropriate for the classroom setting. Not allowed are songs that are offensive or contain inappropriate subject matter such as rape, drug abuse, child abuse, domestic violence, and the like. Some songs and artists used by students in the past include "He Went to Paris" by Jimmy Buffet; "Sorry to a Friend" by Edwin McCain; "Butterfly" by Mariah Carey; "Bridge Over Troubled Water" by Simon and Garfunkel; "Can You Stand the Rain" by Boyz II Men; "Walls" by Yes; "Return to Me" by October Project; "Don't Speak" by No Doubt; and "Best Friend" by Brandy. Songs must be approved by the instructor; if the instructor is not familiar with the song, the student must provide a copy of the lyrics at this step.

2. Obtains the song's lyrics. Students will need to submit the lyrics with their final paper, and will distribute copies to class members during the final presentation. Audio of the song is also required for the presentation.

3. Conducts a thorough analysis of the song. It is important that the analysis focus on the relational messages of the song; that is, the student must be able to explain how he or she sees the song as a reflection of himself or herself as a relational being. Students should be able to explain this connection in their written paper and presentation. Each student's analysis must apply a minimum of six course concepts; for example, transactional communication, gender roles, relational context, life script, relational metaphors, confirming messages, disconfirming messages, proxemics, touch, facial expressions, double bind, gaze, stereotypes, CMM theory, and so on.

4. Gets approval from the instructor for his or her list of six concepts. This step helps students organize their thoughts and the course material.

5. Writes the analysis. The analysis consists of two parts: dissection and explanation. First, the student "dissects" the song on the copy of the lyrics, marking which lines of the song the student believes apply to each concept. Second, the student explains each concept used in the dissection. Each description is limited to one paragraph.

6. Makes a presentation to the class on the song analysis. In their presentations, students must demonstrate their knowledge of the course material as well as effective verbal communication. They also need to explain how the song is a reflection of them as a relational being. Each presentation includes the playing of the song and ends with class discussion.

Assessment

After completing this exercise, students are more willing to participate in discussion, empowered by the untraditional exercise. That discussion can be organized in many different ways. The instructor could categorize songs by themes, and hold one discussion integrating all songs in that grouping; for example, songs about relationship dissolution or an absent parent. This is an effective way to have a cohesive and focused discussion. It also allows students to think about the theme of a particular class and come prepared to discuss. Or, the instructor could decide to hold a discussion after each song. This is time-consuming and probably not as effective a way to discuss song themes.

No matter how discussions are organized, their purpose is to empower each student to discuss his or her perception of the song in the context of interpersonal communication. It is important to remind students that one aim of the exercise is to have them begin to listen to music through educated ears.

Relevant Background

Music can stimulate thought processes and enhance reasoning, and both can improve student understanding of interpersonal communication concepts and encourage student discussion. This assignment is an innovative way to encourage students of color especially because music plays an important role in many cultures. African-American and Hispanic cultures particularly embrace music and use it in many aspects of everyday life. This assignment gives students the power to select a song that is a reflection not only of them but also of their culture.

Group Ceremonial Speeches

Ann Neville Miller

Course

Introduction to Public Speaking

Learning Objectives

Because ceremonial speaking is the most common type of public speech in many cultures, this activity enables many students of color to develop skills in a rhetorical situation already comfortable for them and that does not demand the linear structure characteristic of most speech assignments in the typical Public Speaking course. It also provides an opportunity for the class as a whole to develop an understanding of ceremonial speech patterns of other cultural groups.

Description of the Activity

This activity is nice for the end of the semester, when students have become comfortable with one another and when release from the general stresses of term paper and project deadlines in all their other classes is warranted. (If the class includes a large number of American students of color or international students, the instructor might opt to make this assignment the first of the term in place of the usual introductory speech.)

Students form groups of four or five members each, and are instructed to create a ceremony. They may choose any occasion and may develop the ceremony according to their own tastes. Groups with members from cultures other than Euro-American are encouraged to explore ceremonies in one of those other cultures represented among them if they wish. Some of these occasions will likely occupy speech categories not found in the typical Public Speaking textbook, thus affording the entire class a chance to expand its understanding of ceremonial speaking across cultures.

The sole requirement for the ceremony is that it must be an occasion for which multiple speeches would be given, and each speech must be two to five minutes long. The groups may choose whether or not they wish to use props, but appropriate dress for the ceremony is highly encouraged, as it is a key part of the nonverbal component of such events. Students must also determine whether the use of notes for the speeches is appropriate — that is, whether the audience would typically expect it.

The speeches can be graded or not. Because students view creating a ceremony as an enjoyable activity, they throw the weight of their creativity into it with or without the incentive of grades. As a graded exercise, the entire group could be given one grade, but it is also possible to evaluate how successful each speech is in achieving the general goals of affirming community values and developing the desired atmosphere, as well as whether the speech meets criteria unique to its genre.

Process

1. A week or two ahead of time, put students in groups and give them the ceremony assignment.

2. Groups present their ceremonies one at a time.

3. Following each ceremony, oral critiques can be conducted, focusing both on how effectively the group as a whole created the desired atmosphere in its combination of speeches and on how individual speakers in the group fulfilled their specific roles.

Assessment

The ability of some groups to create a ceremonial atmosphere is remarkable. Instructor and class could well find themselves literally on the verge of tears following eulogies honoring an entirely fictitious "Recently Departed" or tender wedding vows from a couple who have no contact outside of Public Speaking class. Obviously, when the audience is able to enter into the enactment that thoroughly, the speakers have successfully fulfilled the purposes of a ceremonial speech. If the ceremony is set in a culture other than mainstream American, the instructor has the added opportunity to draw the class into a discussion of the decidedly different flavor the event has taken on and why.

Relevant Background

If any speaking assignment is likely to be deleted from the crowded schedules of Introductory Public Speaking, it is the ceremonial, or epideictic, speech. To neglect special occasion speeches seems a sad loss to the course, if for no other reason than it is these very occasions in life where audiences most long for an entertaining and concise speaker to step onto the podium. But for many students of color, the omission is more significant. Most collectivistic cultures and co-cultures, especially the majority that are also high-power distance, are rich with ceremonies to mark significant life events (Hofstede 1991; Triandis 1995). These occasions inevitably require multiple speeches, many of which are not structured in the linear style characteristic of the typical assignments of an Introductory Public Speaking course. By deleting the ceremonial speech, instructors will be overlooking the rhetorical situation with which some students are already most comfortable and denying them the opportunity to practice the type of speaking such students are most likely to use in daily life.

By making ceremonial speeches a group assignment, instructors can include them in the course without unduly sacrificing scarce class hours. Clustered this way, groups of ceremonial speakers require less than half the time it would take for the same number of students to give individual speeches of the same length, because dead time between speakers, set-up time for the next, occasional begging to be the last speaker of the day, and other small time wastages are eliminated. Moreover, critiques of group presentation afford the class an opportunity for reflection on issues of relationships between speeches and the structure of the ceremony itself, as well as on cultural aspects of the rhetorical situation, which would not arise if the speeches were delivered individually. This unusual combination — an activity that provides a higher-quality student learning experience yet frees up class hours — makes the group ceremonial speech assignment a valuable pedagogical addition to multicultural classrooms.

References

Hofstede, G. (1991). *Cultures and Organizations: Software of the Mind.* London: McGraw-Hill.

Triandis, H. (1995). *Individualism & Collectivism.* Boulder, CO: Westview.

Survivor — Everyone Stays on the Island

Promoting Personal Intercultural Skills

Theresa Bridges and Tara Lynn Crowell

Courses

Intercultural Communication, Interpersonal Communication, or Introduction to Communication (hybrid)

Learning Objectives

This semester-long exercise employs cooperative techniques and an instructor-initiated support network to increase students' success in basic Communication courses and develop their intercultural competence skills. It is structured to increase students' cognitive learning through the higher-order processing necessary to teach others course material, as well as to use students' interpersonal relationships to meet the psychological needs that most ensure success. Through exposure to both interpersonal and intercultural scholarship and real-life interaction, students will be challenged to make connective links between these two worlds by critically analyzing and evaluating their own and others' interpersonal skills and intercultural attitudes, beliefs, and values. While all students should benefit from the activity, students of color — both native and international — likely will see additional affective benefits resulting from their interpersonal interactions with classmates.

More specifically, as a result of this activity, students will be able to (1) determine a personal repertoire of effective and appropriate interpersonal skills for interacting with culturally different others, and (2) integrate their personal learning experiences with existing interpersonal and intercultural communication theory and research.

Description of the Activity

This is a semester-long activity that comprises small individual and group assignments as well as a final group assignment. Specifically, this assignment requires (1) individual abstracts of journal articles on intercultural communication; (2) individual journals recording out-of-class intercultural interactions; (3) individual mini-presentations correcting inaccurate perceptions of a culture; and (4) a group paper ("island survival manual" including brief history and overview of a culture, plus culture-specific behavioral advice) and a creative group presentation of the survival kit.

Process

First half of the semester: The instructor breaks up the class into groups of five or six students each, depending on class size. Each group is assigned a culture — ethnic, national, or religious. Because students must actually interact with culture members, cultures should be assigned only if they are sufficiently represented in the local community or student population. No group should be assigned the culture of any of the group members. The instructor frames the assignment to the students as: "You are visiting an island whose entire population belongs solely to the ethnic/national/religious group you have been assigned." Each group should write down everything they collectively "know" about the culture they have been assigned.

Groups investigate their assigned culture in two ways:

1. Each member of the group must locate five academic sources (excluding textbooks) that describe the assigned culture's specific traits and practices, then write a brief summary of the relevant material from each article.

2. Each member of the group must identify one "host" (an actual member of the assigned culture) to introduce the student to the culture. The students may choose someone already known to them or may find someone through a campus or community organization. Students may tell the host that they are working on a class assignment, but they must conduct their investigation through personal interaction, not a formal interview. The student "hangs out" with the host over the course of several weeks, seeing movies, attending cultural events, going out to dinner, or other informal activities. All the while the students are to engage in critical observation, keeping journals of occasions when they feel uncomfortable, misunderstand their hosts, talk about differences in their home cultures, or notice differences in the way they and their hosts communicate. The students should be reflective and expansive in these journals, rather than just making lists of activities.

Second half of the semester: Once they have investigated their assigned culture, the students engage in a version of the "Tribal Council" from the television show *Survivor.* Just as the show's participants voted one member off the island each episode, each class group votes off a "falsity" (myth, stereotype, preconceived notion, idea, attitude, belief) held about its assigned culture that, through this activity, the group now realizes is inaccurate. These "Tribal Council" ceremonies take two forms:

1. In one ceremony per group each week, each member of a group presents a "falsity" about the assigned culture to be voted on by the rest. In accordance with

Survivor's reward challenges, students obtain rewards if they successfully get their "falsity" voted off. The member who most effectively argues for the dismissal of his or her "falsity" is presented with a nominal reward (e.g., candy, hand-made cards, or island jewelry) by the group.

2. In another, larger ceremony each week, one member of each group presents to the class as a whole the "falsity" that that group voted off its island that week. From among these, the class awards one group "immunity" — exemption from a small quiz or daily class assignment, or an award of bonus points.

Toward the end of the semester (two or three weeks left): For their final projects, each group prepares two "island survival kits":

1. The first kit should include general information about the culture: a brief history and overview, rules for what to do and not to do, and unique customs, rituals, and traditions. Most of this information is likely to have come from secondary sources.

2. The second kit is a compendium of advice, gleaned from the experiences of all group members, on interpersonal interactions with members of that culture. This information should focus on the personal, noting similarities and differences among the experiences of the group's members.

The students present their survival course training in both written and speech forms. There are numerous possibilities for the writing assignment; but ultimately, students should integrate their personal experiences with the literature to illustrate that individuals are much more than their culture, even though culture greatly influences their behavior. The students' speech presentations should be professional yet appealing and creative; students might, for example, present a skit, role play, create a survival webpage, compile a three-dimensional survival guide (a suitcase or backpack with objects, pictures, symbols), put a survival song to music, produce a survival video, or compile a picture collage or photo album.

Cautions

Instructors should anticipate a protocol for group members who fail to perform. Possible ways to handle failure to perform (including but not limited to not completing work by the group's deadlines, not coordinating efforts with other group members, in any way impinging upon the educational processes of other group members) are individual point reductions or expulsion from the group. Thus, as the semester unfolds, each group should keep accurate records of its members' attendance and participation; a liaison should be appointed to keep the instructor apprised of difficulties encountered by the group.

Assessment

The instructor has much latitude in evaluating the various individual and group assignments throughout the semester (e.g., to award points for participation/completion of abstracts or to grade based on some objective criteria). Additional activities the instructor can use to assess the students' achievement of the learning goals follow.

Last two or three weeks of the semester: Once all the groups have presented their survival kits to the class, the instructor could reconstitute the groups such that each new group comprises one member from each "island." Over the last few weeks, these new groups could:

- Discuss and compare the different cultures, looking for similarities. Identify general competence skills necessary for interacting with culturally different others.

- Employ specific interpersonal theories/concepts (e.g., self-disclosure, implicit personality theory, attribution theory, uncertainty reduction theory) to explain why some islands had very similar experiences yet others had quite different experiences.

- Reflect upon how students' own cultural background impacted their performance on the islands, and discuss how the activity might have changed how they view their own culture.

Relevant Background

Sedlacek (1983) indicates that the quality of the instructor-student relationship is a critical factor influencing minority students' learning and their comfort level with the educational institution. Unfortunately, due to increasing enrollment in Communication courses, instructors can find it difficult to develop meaningful relationships with each of their students. Much of the literature, however, suggests that students from diverse groups can succeed if (1) they feel welcome, (2) they feel they are being treated as individuals, (3) they feel they can participate fully, and (4) they are treated fairly (McKeachie 1994). One way to achieve these goals is through the use of peer groups in the classroom. While some students could be initially ambivalent toward "groupwork," instructors who effectively design assignments and manage classroom interaction are likely to see increases in students' affective, behavioral, and cognitive learning.

Too often, the classroom study of intercultural communication relies on the identification and analysis of theory and concepts, with little or no attention to pragmatic skills-based outcomes. Certainly, critical thinking, comparative analysis, and hypothetical application are valid learning goals, but they do not give students the behavioral skills necessary to communicate effectively in intercultural encounters. To achieve behavioral learning outcomes, it is essential that students participate in interpersonal interactions with culturally different others, reflect upon effective and appropriate behavior in these encounters, and integrate their conclusions with existing intercultural theory and research.

Note

An earlier version of this paper was presented at the 70th Annual Florida Communication Association Conference, October 2000.

References

McKeachie, W.J. (1994). *Teaching Tips*. Lexington, MA: D.C. Heath.

Sedlacek, W.E. (1983). "Teaching Minority Students." In *Teaching Minority Students: New Directions in Teaching and Learning*, No. 16, edited by J.H. Cones, J.F. Noonan, and D. Jahna, pp. 39-50. San Francisco: Jossey-Bass.

The Cultural Hero Presentation

Navigating Between Exoticism and Assimilationism

Roy Schwartzman and Bayo Oludaja

Course

Any basic course; especially suitable for introductory Intercultural Communication courses.

Learning Objective

Students will develop a better understanding of their own distinctive cultural heritage, while recognizing how different cultures contribute to collective moral goals.

Description of the Activity

Each student investigates his or her own cultural background, then selects an individual from that background who models values that are important in the student's own life. Later, the class generates a consensus list of universally desirable virtues and values. Finally, in a presentation before the class, each student explains how his or her cultural hero both uplifts their cultural group and contributes to their cultural heritage *and* embodies values and qualities that transcend differences among cultural groups.

The emphasis on universal virtues actually complements rather than contradicts affirmations of cultural heritage. As long as the various cultural heroes strive for similar objectives — ends that the students themselves have identified as important and universal — then no path to virtue gets privileged above others. The distinctive cultural features of the heroes show that no one culture is entitled to dominate others (Kincaid and Horner 1997: 19).

Process

Recognizing one's cultural identity. Students are instructed to investigate their own ethnic, racial, and cultural backgrounds:

> Think of the norms, values, and beliefs from this background that have
> shaped who you are and who you aspire to be. Think about how these
> norms, values, and beliefs have given meaning to life among the people of
> your cultural background. Look at history (ancient or recent, written or oral)
> and identify some individuals from your cultural background who have mod-
> eled values that have given meaning to your life.

> Select one of those individuals as your hero. Preferably this person should not be someone who is widely acknowledged in mainstream American culture. Select someone who is less known but who embodies qualities that you believe have universal appeal. In a future class, you will generate as a class a list of universally desirable virtues and values.
>
> [In your presentation,] you will describe the specific ways your cultural hero shows the unique qualities of your heritage and exemplifies at least one of the universal values we identify in class.

As students prepare their presentations, they should be encouraged to recognize the races, creeds, religions, or other group affiliations that inform their own identities. Also, the assessment criteria (see below) should be distributed to students with the assignment guidelines.

Generating universal values. At least one week before the students' presentations are to be delivered, at least 30 minutes (preferably an entire class period) is set aside for students to generate a list of universal values and virtues. This step is critical for the assignment's success. Without this step, nothing in the guidelines for a standard "cultural hero" presentation prevents a student from discussing "Adolf Hitler, My Hero" or other such topics. (Precisely this situation lies at the center of the plot of the film *American History X*, in which an African-American teacher is dismayed that a student uses a cultural hero assignment as a platform for defending Hitler's racist views.)

To generate the universal values, the instructor asks students to specify virtues or behaviors that they believe everyone should try to exhibit. Every suggestion should be recorded. Students should be reminded that these qualities should be considered universally desirable. After a list has been generated, the class votes on which items they want to keep as universal. To stay on the list, that item must be endorsed unanimously. The cultural hero each student has chosen must exhibit one or more of the values from this list.

Such a list should be relatively easy to generate. William Bennett, for example, assembled *The Book of Virtues* (1996) as a compilation of stories that exhibit similar sets of desirable qualities that transcend nationalities and cultures. The list that students generate, however, also has binding force on them because they have identified the virtues themselves. As a result, the question "Whose morals?" never arises, and students do not feel that someone else's morals are being imposed on them.

Delivering the presentation. Each student makes an oral presentation lasting five to 10 minutes. This time limit can be extended, especially if the instructor incorporated a research component in the assignment.

Assessment

An effective "cultural hero" presentation:

- Points out how the hero both fulfills and transcends expected norms of his or her native culture.

- Makes a case for honoring this individual as a cultural hero, since the person is not already in the public eye. (Selecting a widely recognized figure such as Martin Luther King, Jr. or Malcolm X does not offer enough insight about why that figure might be a cultural hero for the student.)

- Explains how the hero explicitly manifests one or more of the universal values identified by the class.

- Includes stories and examples to illustrate how the hero put values into practice. (Students should keep the positive qualities concrete by showing what this person *does/did* to exemplify those values.)

- Characterizes the person as heroic in a way that taps into universal values (to show that different cultures can unite behind shared values).

Relevant Background

A few years ago, at a Communication conference, two bumper stickers distributed by the same vendor lay side by side on a table: "Celebrate diversity!" and "Create community!" How can both objectives be accomplished? John Lucaites (1997) contends that "the primary issue for liberal democracy as it approaches the turn of the century is how to manage the tensions between unity and fragmentation — between collective and individual" that would facilitate collective public action without a dilution of individual identity (283). For the individual in a multicultural society, effective management of diversity implies recognizing and negotiating the many identities in which one participates. Sensitivity thus implies not only appreciating the identities of others, but also seeking "a more dialogical relationship between the individual *qua* human being and the multiple classes of which she or he is a part" (Lucaites 1997: 283).

Many exercises highlight the uniqueness of a student's culture. Although such activities can develop cultural awareness, that heightened consciousness risks exaggerating cultural differences, obscuring the universal human values that cultures share. This tendency to splinter cultures can lead to *exoticism*, which showcases cultural achievements as curiosities without showing how they contribute to moral objectives shared by various cultures. Virtues and accomplishments become compartmentalized and limited in scope: African spirituality, Arabic innovation, and so on.

A second danger, *assimilationism*, stresses cultural similarities to the point of reducing each distinct culture to its role as part of a single cultural mélange. Historically, this extreme was embodied in the melting pot theory that specific cultural markers would "boil away" to form a shared American identity. A more perniciously aggressive version of this idea appears as enforced cultural hegemony, especially in colonialism or the concept of *Kultur*. The German ideal of *Kultur* designated "Nordic" Germans as the sole legitimate proprietors of German identity. Other groups, such as Jews or Roma, simply were not considered "true" Germans (Levin 1968: 285).

References

Bennett, W.J. (1996). *The Book of Virtues: A Treasury of Great Moral Stories.* New York: Simon and Schuster.

Kincaid, T.M., and E.R. Horner. (1997). "Designing, Developing, and Implementing Diversity Training: Guidelines for Practitioners." *Educational Technology* 37(2): 19-26.

Levin, N. (1968). *The Holocaust: The Destruction of European Jewry 1933-1945.* New York: Schocken.

Lucaites, J.L. (1997). "Visualizing 'The People': Individualism and Collectivism in *Let Us Now Praise Famous Men.*" *Quarterly Journal of Speech* 83(3): 269-288.

Appendix

Suggested Readings

Alba, R.D. (1990). *Ethnic Identity: The Transformation of White America.* New Haven, CT: Yale University Press.

Allen, B. (1998). "Black Womanhood and Feminist Standpoints." *Management Communication Quarterly* 11(4): 575-586.

Bennett, W.J. (1996). *The Book of Virtues: A Treasury of Great Moral Stories.* New York: Simon and Schuster.

Blank, R., and S. Slipp. (1994). *Voices of Diversity: Real People Talk About Problems and Solutions in a Workplace Where Everyone Is Not Alike.* New York: American Management Association.

Bosmajian, H. (1983). *The Language of Oppression.* New York: University Press of America.

Brown, C., C. Snedeker, and B. Skyes, eds. (1997). *Conflict and Diversity.* Creskill, NJ: Hampton.

Carlson, D., and M.W. Apple. (1998). *Power/Knowledge/Pedagogy: The Meaning of Democratic Education in Unsettling Times.* Boulder, CO: Westview.

Carr-Ruffino, N. (1999). *Diversity Success Strategies.* Boston: Butterworth Heinemann.

Casbon, J., B.R. Schirmer, and L.L. Twiss. (1997). "Acceptance and Caring Are the Heart of Engaging Classroom Diversity." *Reading Teacher* 50(7): 602-604.

Casse, P. (1982). *Training for the Multicultural Manager.* Washington, DC: Society for Intercultural Education, Training and Research (SIETAR).

Chen, G.-M., and W.J. Starosta. (1998). *Foundations of Intercultural Communication.* Needham Heights, MA: Allyn and Bacon.

Cox, T., Jr. (1994). *Cultural Diversity in Organizations: Theory, Research and Practice.* San Francisco: Berrett-Koehler.

Darder, A., ed. (1995). *Culture and Difference: Critical Perspectives on Bicultural Experience in the United States.* Westport, CT: Bergin and Garvey.

Davidson, A.L. (1996). *Making and Molding Identity in Schools: Student Narratives on Race, Gender and Academic Engagement.* Albany, NY: State University of New York Press.

Delpit, L. (1995). *Other People's Children: Cultural Conflicts in the Classroom.* New York: The New Press.

Foster, M., ed. (1997). *Black Teachers on Teaching.* New York: The New Press.

Gardenswartz, L., and A. Rowe. (1998). "Why Diversity Matters." *HR Focus* 75: 1-4.

Giroux, H.A., and P. McLaren, eds. (1994). *Between Borders: Pedagogy and the Politics of Cultural Studies.* New York: Routledge.

Gonzalez, A., M. Houston, and V. Chen, eds. (1997). *Our Voices, Essays in Culture, Ethnicity and Communication.* 3rd ed. Los Angeles: Roxbury.

Gyekye, K. (1997). *Tradition and Modernity: Philosophical Reflections on the African Experience.* New York: Doubleday.

Haskins, J., ed. (1973). *Black Manifesto for Education.* New York: William Morrow.

Hegde, M.N. (1991). "Diversity and Disorders in Communication." In *Introduction to Communicative Disorders,* edited by M.N. Hedge, pp. 419-438. Austin, TX: Pro-Ed.

Hemphill, H., and R. Haines. (1997). *Discrimination, Harassment, and the Failure of Diversity Training: What to Do Now.* Westport, CT: Quorum Books.

Hendrix, K.G. (1998). "Facilitating Difficult Class Discussions: Creating a Respectful Atmosphere for Discussing Race in Intercultural Communication." In *Teaching Ideas for the Basic Communication Course, Vol. 2.,* edited by L.W. Hugenberg and B.S. Hugenberg, pp. 119-124. Dubuque, IA: Kendall/Hunt.

————. (1998). "Student Perceptions of the Influence of Race on Professor Credibility." *Journal of Black Studies* 28(6): 738-763.

————. (1998). "Teaching Argumentation Perspectives in the Argumentation and Debate Course Using a Nontraditional Exemplar." *The Speech Communication Teacher* 13: 6-7.

————. (2000). "Now What Do I Do?: Advice for Non-ESL Instructors Teaching Courses Requiring Oral Presentations." *The College Student Journal* 34: 641-651.

————. (2000). "Siamiak and Tho: Case Studies in the Assessment and Skill Development of ESL Students in the Oral Performance Course." *Journal of the Association for Communication Administration* 29: 196-212.

Hirabayashi, L.R., ed. (1998). *Teaching Asian America: Diversity and the Problem of Community.* Lanham, MD: Rowan and Littlefield.

Hofstede, G. (1991). *Cultures and Organizations: Software of the Mind.* London: McGraw-Hill.

hooks, b. (1990). *Yearning: Race, Gender, and Cultural Politics.* Boston: South End.

———. (1994). *Teaching to Transgress: Education as the Practice of Freedom.* New York: Routledge.

———. (1995). *Killing Rage: Ending Racism.* New York: Henry Holt.

Houston, M. (1992). "The Politics of Difference: Race, Class and Communication." In *Women Making Meaning,* edited by L. Rakow, pp. 45-49. New York: Routledge.

Jackson, R.L., II. (1999). "White Space, White Privilege: Mapping Discursive Inquiry Into the Self." *Quarterly Journal of Speech* 85: 38-54.

Katz, J.H. (1978). *White Awareness, Handbook for Anti-Racism Training.* Norman, OK: University of Oklahoma Press.

Ladson-Billings, G. (1994). *The Dreamkeepers: Successful Teachers of African American Children.* San Francisco: Jossey-Bass.

Lather, P. (1991). *Getting Smart: Feminist Research and Pedagogy With/in the Postmodern.* New York: Routledge.

Locust, C. (1988). "Wounding the Spirit: Discrimination and Traditional American Belief System." *Harvard Educational Review* 58: 315-330.

Lorde, A. (1984). *Sister Outsider: Essays and Speeches.* Freedom, CA: The Crossing Press.

Lucaites, J.L. (1997). "Visualizing 'The People': Individualism and Collectivism in *Let Us Now Praise Famous Men.*" *Quarterly Journal of Speech* 83(3): 269-288.

McDermott, J.C., ed. (1999). *Beyond the Silence: Listening for Democracy.* Portsmouth, NH: Heineman.

McIntosh, P. (1994). "White Privilege and Male Privilege: A Personal Account of Coming to See Correspondences Through Work in Women's Studies." In *Race, Class and Gender: An Anthology,* edited by M. Andersen and P. Hill Collins, pp. 70-81. Belmont, CA: Wadsworth.

McLaughlin, S. (1998). "Language Differences: Diversity and Disorders." In *Introduction to Language Development,* edited by S. McLaughlin, pp. 399-422. San Diego, CA: Singular.

McLemore, D.S. (1991). *Racial and Ethnic Relations in America.* 3rd ed. Boston: Allyn and Bacon.

McPhail, M. (1994). "The Politics of Complicity: Second Thoughts About the Social Contribution of Racial Equality." *Quarterly Journal of Speech* 80: 343-357.

Minor, V., and S. Sandler. (2000). "Jenny Evans on a Journey Toward Her Students: A Series on Leading and Talking About Race and Culture." *Multicultural Education* 8(2): 38-39.

Moemeka, A.A. (1997). "Communalistic Societies: Community and Self-Respect as African Values." In *Communication Ethics and Universal Values,* edited by C.G. Christians and M. Traber, pp. 170-193. London: Sage.

Orbe, M.P. (1998). *Constructing Co-Cultural Theory: An Explication of Culture, Power and Communication.* Thousand Oaks, CA: Sage.

Quigley, B.L., K.G. Hendrix, and K. Friesem. (1998). "Graduate Teaching Assistant Training: Preparing Instructors to Assist ESL Students in the Introductory Speaking Course." *Basic Communication Course Annual* 10: 58-89.

Richards, J., ed. (1995). *Cambridge Language Education.* Cambridge: Press Syndicate of the University of Cambridge.

Samovar, L.A., and R.E. Porter, eds. (2000). *Intercultural Communication: A Reader.* Belmont, CA: Wadsworth.

Schwartzman, R. (1994). "Can Afro-Americans Be Called Racists?" In *A Legacy Recorded: An Anthology of Martyrdom and Resistance,* edited by H. Rosenfeld and E. Zborowski, pp. 352-353. New York: Athens.

Sims, R.R., and R.F. Dennehy, eds. (1993). *Diversity and Differences in Organizations: An Agenda for Answers and Questions.* Westport, CT: Quorum Books.

Swanson, G.M. (1982). "Say It With Music: An Instructional Technique for the First Course in Interpersonal Communication." *Communication Education* 31(3): 225-230.

Takaki, R. (1993). *A Different Mirror: A History of Multicultural America.* Boston: Little, Brown.

Taylor, O., ed. (1986). *Nature of Communication Disorders in Culturally and Linguistically Diverse Populations.* Austin, TX: Pro-Ed.

Telushkin, J. (1991). *Jewish Literacy, The Most Important Things to Know About the Jewish Religion, Its People, and Its History.* San Diego, CA: College-Hill.

Triandis, H. (1995). *Individualism & Collectivism.* Boulder, CO: Westview.

Williams, R., and W. Wolfram. (1977). *Social Dialects: Difference Versus Disorder.* Rockville, MD: American Speech-Language-Hearing Association.

Wolfram, W., and D. Christian. (1989). *Dialects and Education: Issues and Answers.* Englewood Cliffs, NJ: Prentice-Hall.

Wood, J. (1998). "Celebrating Diversity in the Communication Field." *Communication Studies* 49: 172-178.

About the Editors

Wenshu Lee *(associate editor)* is a professor of Communication, Gender, and Culture in the Department of Communication Studies at San Jose State University. Her recent research interests include politics of identity and representation in transnational and global contexts, and the alliances between Third World feminists and U.S. womanists. Her published works focus on whiteness, postcolonial feminist rhetoric, and critical intercultural communication.

Mark Lawrence McPhail *(associate editor)* is a professor and the chair of Communication at Miami University (Ohio). His research interests include rhetorical theory and epistemology, contemporary race relations, discourse and power, and spirituality. His work has appeared in *The Howard Journal of Communications, Quarterly Journal of Speech, Rhetoric Review,* and *Southern Communication Journal.* He is author of two books, *The Rhetoric of Racism* (University Press of America, 1994) and *Zen in the Art of Rhetoric: An Inquiry Into Coherence* (SUNY Press, 1995).

Dolores Valencia Tanno *(associate editor)* is a professor in the Greenspun School of Communication at the University of Nevada, Las Vegas. Her research interests are in the areas of intercultural communication, communication ethics, and rhetoric. She has coauthored three books, has authored and coauthored articles in various journals and anthologies, and because of her research in intercultural communication has been an invited speaker in Mexico City and in San Jose, Costa Rica.

Orlando L. Taylor *(consulting reviewer)* is the dean of Howard University's Graduate School and a professor in the School of Communications. He is a former president of the National Communication Association. He is currently chair of the Board of Directors of the Council of Graduate Schools and president of the Northeastern Association of Graduate Schools. He is a member of advisory committees for the National Science Foundation and the National Institutes of Health and is the author of numerous publications in the fields of sociolinguistics and intercultural communication leading to the development of new theories and applications.

Judith S. Trent *(editor)* is a professor of Communication at the University of Cincinnati. For 16 years as associate vice president for research and advanced studies she served as the director of the University's graduate minority fellowship program. In 2000, she was the recipient of the University of Cincinnati's "Just Community Award." She is author of numerous books, book chapters, and journal articles in the area of political campaign communication. She served as president of the National Communication Association in 1997 and currently is the director of NCA's Mentor Program.

Carolyn Vasques-Scalera *(AAHE project editor)* is the director of diversity initiatives at the American Association for Higher Education. Her work focuses on the intersections of diversity and democracy, social justice education, intergroup dialogue, service-learning, and the sociology of education. She received her Ph.D. in Sociology from the University of Michigan, where she was also active in the Center for Research on Learning and Teaching, the Center for Community Service and Learning, and the Program on Intergroup Relations, Conflict, and Community.

About the Authors

Kelly Fudge Albada is an assistant professor in the Department of Communication and Broadcasting at East Carolina University. She received her Ph.D. in 1997 from the University of Texas at Austin. Her research interests include the relationship between family communication and media and the influence of media in gender communication. She is involved in a campus initiative on race, and advises a student communication organization.

Cynthia Berryman-Fink is a professor in the Department of Communication at the University of Cincinnati. She has authored five books and more than 30 articles and chapters in communication, psychology, personnel, women's studies, and education publications. She has served as president of the Central States Communication Association, has been a department head and vice provost at the University of Cincinnati, and has provided consulting to dozens of corporate, financial, medical, educational, and government institutions nationwide.

Theresa Bridges is an assistant professor at the University of Central Florida and a doctoral candidate at the University of Oklahoma. She received her M.A. in 1995 from Norfolk State University. Her dissertation focuses on the dialectics of interpersonal negotiation in interethnic friendships. In addition, Bridges combines her interests in intercultural and instructional communication by implementing interactive classroom methods to increase students' critical- and connective-thinking skills with respect to Communication scholarship and their interpersonal relationships.

Aparna S. Bulusu is an assistant professor at the University of Pittsburgh, Johnstown. She is a doctoral candidate at the University of Memphis interested in cross-cultural communication in organizational settings, particularly job interviews. She received her M.A. in 1995 from Western Kentucky University and recently received the Southern States Communication Association's Bostrom Award for excellence in student research.

Nanci M. Burk teaches in the Communication and Foreign Language Department at Glendale Community College (Arizona). She received her M.S. in 1996 from Southern Illinois University, Carbondale, and has taught Speech Communication courses in Arizona since 1996 for Glendale Community College, Phoenix College, Rio Salado College, Arizona State University, and Northern Arizona University. Burk also provides communication consulting for a variety of corporate, industry, and educational organizations in Arizona.

Kathleen D. Clark is an assistant professor in the School of Communication at the University of Akron. She received her Ph.D. in 1995 from the Ohio State University, and conducts research on the sense-making process in communication and in the area of women and spirituality. She recently edited and contributed to *The Electronic Journal of Communication*. She has presented conference papers regionally and nationally.

Tara Lynn Crowell is an assistant professor at the Richard Stockton College of New Jersey. She received her Ph.D. in 1999 from the University of Oklahoma, and her major areas of interest are interpersonal, health, and instructional communication. She explores effective teacher-student communication, while working to develop and implement theoretical and practical communication curricula. She also investigates HIV-positive heterosexuals' communication, attitudes, and behaviors prior to heterosexually contracting the virus, in order to link the communication, attitudes, and behaviors of HIV-positive and uninfected individuals. Her ultimate goal for this research is to motivate heterosexuals to personalize the risk of HIV and engage in safer sexual behaviors.

Dale Cyphert is coordinator of the Business Communication Program at the University of Northern Iowa, where she teaches in the Department of Management. She received her Ph.D. from the Pennsylvania State University and has a broad background in corporate and management communication as a practitioner, researcher, and instructor. Her research involves contrasting rhetorical patterns across cultures, especially the conflict of oral and literate norms in the contemporary workplace.

Celnisha L. Dangerfield is a master's student in Communication Theory within the Department of Speech Communication at the Pennsylvania State University. She is a magna cum laude graduate of Clark Atlanta University and was an undergraduate Summer Fellow of both Brown University and New York University. Her research interests are related to cultural identity negotiations as evidenced in varying contexts from mass media to interpersonal relationships. Dangerfield is also developing a paradigm she has coined "race shock."

Olga Idriss Davis is an assistant professor in the Hugh Downs School of Human Communication at Arizona State University. She received her Ph.D. from the University of Nebraska-Lincoln, and is an alumna of the Juilliard School in drama. As a Rockefeller Fellow, she conducted research on the performative and liberatory nature of black female slave narratives. Her current scholarship extends the role of narrative in the lives of African-American survivors of the Tulsa, Oklahoma, Race Riot of 1921. She is coeditor, with Marsha Houston, of *Centering*

Ourselves: African American Feminist and Womanist Studies of Discourse (Hampton Press, 2001).

Kathleen M. German is a professor of Communication at Miami University (Ohio). She has served as editor of *The Ohio Speech Journal* and as associate editor for numerous nationally recognized Communication journals. She is coauthor of one of the most widely used Public Speaking textbooks in the United States, and has developed a series of innovative media-based ancillaries for the Public Speaking course. Her research interests include World War II propaganda films and other forms of mediated rhetoric surrounding political and social issues.

Cheryl D. Gunter is an associate professor in the Department of Communicative Disorders at West Chester University. A licensed clinician, she previously was an associate professor and clinic director in the Department of Speech Communication at Iowa State University, where she also served as an instructor for the Basic Communication course and the Speech Improvement course in the department. She was a Fulbright Scholar at the University of Malta, where she assisted with the expansion of a new curriculum in Communication Disorders. A member of NCA and ASHA, she is the editor of *ASHA in the World*, the publication of the International Affairs Association. She earned her Ph.D. from the University of Texas at Austin.

Heather E. Harris is an assistant professor in the Department of Communication Studies and a member of the Minority Retention Task Force at Baruch College, in New York City. Born in Montreal, Canada, to Barbadian parents, she studied journalism at Concordia University, received her B.A. in 1988, and during 1989-1994 worked as a news anchor and reporter for the Caribbean Broadcasting Corporation and as a radio producer for the Caribbean News Agency and the Namibian Broadcasting Corporation. She received both her M.A. and Ph.D. degrees from Howard University. During her academic career at Howard, she was a Preparing Future Faculty Fellow, a teaching assistant, graduate assistant, and a Sasakawa Fellow.

Katherine G. Hendrix is an associate professor at the University of Memphis. Her research interests include the scholarship of teaching as it applies to graduate teaching assistants, particularly those of color, and to professors of color at predominantly white postsecondary institutions. She received her Ph.D. in 1994 from the University of Washington.

Patricia S. Hill is an assistant professor in the School of Communication at the University of Akron. Prior to university teaching, she worked several years in the health field. She has contributed to the community as a communication consultant and guest lecturer. Her research is published in scholarly journals such as *Women and Language* and *The Gerontologist*. She has presented numerous convention papers locally, regionally, nationally, and internationally. She received her Ph.D. from Bowling Green State University, with an emphasis in Interpersonal Communication.

Ronald L. Jackson II is an assistant professor of Culture and Communication Theory in the Department of Speech Communication at the Pennsylvania State University. His research interests include the social and intellectual construction and negotiation of cultural, gender, and racial identities with an emphasis on critical white studies, Afrocentricity, and identity negotiation. His theory work includes the development of two paradigms coined "cultural contracts theory" and the "black masculine identity theory." His work has appeared in *Quarterly Journal of Speech, Howard Journal of Communication, International and Intercultural Communication Annual*, and *Communication Theory*. His latest books are the nonacademic *Think About It!: The Question Book for Those Curious About Race and Self-Discovery* (iuniverse.com, 2000) and *The Negotiation of Cultural Identity* (Praeger, 1999). He received his Ph.D. in Intercultural Communication and Rhetoric from Howard University.

Patricia Kearney is a professor of Communication Studies and the codirector of the Hauth Center for Communication Skills at California State University, Long Beach. Her research focuses on communication in the instructional process. She has published several books and more than 60 research articles, chapters, and research reports. She received her Ph.D. in 1979 from West Virginia University.

Yang Lin is an assistant professor in the School of Communication at the University of Akron. He has conducted many studies in the areas of political and intercultural communication, and is also interested in the development of teaching pedagogy, in particular in integrating scholarly research with basic course teaching. He received his Ph.D. in 1997 from the University of Oklahoma.

Jacqueline M. Martinez is an assistant professor in the Hugh Downs School of Human Communication at Arizona State University. She has taught at Purdue University and at Babson College, and was a Chicana Dissertation Fellow in the Department of Chicano Studies at the University of California at Santa Barbara. She writes in the area of Intercultural Communication. She is the author of *Phenomenology of Chicana Experience and Identity: Communication and Transformation in Praxis* (Rowman and Littlefield, 2000). She received her Ph.D. from Southern Illinois University.

Ann Neville Miller is a lecturer in the Department of Communication at Daystar University, Nairobi, where she is also founding director of the only writing and speech center in East Africa. She received her M.A. from Wheaton College Graduate School and has taught Speech Communication both in the United States and in Kenya.

Diane M. Monahan is an assistant professor of Communication at Keene State College, where she teaches classes in Interpersonal Communication, Nonverbal Communication, and Research Methods. She has a strong interest in effective teaching and assessment, and has conducted workshops on teaching effectiveness for both gradute teaching assistants and professors. Additionally, she has conducted an inservice for university employees on issues of diversity. Monahan has presented several papers at the National Communication Association and the International Communication Association conferences. She received her doctorate from Temple University in Communication Sciences.

Carlos D.J. Morrison is an assistant professor of Speech Communication and Theatre Arts at Clark Atlanta University. He teaches courses in African-American Rhetoric and Communication, Persuasion, Public Address, and Communication Theory. His research focuses on black popular culture and rhetoric, social movements, Afrocentricity, and African-American rhetoric. His most recent publication examined the rhetorical meaning of Louis Farrakhan's song "White Man's Heaven Is a Black Man's Hell." He received his Ph.D. in Intercultural Communication and Rhetoric from Howard University.

Thomas K. Nakayama is a professor in the Hugh Downs School of Human Communication and director of Asian Pacific American Studies at Arizona State University. He has been a visiting faculty member at the University of Iowa and the University of Maine, and was a Fulbright Scholar at the Université de Mons-Hainaut, in Belgium. He writes in the areas of Cultural Studies and Critical Communication Studies, focusing particularly on issues of race and sexuality. He is coeditor, with Judith Martin, of *Whiteness: The Social Communication of Identity* (Sage, 1999). He received his Ph.D. from the University of Iowa.

Bayo Oludaja is an assistant professor of Communication at Northwest Missouri State University, where he teaches Intercultural and Interpersonal Communication courses. His research interests include listening and ethical issues relating to globalization and business. He received his Ph.D. from the University of Kansas.

Victoria O. Orrego is an assistant professor in the School of Communication at the University of Miami (FL). Her research interests include persuasion, interpersonal communication, academic mentoring relationships, health communication, and instructional communication. She received her Ph.D. in 1999 from Michigan State University.

Dorthy L. Pennington is on the faculty at the University of Kansas, where she earned her Ph.D. She teaches courses in Intercultural/Interracial Communication, Rhetoric, and Cultural Studies. Her research and publications address these areas and also African-American women in the workplace. She is the coauthor of one of the earliest books in interracial communication, *Crossing Difference . . . Interracial Communication* (with Jon Blubaugh; Merrill, 1976). She has contributed to the *Handbook of Intercultural Communication* and to the *Handbook of International and Intercultural Communication.* In 1995, she was given a convention program in her honor as a "Teacher, Mentor, and Intercultural Scholar" by the Feminist and Women's Studies Division of the National Communication Association. In 1997, she was given a convention program in her honor and an award by the Teachers on Teaching Series of the National Communication Association, in recognition of outstanding contributions to the philosophy and methodology of the teaching of speech communication.

Timothy G. Plax is a professor of Communication Studies at California State University, Long Beach. His research focuses on social influence and communication in instruction and training. He has published several books and more than 100 research articles, chapters, and research reports. He received his Ph.D. in 1974 from the University of Southern California.

Roy Schwartzman is an associate professor of Communication and Basic Course director at Northwest Missouri State University. His primary research interests are Holocaust studies, communication pedagogy, and rhetoric of inquiry. His research on metaphors in education won a 1996 Special Merit Award for Excellence in Educational Research from the editorial board of *Education.* He received his Ph.D. from the University of Iowa and was a winner of the 1994 Speech Communication Association Outstanding Dissertation Award.

Ronald B. Scott is an associate professor of Communication at Miami University (Ohio), an affiliate professor in Black World Studies, vice chair of the Film Studies Program, and director of the College of Arts and Science Diversity Seminars for First Year Students. His research and publications focus on representations of African Americans in film and television, and his current scholarship addresses issues of race, gender, and diversity in mediated and educational contexts.

Linda G. Seward is currently teaching in the Department of Communications at John Carroll University. She earned her doctorate from Purdue University.

Thomas J. Socha is an associate professor and University Professor in Old Dominion University's Department of Communication. He is the founding editor of the *Journal of Family Communication* and has published two books and numerous chapters and articles focusing on family communication, children's communication, and group communication. His most recent book, *Communication, Race, and Family: Exploring Communication in Black, White, and Biracial Families* (with Rhunette Diggs; Lawrence Erlbaum, 1999), breaks new ground by studying race relations in the context of families communicating at home. He received his Ph.D. from the University of Iowa.

Julia A. Spiker is an assistant professor in the School of Communication at the University of Akron. She conducts research in the areas of political communication and instructional communication, specifically political malaise, the Internet, learning communities, and service-learning. She received her Ph.D. in 1998 from the University of Oklahoma.

Mary E. Triece is an assistant professor in the School of Communication at the University of Akron. Her areas of expertise include rhetorical theory and criticism, with an emphasis on social movement rhetoric, feminist theories, and popular culture. She recently published her first book, *Protest and Popular Culture: Women in the U.S. Labor Movement, 1894-1917* (Westview, 2001). She has also published articles in *Critical Studies in Mass Communication* and *Women's Studies in Mass Communication* and has presented numerous conference papers both regionally and nationally. She earned her Ph.D. in 1997 from the University of Texas at Austin.